D1277086

HARRAP'S

English Punctuation & Hyphenation

William Gould

HARRAP
London Paris

First published in Great Britain 1990
by HARRAP BOOKS Ltd
*Chelsea House, 26 Market Square, Bromley,
Kent BR1 1NA*

© *Clark Robinson Limited* 1990

All rights reserved. No part of this
publication may be reproduced in any
form or by any other means without the prior
permission of Harrap Books Ltd.

ISBN 0-245-60020-5

*Typeset by Action Typesetting, Gloucester
Printed in Great Britain by
Richard Clay Ltd,
Bungay, Suffolk*

Preface

This book has been conceived and produced to meet a dual need. For users and learners of English, the 19 chapters on Punctuation deal with all but the most technical applications of punctuation marks and their accessories, such as spacing and the use of boldface and italic letters. The Punctuation section concludes with a chapter on Hyphenation, with advice on how to solve the knotty problem of where to split a word that is too long to fit at the end of a line of text. This is followed by a Hyphenation Dictionary, which lists 12,000 words of more than one syllable with indications of where they can be hyphenated if necessary. Finally there is a Glossary of grammatical terms.

The production of this book has required two specialist skills, and the publishers wish gratefully to acknowledge the people who supplied them. The knowledge of grammar and working practice of modern English usage − essential for the creation of the chapters on Punctuation − was contributed by William Gould. His in-depth experience gained while writing and editing various dictionaries and encyclopaedias has enabled him to provide a comprehensive and definitive account of the latest views on English punctuation.

Correct hyphenation practice is also an editorial skill, but one that has now become part of the province of the experienced proofreader. For many years, Fred Gill has fulfilled this role for publishers, typesetters and printers, and has used his extensive experience in compiling the Hyphenation Dictionary.

J.O.E.C. − London, 1990.

Contents

Introduction

> For truly, I say to you, till heaven and earth
> pass away, not an iota, not a dot, will pass
> from the law until all is accomplished.
>
> – Matthew 5:18

Punctuation and hyphenation are not all-powerful, but they are both a good deal more important than some people think. In relation to punctuation, the late Eric Partridge, whose book *You Have a Point There* is one of the few classic studies of the pure art of using punctuation marks, was not far wide of the target when he wrote:

> The ability to write a letter is extremely important; and if you think that you can write an even passable letter without knowing how to use [apart from the full point] one and preferably two other stops (comma and semicolon), you are making a grave mistake. To go further: if you think you can write a good business report or an essay or an article, without also knowing how to employ at least two of the remaining stops – the colon, the dash, and the parenthesis – then you are probably overestimating your own abilities as a writer and the intelligence of your readers.

Partridge was writing in 1953, when punctuation was rather more in evidence than it often appears to be today. Even though throughout the twentieth century writers have been scaling down their use of punctuation marks, particularly commas, the general trend of Partridge's argument is not invalidated. But we have not yet reached a time when we can do without stops altogether, and probably we never shall.

1

The Purpose of Punctuation

Punctuation is an essential part of good writing that we all have a duty to master: without it, we cannot make our meaning fully clear; with it, we can enhance the elegance and subtlety of our use of language.

Hyphenation is a branch of punctuation, but it is almost a subject in itself. It is idiosyncratic in operation, but its underlying principles can be learned. The term means not only the insertion of a hyphen into a word or the joining up of two or more words with a hyphen or hyphens, but also the breaking of a word at the end of a line of text, whether handwritten, typed or typeset. Such a break is signalled with a hyphen, and end-of-line hyphenation is an essential ingredient that gives a piece of typed or printed copy that professional look. It is not, therefore, something to be taken for granted or ignored. If you produce justified text (that is, text that has an even appearance on both the left- and the right-hand margins) on your typewriter, word processor or typesetting machine, then familiarity with hyphenation is a skill that you really ought to acquire.

The computer software that runs sophisticated word processors and typesetting equipment these days almost always contains a hyphenation and justification (H & J) program. This is a computer routine that automatically breaks words at the end of a line when necessary in accordance with preset instructions. But often these instructions are geared to American demands and solutions to end-of-line hyphenation problems. What happens if you want to hyphenate according to a different set of rules? What happens when the H & J program breaks down?

The purpose of the second part of this book is to explain the recommended principles of end-of-line hyphenation and to provide a comprehensive word list showing how words should be broken according to the most widely held practices.

It is preceded by a guide to all the other marks of punctuation taken in logical order from the indispensable (the full point) to the arcane (accents, reference symbols and the like). Each topic is explained as clearly as possible, and the uses of every punctuation mark and other sign are illustrated with examples. We also discuss such matters as capitalization, typographical emphasis, and numbers in text. We end our survey with sections on paragraphing, spaces and the hyphen, which serves as an introduction to the extensive word list.

This book is designed for everybody who writes or is connected, however remotely, with the business of putting words on paper — somebody writing a letter to a friend or to the bank manager; an author tapping out a novel or technical manual; an executive responsible for producing a cogent report; a busy secretary who might have to type that report or generate one of his or her own; and a student with an essay or term paper to hand in. We hope that the book will appeal particularly to those with only a sketchy knowledge of the guidelines of punctuation and hyphenation. But we also hope that it will be of value to a busy editor or typesetter who may need a reminder of some of the less common aspects of the subject.

Whether you belong to any of these categories or to none of them, we sincerely hope that you will find this book both instructive and enjoyable. Everybody should be able to punctuate and hyphenate adequately. We trust that this book will provide a way of discovering the principles involved.

A Brief History of Punctuation

Punctuation (or pointing, as it was once called) is the use in handwritten, typed or printed matter of a standard set of signs, symbols and typographical devices (such as capital letters, bold or italic type, etc.) by which meaning is clarified and sentences are split into their grammatical or structural elements. The system of conventional punctuation marks that we now use has evolved since the sixteenth century to divide off words, phrases and clauses from each other within the sentence and to indicate where one sentence ends and the next begins. But those same punctuation marks also serve to indicate pauses in reading, both silently and aloud, and some of them, notably the exclamation mark and the question mark, are tones of voice written down.

Punctuation Before the Age of Printing

Punctuation in its modern form is a by-product of the birth of printing, when the characters and symbols that we use to represent our language first began to achieve their mass-produced, standardized forms. But the use of special signs to indicate pauses in writing is far older than the fifteenth and sixteenth centuries, the era of the earliest printers. Our notions about punctuation were borrowed, along with terms such as colon, comma, and period, from the Greeks. Their punctuation was in practice quite different from ours. But even the Greeks were not the first to break up their written texts with what we might call punctuation marks.

The most ancient instance of a 'punctuated' text so far known is an inscription in the Canaanite language (a Semitic tongue related to Hebrew) dating from the ninth century BC. The 34-line inscription, preserved on the so-called Moabite Stone, is written in an alphabetic script from right to left and tells of the wars fought by King Mesha of Moab against the

Israelites and Edomites. The words of the inscription are separated by dots, and what we might call sentences are marked off from each other by vertical lines. The Moabite Stone was discovered at Diban, east of the Dead Sea, in 1868 and is now in the Louvre, Paris.

Greek alphabetic inscriptions that survive from the sixth century BC and later were mostly carved as continuous lines of capital letters with no separation of words and no punctuation marks. The lines of text often ran in alternate directions, first right to left, then left to right. If the Greeks had been writing modern English, the opening of the American Constitution might have looked like this:

REDRONISETATSDETINUEHTFOELPOEPEHTEW
TOFORMAMOREPERFECTUNIONESTABLISH
YTILIUQNARTCITSEMODERUSNIECITSUJ
PROVIDEFORTHECOMMONDEFENSEPROMOTE
EHTERUCESDNAERAFLEWLARENEGEHT
BLESSINGSOFLIBERTYTOOURSELVESAND
SIHTHSILBATSEDNANIADROODYTIRETSOPRUO
CONSTITUTIONFORTHEUNITEDSTATESOF
ACIREMA

The modern version is of course this:

We the people of the United States, in order to form a more perfect union, establish justice, insure domestic tranquillity, provide for the common defense, promote the general welfare, and secure the blessings of liberty to ourselves and our posterity, do ordain and establish this Constitution for the United States of America.

This example demonstrates why punctuation is so necessary to us. But for the Greeks, unseparated words posed less of a problem than they do for us because the Greek language, being inflected, had more regular word endings than an uninflected language such as English does. The *-os, -a, -on,* etc., of Greek nouns, for instance, functioned almost like word spaces. Nevertheless, in a few inscriptions dating from before the fifth century, groups of words were separated by a vertical row of two or three dots. In the famous Law Code of Gortyn, found on a site in Crete, a single sign consisting of two triangles placed horizontally with their apexes touching is used once to separate a pair of clauses in the code.

The earliest surviving Greek texts written on papyrus date from the fourth century BC. They too are written in undivided capitals. A horizontal line was drawn under the beginning of a line of text in which a new topic was brought in. This mark was called the *papagraphos* and is the origin of our English word *paragraph*.

The Greeks were far more interested in splitting, not words, but whole sections of text that formed discrete units of thought or argument in a piece of writing as defined by the rules of rhetoric. The shortest such unit was a *komma*, the next a *kolon*, and the longest a *periodos*. This approach opened the way for the development of a coherent punctuation system and ultimately led to the one that we know today.

The credit for the invention of the Greek punctuation system is usually assigned to Aristophanes of Byzantium, a scholar who became head of the great library at Alexandria in about 190 BC. He invented a three-point system, in which a point or dot placed high in relation to the letter that it followed signalled the preceding rhetorical unit as being a periodos (period), a centrally placed point indicated a komma (comma), and a point written after the bottom of a letter signalled a kolon (colon). Aristophanes was also said to have invented the system of accents, breathings, and other signs still used in the printing of classical Greek today. His set of symbols included one for a hyphen, which was a curve joining the bottom of the last letter of a word with the bottom of the first letter of the next word. Sadly, the three-point system of Aristophanes was rarely employed, except in a debased form using only two points.

Roman inscriptions, from the earliest to the latest, separated words with points or dots. They also used a large number of abbreviations, a fact which may account for the presence of full points in abbreviations today. Latin manuscripts surviving from the period between the first century BC and the second century AD also show the use of dots to separate words, although this practice was subsequently abandoned in favour of unseparated capitals. The introduction of a new topic was sometimes signalled by a new paragraph, the first letter of which was enlarged and sometimes decorated and projected into the margin. The use of enlarged letters in this way reached artistic heights in the illuminated manuscripts of the Middle Ages and survives today in the use of an enlarged capital to introduce a chapter or lead off a magazine or newspaper article.

From the third century BC, a tally was kept of the number of lines in a manuscript, probably as a way of working out the copyist's fee. A standard line was counted as being about 15 or 16 syllables long. In the course of time, manuscripts began to be written in 'sense lines', with each line representing a coherent thought or complete step in the argument of a piece of writing. St. Jerome, who supervised the Vulgate (the Latin translation of the Bible) between 382 and 405 AD, arranged the manuscript into cola (lines of 8 to 17 syllables) and commata (lines of less than 8 syllables). This arrangement was like that found in the speeches of the great classical orators Demosthenes and Cicero, and was specifically designed to help someone reading the text aloud. Cola and commata (what we might call clauses and phrases) were the origin of the division of each chapter of the Bible into verses. The first letter of each clause or phrase projected

7

into the margin, and the reader was expected to take a breath before each one. Successive editions of the Vulgate preserved this careful punctuation.

In the seventh and eighth centuries, the form and style of lettering changed in manuscripts. Until then, scribes had broadly used undivided capitals known as majuscules. Now copyists introduced minuscule letters, which had parts that projected above or below the average vertical extent of a line of text. We now call these parts ascenders and descenders. Minuscule letters resembled modern lower-case letters.

Now also, for the first time, words were divided from each other by spaces. Anglo-Saxon, German and Irish scribes, to whom Latin was a foreign language, were chief among those who introduced this practice. Spaces were always left at the end of a sentence, and an enlarged letter, usually a majuscule, was used to start a new sentence as well as a new paragraph. A point, placed high or low, was written inside or following a sentence, and a compound point (two or three points written together) might signal the end of a sentence.

Towards the end of the eighth century, Charlemagne, King of the Franks and Holy Roman Emperor, presided over an educational revival led by his Anglo-Saxon adviser Alcuin. The revival laid stress on improvements in spelling and punctuation in Biblical and liturgical manuscripts. Over the next century, new marks appeared: the primitive comma (in fact just a plain point), the question mark and the punctus elevatus (a kind of inverted semicolon). An arrow-head was commonly used to signal a quotation.

The end-of-line hyphen (often doubled) appeared towards the end of the tenth century. By the twelfth century, a mark resembling a figure 7 (known as a punctus circumflexus) came into use to indicate a pause and a rise in the pitch of the voice at the end of certain clauses. In the thirteenth and fourteenth centuries, the virgule or solidus (/) came into use as a pause mark. It proved to be the forerunner of the modern comma. The simple point was finally emerging as the end-of-sentence marker.

During the fifteenth century books appeared in a new form of script known as the Italian humanist style. After 1450 the punctus elevatus and punctus circumflexus fell out of use, and the virgule was widely used along with what we now think of as the colon (:) to mark slight pauses. Parentheses (round brackets) appeared in 1500, and the earlier printers, notably those in Italy, borrowed the Greek question mark for use as a pause mark between the comma and the colon. This eventually became known as the semicolon (;).

By the time printing had got under way, most of the elements of our punctuation system had been finalized. In 1566 Aldus Manutius the Younger (1547–1597), grandson of the famous printer of Venice whose name he shared, published *Orthographiae Ratio*, a Latin spelling system in which he described, under different names, the modern comma, semicolon, colon and full point. By the end of the seventeenth century all the punctuation marks now in use had acquired their modern names, and the apostrophe, dash, exclamation mark and quotation marks had been added to the punctuation 'pantheon'.

The Approaches to Punctuation

The Greeks and Romans punctuated their writing in accordance with rhetoric and oratory. Initially, texts were broken up in a way that helped to get the argument across in manageable 'chunks' of clear and consistent thought. Later the punctuation was designed to mark off breathing points to aid the reading out loud of a speech or other public utterance. In the Middle Ages, the most accurate punctuation was reserved for Biblical, liturgical and other religious texts that might have to be read out loud as part of Christian ritual. The punctuation marks signalled pauses of differing lengths, for breath or for dramatic or oratorical effect.

Punctuation up to the beginning of the age of printing was haphazard. The symbols used were rarely consistent: often a simple point meant a short pause, such as that signalled by a comma, as well as a long pause, indicating the end of a sentence. Moreover, the virgule and the simple point might mean the same thing − i.e. a short breath mark.

The confusion did not end with standardization of the system in the sixteenth and seventeenth centuries. Although widely accepted relative values were assigned to the main punctuation marks or stops (so that one full point was considered equal to two colons, three semicolons or four commas), the use of punctuation marks in written texts veered between two extremes − the elocutionary or rhetorical, in which the marks, employed quite freely, stood for the different lengths of pauses observed by someone reading aloud to an audience or congregation, and the syntactical, in which the marks were used more systematically to separate out from each other the grammatical building blocks that made up the structure of a sentence or paragraph.

In regard to English punctuation, the syntactical approach had won the day by the end of the seventeenth century. Among its proponents had been the dramatist Ben Jonson, whose *English Grammar*, written in about 1617, was published posthumously in 1640. From about 1660 onwards, syntactical punctuation was the norm. But rhetorical or elocutionary pauses often coincide with breaks required by syntax, and modern punctuation, although basically syntactical, also takes note of the subtleties of rhetoric.

Heavy and Light: Close or Open Punctuation
During the eighteenth century, excessive, or 'close' punctuation became endemic. Alexander Pope wrote in the

Prologue to his Satires:

> Commas and points they set exactly right,
> And 'twere a sin to rob them of their mite.

The worst offenders in this respect used a comma to introduce every subordinate clause or separable phrase. Pedantic writers on grammar made up rules for correct punctuation. One author gave 40 rules governing the use of the comma.

It was not until 1906 that the brothers H.W. and F.G. Fowler, in their book *The King's English*, outlined a rational punctuation system in which the light, or 'open', use of stops was recommended. Since then the trend has continued in the direction of 'open' punctuation, reducing the use of punctuation marks to a minimum. As G.V. Carey put it in his short guide to punctuation *Mind the Stop*: 'At its best . . . modern punctuation uses no more stops than are needed to give immediate clarity and force to the sense; and beyond that point it can hardly go.'

Chapter 1

Full Point

The symbol . (⊙ in a proof correction or typescript amendment) represents the full point, full stop, or period. This is the one punctuation mark whose presence is obligatory in every sentence that is not a question or an exclamation. Obligatory, that is, unless you happen to be James Joyce, for example. Joyce wrote the last 46 pages of his epic *Ulysses* without using any punctuation at all. However, not everybody is an experimental writer like Joyce, and most people work on the principle that all non-interrogative, non-exclamatory sentences end in a full point. The sentence that you are reading now ends in one. So does this one. In the United Kingdom, the full point is generally known as the full stop, except among printers and typographers. In the United States, it is called a period.

Full Point at the End of a Sentence

Three main types of sentences end in full points. They are direct statements, indirect questions, and polite or formal requests.

1. Direct Statements. The full point is the mark that rounds off a sentence, pure and simple. These examples illustrate its use:

Anne arrived at the office early.

She took off her raincoat and sat down at her desk.

Tom will be in town again on Thursday.

History of the Full Point

The use of a single point to end a sentence grew up gradually as part of the great medieval punctuation system. It was general practice by the 14th century: witness a closing line from the Canon's Yeoman's Tale by Chaucer: "And ther a poynt; for ended is my tale." The full point emerged in the punctuation of the 16th century at the top of a hierarchy of stops. We can think of it as being equivalent in terms of time units to two colons, three semicolons or four commas. Today the idea of time units may have gone, but we still consider the full point as primarily a pause mark − in fact, the most emphatic pause mark of all.

The word *period*, the regular term for the full point in the United States, looks back over more than 2,000 years to the punctuation system attributed to Aristophanes of Byzantium. Aristophanes used a simple point to mark the end of the *periodos*, the longest and most complete division of rhetorical discourse. A long, involved complex sentence is still called a period, and it is natural that the stop signalling the end of such a sentence should also take this name.

The defective sentence. Certain utterances that lack a finite verb or obvious subject, and therefore not strictly allowable as sentences, nevertheless end in a full point as if they were sentences. The second "sentence" in each of these examples is typical of what we might call the defective sentence.

Angela did not dislike her job. Far from it.

Tom would never say such a thing. Of course not.

Defective sentences such as these almost always have a strong connection with what has gone before, either as answers to questions or as contradictions or reinforcements of a previous statement. Generally they are elliptical expressions, and a main subject or finite verb is readily understood in working out their meaning. For example:

Where's the car? In the garage.

I believe he's gone to China. Quite right.

Here we could have written "It is in the garage" or "That is quite right".

Defective sentences can be as short as one word and still take a full point. For example:

What's for breakfast? Toast.

Was he willing to be chairman? Certainly.

Is there life on the Moon? No.

We'll have to dismiss him. Agreed.

Greetings or salutations, such as "Hello", "Cheers", etc., although strictly exclamations, may be written with a full point, especially when no emotional or dramatic connotation is involved.

Defective sentences lacking a subject are illustrated by the following examples. In each case the missing subject of the second sentence is understood to be the same as that of the first.

She enjoyed her work. Loved it, in fact.

His patriotism was not in doubt. Was not even to be suspected, since he had performed many deeds of heroism for his country.

14

Full points used in this way provide a clear break that lends weight to an emphatic or rhetorical effect. Such a mode of expression is likely to be used by journalists or political speech-writers. In ordinary writing, however, a different kind of punctuation is to be preferred, as in:

She enjoyed her work — loved it, in fact.

His patriotism was not in doubt: was not even to be suspected, since he had performed ... etc.

A few writers indulge in defective sentences in writing descriptive or racy passages. For instance, a string of noun phrases might be separated by full points, as in:

The beach was crowded with every example of the British holidaymaker. Little girls with buckets making sandcastles. Horrid little boys knocking the sandcastles down or playing French cricket with reluctant fathers. Young bikini-clad beauties worshipping the sun. Old men snoozing in deck chairs. Homely women eating candy floss.

The sequence could easily be extended.

Conservative authors and editors frown on this kind of writing. In the United States it is known as the period fault. Careful writers would probably prefer to punctuate the above example as one sentence using commas or semicolons, yet full points in such passages are great attention-getters, purely because their use is unorthodox.

2. Indirect Questions. An indirect question is a statement with a question embedded in it. So the correct punctuation for an indirect question is a full point, not a question mark. Note the difference between these two examples:

What time is the train due to leave?

She asked what time the train was due to leave.

The first is a direct question and takes a question mark. The second, being an indirect question, takes a full point.

As we shall see in a later section on quotation marks, thought can be represented verbatim, as it were, without the quotation marks being present. So sentences like this are not uncommon:

What would he be like? she wondered.

This is a sentence containing a quoted question, but there are no quotation marks round the question itself. However, the position and even the presence of the question mark is open to some controversy. Omission of the question mark and its replacement by a comma is probably the most usual form of punctuation in this kind of sentence:

What would he be like, she wondered.

We shall discuss this aspect of the question in detail in the sections on the question mark and exclamation mark.

3. Polite or Formal Requests. These are logically not questions but very weak commands. They therefore end with a full point.

Could you please send me a copy of your latest catalogue.

May I draw your attention to the mistake on page four.

Full Point and Quotation Marks

Writers and editors in the United States generally place a full point inside quotation marks regardless of whether the full point belongs to the quoted material or not. British writers and editors place the full point inside the quotation marks if it ends the quotation and outside if not. These examples illustrate the idea:

American usage:

> "Sheila," said John, "I love you."

> Tom's ideas were not crazy. He liked to think of them as
> "modern."

British usage:

> "Sheila," said John, "I love you."

> Tom's ideas were not crazy. He liked to think of them as
> "modern".

Note that the only difference between these pairs of examples
is the placing of the full point in the last one.

An important principle to bear in mind is that when the
end of a quotation coincides with the end of the whole
sentence, the full point ending the quotation goes inside the
quotation marks and the full point ending the whole sentence
is suppressed. For a full discussion of all punctuation in
relation to quotation marks, see the chapter on Quotation
marks later in this guide.

Non-punctuational uses

Three categories of the non-punctuational use of the full
point are discussed here: its employment in abbreviations,
with initials and with numerals.

1. Abbreviations. Some publishers continue to follow H.W.
Fowler, who in his book *Modern English Usage* suggested
that if an abbreviated word consists of the first and last
letters of that word, then the full point ought to be omitted
after the abbreviation; otherwise it should be included. First-
and-last-letter abbreviations are sometimes called
contractions. Following Fowler, we are supposed to write, for
example, Capt. (with a full point) for Captain, but Cpl (with
no full point) for Corporal. Another recommendation is that

of the compilers of *The Oxford Dictionary for Writers and Editors*, who say that single-letter abbreviations and abbreviations consisting of a mixture of upper- and lower-case letters should (with certain exceptions) take a full point. Thus we should write Jan. for January and Yorks. for Yorkshire, but Hants (no full point) for Hampshire.

Whatever the established authorities say, however, the modern trend in the United Kingdom is now towards an "open" style for abbreviations, in which there are few full points. A more conservative approach predominates in the United States, where full points are still required in many abbreviations.

It is impossible to make hard and fast rules on the use or omission of a full point in a given abbreviation. The best recommendation is to follow the house style if you are writing for publication, avoid ambiguity and be consistent. The following brief selective lists of common abbreviations are based as far as possible on present-day usage. Remember too that if you are writing for publication, some abbreviations derived from foreign words ought to be set in italic.

Use a full point in the following:

anon. (for anonymous)
approx.
c., *ca.* (for *circa* - prefer *c.*)
Co.
et al.
etc. (prefer this form to the now old-fashioned &c.)
ibid.
in. (for inch)
mi. (for mile)
No. or no. (for number – plural Nos., nos.)
op. cit.

p. (page)
pp. (pages)
viz.

In the United States the symbol # is commonly used for
number. The abbreviation No. or no. ought, however, to be
substituted in what you write in order to prevent readers
outside the United States being puzzled and to avoid
confusion with the proof-reader's symbol still regularly used
in Britain to mark a space.

For abbreviations of the names of states in the United
States, follow American traditional practice and use a full
point, e.g. Pa. for Pennsylvania, and Mo. for Missouri. For
addresses the US postal service uses capital letters and no full
points – PA and MO.

Do not use full points in the following:

C (Celsius or centigrade, used in quoting temperatures)
Dr (Doctor)
E (east)
f or ff (following)
K (kelvin temperature)
Ltd (limited)
M
Mlle } (modes of address in French)
Mme
Mr
Mrs } (modes of address in English)
Ms
N (north)
NE (north-east)
NW (north-west)
p (pence)
per cent
Rev or Revd (Reverend)

Rd (Road)
S (south)
SE (south-east)
St (Saint, Street)
SW (south-west)
W (west)

Do not use a full point with scientific units or weights and measures, except for in. (inch) and l. (litre), where ambiguity might arise (see the section on numbers in text).

Do not use a full point with chemical symbols or formulae: Au, C, Ca, H, N, O, Pb, H-16−2-16-O.

For a note on the plurals of abbreviations, *see* the section on the Apostrophe.

2. Initials. The coining of initials, in particular those that stand for organizations, is one of the biggest growth industries of our generation, and a selective list is hardly likely to scratch the surface. Suffice it to say that for initials involving capitals the full point is now very much the exception rather than the rule. B.B.C. is old hat and BBC is now widely accepted, even by the BBC.

When it comes to company names, the conscientious writer and editor will find out the preferred abbreviation from the firm concerned. Thus British Petroleum itself prefers BP, not B.P., and AT&T is what the American Telephone and Telegraph Company likes to be called.

"Euro-abbreviations" such as CAP, EEC, EFTA, MEP and so on, do not take full points. With regard to other organizations, write, for example, PLO, KGB, not P.L.O., K.G.B.

Capital initials can, if the typography allows it, be rendered by small capitals. The forms AD and BC, rarely seen with full points these days, regularly appear in small capitals. So too do academic qualifications, such as BA or DD, and the designations MP or PC (Privy Councillor), when written after somebody's name.

Lower-case initials tend to cling to their full points, notably i.e, e.g., a.m., p.m., q.v. and the like. But the form emf (for electromotive force) is replacing e.m.f. The abbreviations ecu (European currency unit) and plc (public limited company – also written PLC) have never had full points.

Initials that form pronounceable words are known as acronyms, and some well-known examples are ACAS, ANZUS, GATT, NATO, NATSOPA, SOGAT, UCCA, UNESCO and VAT. Some of these forms can be written as words with an upper-case initial, e.g. Nato, Unesco and Sogat. Full points are still the norm when quoting the initials of a person's name. H.G. Wells (not HG Wells, although some publishers do like H G Wells). How the initials in a name should be spaced is a matter of debate. H. G. Wells (with a space after each point) is still the general custom, but the closing up of initials with full points has become common practice with the introduction of word processors.

If an abbreviation or set of initials closing with a full point comes at the end of a sentence, do not put in another full point to finish the sentence off. All the other stops, however, follow a full point when it closes an abbreviation or set of initials.

For forty years Henry had been employed by the firm of Trotter & Co. (not "Trotter & Co..")

Come to my office at 5 p.m., Jones.

3. Numerals. A full point may be used after Arabic or Roman numerals in a list.

The agenda is as follows:

1. Minutes of the last meeting

2. Matters arising
3. Secretary's report
4. Any other business

or:

The four states of matter encountered in nature are:
I. Solid
II. Liquid
III. Gas
IV. Plasma

Alternatively, the numerals can be enclosed in parentheses or followed by a half-bracket, in which case they should not take a full point: (5) or 5); (v) or v).

Decimal Point. A full point is commonly used in printed text to precede a decimal fraction. It is also used in quoting sums of money:

    2.5   0.428571   £30.62 $120.79

Mathematical texts may use a centred point for a decimal point:

    2·5   0·428571   £30·62 $120·79

In Britain a full point is often used when quoting the time in the hours-and-minutes format.

10.25   6.05 p.m.   8.00 a.m. (or 8.0 a.m)   19.45

In North America a colon is commonly used instead of a full point in quoting the time in the above form.

All-figure formats for dates usually take full points or slashes (solidi), but remember that the British and American formats differ. See the chapter on Numbers in text.

22

```
29.5.89   or   29/5/89 (UK)

5.29.89   or   5/29/89 (USA)
```

In both of the above examples, the date rendered is 29 May, 1989.

4. Leaders. Widely spaced groups of two or three full points used in tables to guide the eye when reading related items are called leaders. They can be useful in helping to make a complex table more readable, but care should be taken to avoid a cluttered effect. Leaders should be used only when absolutely necessary. They should also be carefully positioned, one group of dots lying directly above the other:

Table of Contents

For the use of three and four full points to denote missing text or faltering dialogue, see the section on the ellipsis. *See also* the chapter on the Paragraph for full points in headings.

Chapter 2

Comma

From the full point, the most emphatic of stops, we turn to
the comma, the least emphatic but the next in importance.
The sign for this punctuation mark is , (⸲ or ⊙ in corrections
to proofs or handwritten amendments to typescripts).

The comma is the most ubiquitous and, it would seem, the
most misused of all punctuation marks in English. G.V.
Carey, in *Mind the Stop*, called it 'Punctuational Enemy No.
1'. Putting a comma in the wrong place or not putting it in
the right one certainly accounts for a lot of the mistakes in its
use. But peppering one's text with commas is a far worse
error; as one writer has succinctly put it: 'Commas are for
sense not decoration.'

In line with a modern tendency to reduce all punctuation to
a minimum, experienced writers today use far fewer commas
than their predecessors ever did. Their practice is governed by
a desire not to slow down the pace of the text and a belief
that the reader will be distracted — even irritated — by being
brought up short too many times by too many commas. They
emphasize the role of the comma as a way of marking out the
syntax or grammatical structure of a sentence rather than as a
pure stop. This grammatical approach to the comma is
especially important in writing non-fiction. But all careful
writers are sensitive not only to the comma's purely
grammatical applications but also to its rhetorical or
elocutionary use in marking a short but often crucial pause.
For example, the sentence

History of the Comma

A mark looking more or less like a comma or a modern figure 7 was in use in medieval times, but its function as a stop was not consistent. Often a single point served to mark a pause that would now be rendered by a comma.

The modern comma symbol dates from the fifteenth century. It was descended from the virgule or solidus (/), which up until then had been used to denote a brief pause in text. Scribes placed the virgule next to the upper part of a preceding letter. In the course of time, however, it sank to the baseline and became curved, thereby giving rise to the comma as we know it today. The virgule persisted as a stop into the age of printing: it can be found in a number of early sixteenth-century books. (It is perhaps worth noting that the modern French word for comma is indeed *virgule*.)

The word comma itself comes through Latin from the Greek word *komma*, a noun formed from the verb *koptein*, 'to cut'. *Komma* meant, in effect, 'a part cut off'. The ancient Greek grammarians used this word to denote the shortest section of a piece of rhetorical text and, by transference, the symbol signalling the end of such a section. Thinking of the present-day comma as a mark that 'cuts off' sections of text is still a valid guide to its modern punctuational usage.

She walked into the room and found her husband there.

is a matter-of-fact statement, but

She walked into the room, and found her husband there.

conjures up a *double entendre* or a layer of meaning that could be rather sinister. Using the comma properly needs a

feeling for both good grammar and good taste — backed up
with common sense and a little observational skill.

Commas between Clauses

A comma marks off discrete sections of a sentence, or to put
it another way, a comma helps to parcel up the bits of a
sentence that belong together and keeps them apart from the
bits to which they do not belong. The most significant
components of a sentence are clauses.

1. Between Independent Clauses. Independent clauses are
clauses that can stand alone as separate sentences without any
grammatical connectives (such as conjunctions) but are
nevertheless linked by sense or logic. Independent clauses can
be treated as separate sentences, being separated by full
points, as in:

> I came. I saw. I conquered.

The cumulative effect of these statements is better seen,
however, if they can be put into a single sentence. But how
should we punctuate this sentence? The answer is to use
commas:

> I came, I saw, I conquered.

In choosing this well-worn example, we have probably lighted
upon the only general instance when commas between
independent clauses are regarded as permissible — that is, the
situation in which three or more independent clauses are
linked together. We can justify it mainly on the ground that
words or short phrases in a list are separated by commas. We
shall come back to lists later.

The placing of a comma between two independent clauses
in a sentence is a practice frowned on by most writers,
especially in the United States, where it is considered a
'comma fault'. So there is a ban on such sentences as:

They could not go on, the road was blocked by a fallen tree.

The explanation for the prohibition is that a comma, being the weakest stop available, is too brief a pause between two stand-alone statements that would in the normal course of events be separated by a full point but are in this case too closely connected for a full point to be used. The connection between them ought to be signalled by a conjunction or, failing that, another stronger stop — namely, a semicolon. The sentence should therefore be punctuated:

They could not go on; the road was blocked by a fallen tree.

(Incidentally, we could have written earlier 'I came; I saw; I conquered'. Such a form is allowable but rather literary. *See* the chapter on Semicolon.)

2. Between Co-ordinate Clauses. The use of a comma between co-ordinate clauses in a sentence — i.e., clauses of equal status connected to each other by co-ordinating conjunctions such as *and, but, for, neither, nor, or*, etc. — depends (in British English, at least) on the length of the clauses, the closeness of the link between the clauses, and the writer's overriding duty to eliminate all ambiguity from the mind of the reader, however fleeting that may be.

On purely syntactical grounds, no commas are needed in the following plain statements:

John has bought a computer and is using it for work.

John has bought a computer but can only use it for work.

In these two sentences, both clauses share the same subject, and because the clauses are short, there is no need to repeat the subject or commute it to the corresponding pronoun. Even if we had made the sentences read:

John has bought a computer and he is using it for work.

John has bought a computer but he can only use it for work.

there would clearly still be no need for a comma between the two clauses, mainly because the links between them are so close.

When the subject is different, however, notions of contrast arise. Many writers under these circumstances, especially those in the United States, feel that a comma before the conjunction is required, as in:

John has bought a computer, and Jane has bought a typewriter.

John has bought a computer, but Jane is using it all the time for her word processing tasks.

Some British writers might balk at using a comma in sentences such as these, but a comma before a clause in which the matter is significantly different is usually essential:

Helen thought of herself as photogenic, but the camera doesn't lie.

He was dying to go out to the pub for a drink, and the dog obliged him by asking to be taken for a walk.

If you are seeking guidelines, the tag 'Change the subject; chuck in a comma' might not be a bad rule of thumb. Although not expressed in the most refined terms, it does have the important merit of being clear and consistent — something punctuation rarely is but always should be.

In the next, more complicated, sentence we insert our first comma mainly in order to clear up doubt — in this case, to stop the reader from momentarily thinking that John and David want to develop a brewery as well as the site. But what we said earlier about changing subjects reinforces our need for both commas here.

John and David want to develop the site, and a brewery is backing their challenge, but the owners of the land are trying to put off making a decision until next year.

Commas between co-ordinate clauses where subjects change are, however, not necessarily obligatory. At the risk of taking back our rule of thumb, we must concede that in the next examples, even though the subjects change, adding a comma is superfluous:

The band played and everyone danced.

Tessa sings quite well but Caroline is tone-deaf.

She agreed with them but I did not.

No commas are needed here for three very good reasons:

1. All the clauses are short
2. They are closely linked with each other
3. None of the sentences is likely to be misleading or ambiguous for readers

In the light of all this we have to restate our rule of thumb relating to commas between clauses linked by a co-ordinate conjunctions: 'Change the subject, chuck in a comma, but check for linkage, brevity and clarity first'.

3. Between Main and Subordinate Clauses. Every normal sentence must have a subject and a main finite verb, a verb whose special distinguishing features — tense, mood, person, etc. — tie it to that subject. The clause containing the subject and the main verb, together a predicate that may or may not be present (depending on the nature of the verb), is known as the main clause. Other clauses may be dependent on the main clause or some of its components: these are known as subordinate clauses and are introduced by subordinating conjunctions, such as *after*, *before*, *that*, *who*, *which*, *when*, etc.

In the golden age of the over-punctuator, back in the eighteenth century, a comma was virtually obligatory between a main clause and a subordinate clause. Noun clauses introduced by 'that' were always preceded by commas. These days the best writers generally avoid commas — they never use them before 'that' clauses at all. Any commas that are used are there for rhetorical purposes or for making vital grammatical distinctions and eliminating doubt. The latter, non-rhetorical, uses of the comma are in fact mandatory.

Each of the following examples consists of a main clause followed by one subordinate clause. All are plain statements. None of them contains ambiguities, none of them poses a grammatical problem, so none of them requires any commas.

She left the office early that day because she was going out to the theatre in the evening.

I'd love to read that book when you've finished with it.

He said that he would come.

No commas are needed when two subordinate clauses follow the main clause, provided that each clause is dependent on the one before:

He said that he would come when he could.

John said that Jane could use his computer whenever she liked.

When more than two subordinate clauses follow a main clause, however, a comma is usually advisable:

John said that Jane could use his computer whenever she liked, as long as she was careful with it.

30

A comma may separate a main clause from a subordinate clause for various reasons, mostly to do with the comma's rhetorical uses. However, a comma is valuable in denoting certain shifts of meaning that may be rather subtle. Compare these pairs of examples:

a) I am doing this job because I need the money.

Don't lecture me, because I won't stand for it.

b) He would be able to have some coffee when the milk arrived.

He had just resigned himself to having black coffee, when the milk arrived.

Since. A significant use of the comma in this connection is encountered in distinguishing between the two senses of *since*: the causal sense, in which since equals 'because' or 'for', and the temporal sense, in which since means 'during the period following the time when'. A comma is regularly used to signal the causal since; the absence of a comma usually indicates the temporal since. Thus the comma is essential in sorting out these two sentences:

I haven't seen her in London, since she got married last year. (causal)

I haven't seen her in London since she got married last year. (temporal)

Using a comma between a main clause and a following subordinate clause is generally restricted to the instances we have already described. When a subordinate clause precedes a main clause, a comma is much more likely to be used. But such a comma can be left out if the subject of both clauses is the same and especially if the subordinate clause is short. No commas are needed in these two sentences:

When he moved to Berlin he bought a flat.

Before I go I must tell you this joke.

But commas are needed in these:

Whether you like it or not, she will have to go.

As I told you yesterday, we have asked Smith to accept the position of chairman.

When John left, the house was all locked up securely.

If he dies, there will have to be a post mortem examination.

In the last two examples, the comma is essential in stopping the reader from assuming at first sight that (a) *the house* is the object of the verb *left*, and (b) *there* functions as an adverb modifying the verb *dies*.

If you are in doubt about using a comma between a subordinate clause and a following main clause, you should feel free to use one. Such commas are not wrong, always provided of course that they do not cause confusion in the reader's mind. Using commas between a main and a following subordinate clause, however, needs careful thought. Ideally, the comma should be reserved for clarifying doubt, marking distinctions in sense, and only rarely for achieving subtle rhetorical effects.

Commas and Relative Clauses
Relative clauses are adjectival subordinate clauses that qualify a noun. There are two types: specifying relative clauses define or specify the noun, picking it out, as it were, from a host of others of its kind; non-specifying relative clauses add extra information about a noun that has already been implicitly or explicitly specified or identified.

One of the few but also one of the most important genuine

rules of punctuation is that a comma must never be used with a specifying clause but must always be used with a non-specifying clause. Here are some examples:

He is the man who came looking for you yesterday. (specifying)

The car that I bought from the garage up the road has broken down three times in the past month. (specifying)

The statement that she made to the police turned out to be false. (specifying)

America's third man in space was John Glenn, who made three orbits of the Earth in February 1962. (non-specifying)

The postman, who had lived in the village all his life, greatly resented the newcomers. (non-specifying)

The mole, which spends nearly all its life underground, has very poor vision. (non-specifying)

It is hard to overstress the importance of the job that the comma performs in distinguishing between specifying and non-specifying clauses. If a writer fails to use the comma properly in this respect, he or she is likely to be misunderstood. A wrongly placed comma, or the absence of a comma when it should be there, can change the meaning of a sentence completely, often with results that are at best embarrassing, at worst insulting or insensitive:

This exacting career requires intelligence and is unlikely to appeal to women, who feel that their place is in the home. (Remove the comma to remove the insult.)

The pope who is Bishop of Rome is the head of the Roman Catholic Church. (How many popes are there? Insert a comma after *pope* to show that there is only one and we are adding extra information about him.)

33

We have so far skated over the fact that in a couple of our examples the relative clause has been 'embedded' in the main clause. When the relative clause is a non-specifying one, we need not one but two commas to mark it off from the surrounding main clause. Remember what we said earlier about cutting off or 'parcelling up' the parts of a sentence that should be taken together. In our next example, correctly comma'd, we note the two commas that mark off the non-specifying clause from the rest of the sentence:

The pope, who is Bishop of Rome, is head of the Roman Catholic Church.

The fact that the pope is Bishop of Rome is a piece of extra information about him that can, grammatically at least, be dispensed with. The words:

The pope is head of the Roman Catholic Church.

still make a coherent sentence. There is a loss of information but not a change in meaning. The clause 'who is Bishop of Rome' stands outside the main sentence structure in terms of grammar and is also peripheral to the meaning of the sentence. It is a parenthetical phrase and as such is marked off by commas.

These comments provide a useful test for whether one is dealing with a specifying or non-specifying relative clause. In the example just discussed, a non-specifying clause, comma'd off from the rest of the sentence, can be removed without losing the basic meaning of the sentence because it adds extra detail that is marginal to the issue. In the case of a specifying relative clause, however, the detail contained in the clause is anything but marginal. Consider an earlier example:

The car that I bought in the garage up the road has broken down three times in a month.

If we take out the relative clause, we are left with 'The car has broken down three times in a month.' This immediately begs the question 'Which car?' Something material has been lost: namely, the information identifying or specifying the car. The missing clause is therefore a specifying relative clause and should not have commas around it.

Parenthetical Commas

Any word or group of words that naturally stands outside the main framework of the sentence is parenthetical. In practice, this means an adverb or adverbial phrase that modifies a clause or part of a clause; a certain type of subordinate clause that lies within a main clause upon which it depends (a non-specifying relative clause, for example); and even an independent clause or sentence introduced into another sentence as an aside.

Punctuation provides a number of different ways of signalling the breaks between the parenthetical and the main material, ranging from nothing at all to the abrupt interruption of the dash.

The comma is, next to the use of no punctuation at all, the lightest and least disruptive way of signalling parenthetical material. For example:

> Mr Harrington, the owner of the painting, was surprised that it had fetched such a high price at the auction.

> Everyone remarked that Thomson, not usually given to expressions of emotion, had cried like a baby on the night of his mother's death.

> He was, poor fellow, completely distraught.

When the parenthetical material comes in the middle of a sentence, it must be both introduced and followed by a comma, as in these examples. Writers sometimes forget this and use only one comma:

The mole, which spends most of its life underground has very poor vision. (Insert a second comma after *underground*.)

The day when it finally came, dawned like any other. (Insert a comma after *day*.)

A parenthetical phrase at the start of a sentence takes only one comma — that is, the one that follows it and cuts it off from the main sentence:

In an open letter to the prime minister, the leader of the opposition accused her of being anti-European.

Apart from a childhood interest in stamp collecting, he had had few hobbies in his life.

A modern tendency is to use no commas after short introductory phrases or one-word sentence modifiers, except to avoid any ambiguity. Thus no comma is now normally needed in the following:

Normally I do not write sentences like this, but my editor insists upon them. (No need for comma after *normally*.)

As far as I know he doesn't live in London any more.

But commas in the following examples help the reader to avoid comprehending the adverbs in the opening phrases as prepositions or conjunctions.

Inside, the house had been decorated in the most modern style.

A few weeks before, the event had already been advertised in the local newspapers.

On the morning of 30 January 1649 King Charles I walked and talked; half an hour after, his head was cut off.

The last example, rather an old chestnut, also serves to illustrate the modern practice of no longer following dates with commas. The same is true of simple year dates used in introductory parenthetic phrases. Thus we now write:

In 1989 Konrad Lorenz, the famous behavioural scientist, died.

A comma after 'In 1989' would now be considered unacceptably fussy or old-fashioned, except when another number follows it, as in this example:

On 8 January 1989, 47 people died when a Boeing 737 airliner crashed onto the M1 motorway near Kegworth, Leicestershire.

Parenthetic words or phrases at the end of a sentence take only the introductory comma. The second comma coincides with and is absorbed by the final full point of the sentence. Note the last word in the above example. Note also the following:

He was met at the door by Jarvis, a tall handsome man in his early 40s.

A parenthetical phrase at the end of a clause separated from the next clause by a semicolon or colon also loses its second comma by the same rule, as in these examples:

The report is concise, as we have already explained: it presents its case in only 32 pages.

She was overburdened with worries, poor girl; yet she bore them all with uncomplaining fortitude.

Conjunctive adverbs — words such as *moreover*, *however*, etc., that connect sentences or clauses to previous sentences or clauses in the manner of conjunctions — are traditionally set off by commas from the rest of the clause or sentence that they modify. We shall have more to say about conjunctive adverbs when we discuss the semicolon. Meanwhile, we shall provide just two examples here:

Moreover, there is little doubt that this man is a scoundrel.

Much can be said, however, for his inspirational qualities as a writer.

or:

However, much can be said for his inspirational qualities as a writer. (Note that a comma after 'However' is obligatory here because of the confusion with 'However much'.)

1. Commas with Participial Phrases. A parenthetical adjectival phrase containing a participle – a verbal adjective – is generally set off from the rest of a sentence by commas:

Walking into town the other day, I was stopped by a man driving a large black car, who asked me for directions to the nearest garage.

John, seeing Helen unconscious on the floor, immediately phoned for a doctor.

Not all participial phrases are parenthetical, however. No commas are needed in the following examples, where the participial phrase is integral to the sentence and not peripheral to it.

John saw Helen lying unconscious on the floor and immediately phoned for a doctor.

He saw the men tearing down the poster.

Note the comma-ing in this sentence:

John, seeing Helen lying unconscious on the floor, immediately phoned for a doctor.

Using participial phrases can hold traps for the unwary. Do please avoid absurdities like these:

Driving through the desert, the sun beat down relentlessly.

Hurrying down the street, her handbag fell into a puddle.

2. Absolute Constructions. One of the trickiest aspects of using the comma in parenthetical phrases concerns the so-called absolute construction. An absolute construction is a phrase containing a present participle and a subject and/or predicate that stands outside the grammatical framework of a sentence. It is very easy to get the commas wrong in a sentence containing such a construction. The following example is incorrect:

Liverpool, having won the FA Cup, their match against Arsenal assumed great importance because a win would give them the League championship as well.

The first comma is wrong because the absolute construction in this sentence is the phrase 'Liverpool having won the FA Cup'. The sentence, correctly punctuated, reads:

Liverpool having won the FA Cup, their match against Arsenal assumed great importance because a win would give them the League championship as well.

Here is one more example of an absolute construction, with the commas placed correctly:

The protesting students having taken over the main square of the city, the authorities retaliated by sending in troops against them.

3. Appositional and Restrictive Uses. Parenthetical phrases that stand in apposition to a noun or serve to restrict its meaning or application are regularly marked off from the rest of a sentence by commas. This example illustrates both apposition ('a grocer's daughter from Grantham, Lincolnshire') and restriction ('Grantham, Lincolnshire', not any other Grantham):

Margaret Roberts, a grocer's daughter from Grantham, Lincolnshire, dreamed of someday becoming prime minister of Great Britain. (Note that the second comma required for the whole appositional phrase and the second comma needed after the restrictive phrase coalesce into one.)

Whether one uses commas to mark appositional nouns and phrases these days is increasingly a matter of taste. Eric Partridge claimed to see a difference in meaning between 'This is my cousin, John Smith.' (= this is my only cousin, and his name is John Smith) and 'This is my cousin John Smith' (= I have several cousins, and this particular one is named John Smith). Few people now subscribe to this distinction, and one can use a comma or not. On the whole, journalists not wishing to have too many commas slowing down their snappy prose will go for 'My cousin John Smith', just as they write of 'Prime minister Margaret Thatcher'. However, no journalist or any other writer is likely to omit the commas in this example:

Margaret Thatcher, Britain's prime minister, visited Paris on the 200th anniversary of the French Revolution.

The purely restrictive use of commas, especially in place names and identifications, is retained by today's writers; the forms 'Kegworth, Leicestershire', 'Paris, France', and 'London, Ontario' are still the norm. But beware the omission of that all-important second comma in the middle of a sentence. These examples are correct and should be followed:

He was born in Paris, Texas.

After moving to Shaftesbury, Dorset, in the 1950s, Mr Jones became a well-respected member of the community.

She attended school at Cheltenham, Gloucestershire.

This example is wrong but amazingly prevalent among all writers:

She was born at Grantham, Lincolnshire and educated at Somerville College, Oxford during the 1940s. (We need commas after both 'Lincolnshire' and 'Oxford'.)

The Vocative Comma, or Comma of Address. One final parenthetical use of commas needs to be mentioned. The name of a person or thing addressed or apostrophized in a speech, piece of dialogue, poem, etc., is set off with commas:

Come on, Jones. Get a move on.

You, sir, are a scoundrel.

Where do you think you're going, dog?

'Lord, thou hast been our refuge in every generation.'

Commas in Quotations

The entire question of where one places other punctuation marks in relation to quotation marks is dealt with in the chapter on Quotation marks later. Here all we need do is say that, among British writers, commas are included inside quotation marks if they form part of the original quotation or if they mark a significant pause within it. We shall elaborate on this in the later chapter just mentioned. Meanwhile, a few examples will suffice. (Note that United States usage requires that the comma be placed inside the quotation marks as a matter of course. Here we shall illustrate non-US practice only.)

'Well, Jane,' said Tom, 'here we are.' (Tom's actual words were 'Well, Jane, here we are.')

'Come in', said Dick, 'and have a drink.' (What Dick said was 'Come in and have a drink.' Because there is no pause in the original quotation, the comma is placed outside it.)

Lennon and McCartney's most famous songs include 'Please please me', 'Can't buy me love', 'Eleanor Rigby' and 'Yesterday'.

Commas in Lists

Three or more items in a list or nouns and phrases in a series are normally separated by commas.

A musical sound is defined in terms of its pitch, duration, tone colour and volume.

Among the stalwarts in the tenor section of the choir were Martin Miller, Tom Taylor, Michael Wright and Martin Hart.

Old boots, tin cans, cigarette packets, non-biodegradable sweet wrappers were all deposited in the entrance to the building.

The vexed question here is whether, in a cumulative list in which the last item is introduced by 'and' or 'or', a comma should be included or omitted before the 'and' or 'or'. The habit among British writers has generally been to omit, as in the first two examples just given. American writers, on the other hand, have tended to include the comma before 'and' or 'or', and it is hard to see why one should not do this. Where phrasal items in a list themselves contain conjunctions such as 'and' or 'or', a comma before the final 'and' or 'or' in the list is a mandatory aid to clarity. These examples show the recommended use of the comma in such lists:

Dostoevsky's greatest books include *The Idiot*, *Crime and Punishment*, and *The Brothers Karamazov*.

My favourite meals include bacon and eggs, fish and chips, steak, cheese on toast, and sausage and mash. Lovely!

I do not like peanut butter, chicken and ham paste, or mustard and cress in my sandwiches

Putting a comma before 'and' or 'or' in a simple list is not wrong. Sentences such as this are quite acceptable:

The car park contained three Toyotas, a Nissan Cherry, a Ford Fiesta, and a Mercedes.

If, however, you write for publication, you should first find out your editor's preference before putting commas in front of all your 'ands' and 'ors'.

Comma with 'etc.' Some editors have a liking for a comma both before and after etc., when it precedes another part of the sentence. The word etc., like 'and so on', is properly thought of as a parenthetical element in a sentence and can therefore be legitimately 'comma'd off':

Lions, tigers, jaguars, etc., all belong to the cat family.

Each child brought his or her books, pencils, erasers, compasses, etc., into the classroom.

Commas between Adjectives

When two or more adjectives modify the same noun, are they or are they not separated by commas? This is a difficult problem that does not allow of an easy solution. Rules have been suggested covering this question. G.V. Carey, for instance, recommended that commas should be included if the adjectives 'are, so to speak, cumulative, but not otherwise'. Thus he was able to distinguish between 'a dazzling, luxurious limousine' and 'a large grey sports car'. In *You Have a Point There*, Eric Partridge gave an example that used a list of adjectives with the last preceded by *and*; so, presumably, he supported the use of commas: 'An odd, strange, curious and queer creature.' Other authorities say that if *and* can be placed 'meaningfully' between each adjective and the next, commas should be used, but not otherwise. But what do they mean by 'meaningfully'? Unfortunately, we are dealing here with one of the most subjective aspects of punctuation. Nevertheless, it is our duty to make some recommendations, so here goes.

1. Absence of Commas. We do not use commas in these sentences:

He wore a pale blue shirt and a dark red tie and light green socks.

Outside the graceful Georgian house stood a large black Mercedes.

In the first sentence the colour names are in fact nouns used as modifiers. We can prove this by turning the sentence to read: 'He wore a shirt of pale blue ...' or 'The colour of the shirt he wore was a pale blue ...' The adjectives 'pale', 'dark', etc., go with the colour names and not the nouns that the colour names modify.

In the second sentence, 'Georgian house' can be thought of as a linguistic unit that is modified by 'graceful'. Other similar linguistic units might be 'old man' or 'young woman', as in 'a kind old man' or 'a beautiful young woman'. The two adjectives 'large' and 'black' both say something about the physical appearance of the Mercedes. We can signal this fact by not using commas between them.

2. Presence of Commas. We use commas in these sentences:

Our Galaxy contains dwarf, giant(,) and supergiant stars.

He lived in a large, comfortable house on the outskirts of the city.

In the first sentence, the adjectives amount to a straightforward list, and the recommendations already made under 'Commas in Lists' apply here. The comma in parentheses is optional.

In the second sentence, the two adjectives, 'large' and 'comfortable' describe different aspects of the noun 'house'. One says something about its physical appearance; the other refers to its qualities as a place of residence. Because the adjectives describe different aspects of the noun, we separate them with commas. Further examples of this use of the comma might be given by the phrases 'a tall, kind old man', 'a large, smoke-filled room' or 'her long, slinky dress'.

Before we leave the punctuational uses of the comma, it is worth making two general points.

First, never let a comma come between the subject of a sentence and its verb, or the verb and its object, except when you are introducing a parenthetical phrase. The most careful writers have done this in the past, but it is a fault. These sentences are wrong:

The debate over whether the modern teaching of English should or should not stress the need for good punctuation, has barely got off the ground.

The answer to the question of whether punctuation should be formally taught in our schools today must surely be, yes.

No comma is necessary in either of the above sentences. However, commas are rightly inserted in this sentence:

45

The second largest party in the House of Commons, which during the 1980s was the Labour Party, forms Her Majesty's Opposition.

Second, if you find yourself having to use too many commas and the commas are all justifiable on any of the above grounds, you should still avoid an excess of commas by changing some of the parenthetical ones to parentheses or dashes or by rewording your sentence. Commas have a duty to clarify not clutter the text. When they do clutter it, they cause a barrier to communication and ought to go. If that means recasting your thoughts, so be it.

Non-Punctuational Uses

The most frequently encountered non-punctuational use of the comma is in alphabetically arranged lists of personal names using the surname-first system, such as those found in biographical dictionaries or encyclopaedias. Other uses of the comma are those found in simple bibliographies, in personal and business letters, and in the writing of numbers.

1. Alphabetical Lists of Personal Names. In most lists of this kind, the surname is followed by a comma and then by the forenames or initials. Any additional information is also preceded by a comma, although other punctuation may also be used. For example:

Bach, Johann Sebastian, German composer: b. Eisenach, 21 March 1685; d. Leipzig, 28 July 1750 . . . .

2. Simple Bibliographies. The simplest way of presenting a bibliography, especially a brief reading list attached to an article in a book or magazine, is to use a form where author, title, publisher and year are set off from each other by commas. This example will demonstrate:

Paul Johnson, *The National Trust Book of British Castles*, Weidenfeld & Nicolson, 1978.

An alternative way of presenting bibliographical information, but one which requires additional punctuation, is as follows:

Johnson, Paul. *The National Trust Book of British Castles*. Weidenfeld & Nicolson, 1978.

A way of presenting a brief book list continuously is illustrated as follows:

Johnson, Paul: *The National Trust Book of British Castles*, Weidenfeld & Nicolson, 1978; Warner, Philip: *Guide to Castles in Britain*, New English Library, 1981.

Other bibliographical formats are possible.

3. Personal and Business Letters. A comma is used in the following circumstances:

(a) In addresses. A comma is usually placed after each element of an address or name and address written at the top of a letter. The format of the name and address of the recipient on business letters is usually as follows:

Mr Thomas Smith,
'Sunnyview',
Elmers End Road,
Beckenham,
Kent BR3 4SZ.

A quoted name and address may be written out continuously in this form:

Mr Steve Mason, 106 Roslyn Hill, London N15.

Note that commas are no longer used to separate house numbers and street names and are not used to set off postcodes:

30 Eden Park Avenue, Beckenham, Kent BR3 3HN.

If the person identified in the name and address has a title or set of letters after his name, the use of a comma may be regarded by some people as unclear:

John Smith, MA, Esq., 75 Cornwall Gardens, London SW7.

An alternative way of representing this, noted by Eric Partridge, employs the use of colons:

John Smith, MA, Esq.: 75 Cornwall Gardens: London SW7

A more modern method might be to include extra spaces:

John Smith MA   Esq. 75 Cornwall Gardens   London SW7

This last style might work well for letterheads, but for general purposes the all-comma format is usually adopted.

Note that in informal letters on unheaded notepaper it is still the norm to write the sender's address in the top right-hand corner.

(b) In salutations. The style common in countries such as Britain is to begin letters with a salutation followed by a comma:

Dear Jane,

How lovely it was to go with you to the concert last week. I can't wait until we see each other again . . . .

Dear Mr Smith,

Thank you for your recent enquiry about our hotel . . . .

Dear Sir,

Further to our letter of 16 July, I am sorry to have to inform you . . . .

Sir,

May I through your columns express my opinion that Prof. Ramsbotham's theory concerning the use of the letter v in Middle English is utter nonsense . . . .

Note that in the case of formal and business letter-writing, the American practice is to follow the salutation 'Dear Mr Smith' or 'Dear Sir' with a colon:

Dear Sir:

Since you have not replied to our letter of 16 July, it is my duty to inform you . . . .

Informal private letters, however, follow British practice in using a comma. *See* the chapter on Colon.

At the end of a letter, before the signature or name of the writer, it is customary to write 'Yours sincerely' (for personal letters or business letters where the name of the recipient is stated in the salutation) or 'Yours faithfully' (where the recipient is addressed as 'Dear Sir', 'Dear Sirs' or 'Dear Madam'). Other variants, such as 'Yours truly', 'Best wishes' or 'With all my love', are also found. A comma usually immediately follows this closing tag.

Yours sincerely,

Jane

Note that some offices follow the practice of placing the closing tag, signature and name on the right of the page at the foot of a letter when the paragraphs of the letter are indented. When they all start flush left, the closing tag, name and signature are also placed flush left.

4. Numbers. Numbers of four or more digits are normally 'comma'd off' in groups of three digits moving leftwards from the implied or actual decimal point:

5,000 years ago.   £27,642.50   population 12,865,370

However, if you are writing a technical report or an article for a science magazine, you may be asked to write four-figure numbers without a comma:

5000 metres   2361.75   8000°C

In technical or scientific papers numbers containing more than five digits before the decimal point may be marked off not with commas but with spaces (in printed matter, these may be thin spaces):

22 584 631   50 000 km

Years consisting of four digits do not contain a comma:

1989   2000 BC   AD 1645 (not 1645 AD)

On the European continent, the comma is generally used as the decimal point, with the space used to group the digits in a number with five or more figures:

263,8   56 421,75

For further information, *see* the chapter on Numbers.

Chapter 3

Semicolon

Although the semicolon is now probably not as neglected as its more emphatic brother the colon, it is rare enough in ordinary writing to be considered something of a bogey. Most people who do not write for a living — and a few who do — hardly use it at all. Some people seem to be afraid of it; others are clearly prejudiced about it. It is certainly possible to overwork the semicolon, and some experts on English, notably H.W. Fowler, were perhaps overfond of it. But our stock of punctuation marks is not so rich that we can do without it. In fact, we ought to welcome the semicolon rather than distrust it; in the right place it can add freshness and subtlety to the most tired and pedestrian prose.

The semicolon is now no longer seen principally as a weak form of colon. In its strictly punctuational uses, it occasionally duplicates the duties of the colon, which has itself become much more important as a non-punctuational device. The fortuitous appearance of the semicolon as a combination of full point and comma advertises exactly what the semicolon now is — a cross between a comma and a full point, signifying a more significant break than the former but altogether lacking the finality of the latter.

Semicolons between Clauses

The semicolon's modern status as a strong comma or weak full stop is amply demonstrated in its chief use within the sentence, that of separating clauses. A semicolon may separate clauses with or without connecting conjunctions.

History of the Semicolon

We use the symbol ; to represent the semicolon, a sign
derived not from the full point and comma, as one might
expect, but from the Greek question mark. Anglo-Saxon
manuscripts from the eighth and ninth centuries used a
symbol known as the punctus elevatus, which, as a stop,
had a value similar to our semicolon. Modern printed
editions of Old English texts sometimes render this mark
as a reverse semicolon (⁏), but early printers required
something neater and tidier, and the Greek question mark
filled the bill admirably.

Although it formed part of the hierarchy of stops in use
during the sixteenth and seventeenth centuries, the
semicolon was dominated by the colon until the 19th
century. Now the roles have almost been reversed: the
semicolon predominates over the colon, although both
remain under-utilized.

1. Without Connecting Conjunctions. We said earlier that
one of the 'thou-shalt-nots' of using the comma was the
placing of it between two independent clauses not linked by a
co-ordinate conjunction. A comma in such a position is felt
to be too weak a break. Normally, syntax would require a
full point. But if the clauses are close to each other in sense
– so that the second or subsequent clauses represent logical
additions to, restatements of, or marked contrasts with the
first – then a full point might be too disruptive a break. The
mark that shows the connection in the absence of an
appropriate conjunction is the semicolon.
We therefore avoid this kind of sentence:

The sky was black, the rain fell continuously.

From what has just been said, a comma is not allowable after 'black'. A full point is acceptable, but a semicolon is better because it establishes the logical link between the two clauses:

> The sky was black; the rain fell continuously.

The following examples illustrate the types of independent clauses so far mentioned that can be linked by semicolons:

> He was born in the seaside town of Lowestoft; he died in Aldeburgh, another town by the sea. (Logical addition)

> He lived a life of debauchery; wine, women and gambling were his constant pursuits. (Restatement)

> He lived in London all week; he spent his weekends in the country. (Contrast.)

The use of semicolons between independent clauses gains maximum impact and effect when the clauses are short and employ parallel constructions:

> He lived in the town; she lived in the country.

> Describe it you may; explain it you cannot.

When the independent clauses share a main verb, that of the first does not have to be repeated in subsequent clauses. We may or may not signal its presence with the use of a comma:

> To err is human; to forgive, divine.

> The sun shines by its own light; the moon by reflected sunlight.

2. With Connecting Co-ordinate Conjunctions. Co-ordinate clauses linked by conjunctions, when they need to be punctuated, are normally marked off by commas. But we may need to strengthen the comma by replacing it with a semicolon to achieve a rhetorical effect, especially to emphasize a contrast:

He was brave; but he feared the thought of entering the forest at night.

He hated commuting; and he hated the office even more.

His novels were much admired; yet his poetry attracted nothing but caustic criticism.

Give me liberty; or give me death.

He would do anything for her; for he loved her beyond all reason.

When co-ordinate clauses in a sentence each contain several internal commas, the break between them is signalled not by another comma but by a semicolon.

The doctor took off his hat and coat, removed his gloves and went upstairs; but he could not find the room in which his patient lay.

Time, we all know, is a great healer; and, despite all the anguish and suffering she had endured, it eventually worked its miracle for Jane.

3. Semicolons Before Conjunctive Adverbs. In the earlier section on commas, we touched on a group of linguistic forms called conjunctive adverbs. These are a group of adverbs and adverbial phrases that are used parenthetically in a clause and serve to mark some form of connection with a previous clause. Many of these conjunctives are not restricted to the beginning of the clause they modify and can appear some way into it. Typical conjunctives are the following:

accordingly   in addition
also   indeed

anyway, anyhow	in fact
as a result	likewise
at least	moreover
besides	nevertheless
consequently	still
even so	then
furthermore	therefore
hence	thus
however	yet (and yet, but yet)

A few examples will illustrate the use of the conjunctives:

He bought the car in Belgium; at least, that's what he said.

No one died or was hurt in the shooting incident; in fact, the only real damage was to a few panes of glass.

He considered himself a talented writer; the critics, however, did not agree with him.

A couple of important conjunctives are the phrases 'for example' and 'that is':

None of her relatives liked her; her aunt, for example, refused to communicate with her or mention her at all.

He was believed to have flown to Paris; that is, a ticket for a flight bound for Orly Airport had been booked in his name.

Note that the abbreviated forms of 'for example' and 'that is', e.g. and i.e., may also be preceded by semicolons:

The terrestrial planets have relatively slow axial rotation periods; e.g., Mercury completes one rotation every 59 days.

A fugue is a musical form that is based on imitative counterpoint; i.e., each part follows the one before, presenting broadly the same melodic theme.

4. Between Main and Subordinate Clauses. In general, it is wise to steer clear of using semicolons between main and subordinate clauses. However, subordinate clauses introduced by the word *because* occasionally benefit from being prefaced by a semicolon, which emphasizes the decisiveness of the clause:

Davidson was certainly grateful to Dr Boone; because without that good doctor's skills as a healer he would surely have died.

He rushed to carry out the captain's command; because he knew that disobedience meant certain death.

The conjunctions *because* and *for* are virtually interchangeable. Because *for* is a co-ordinate conjunction, it will take a semicolon, as in our earlier example:

He would do anything for her; for he loved her beyond all reason.

Its counterpart *because* is traditionally regarded as a subordinate conjunction and should not normally be preceded by a semicolon — at least, so the pundits say. However, sensible writers who adhere to the spirit of written communication rather than the law of grammar see no reason why *because* and *for* should be treated differently from each other and use a semicolon with both when they feel it appropriate to do so. Apart from this one exception, though, do follow the pundits and keep semicolons for separating co-ordinate clauses only — unless you have some extremely subtle or dramatic effect in mind.

5. Between Complex Sentences. Semicolons can be placed between independent clauses, as we have seen; they can also be put between whole sentences that contain a main and subordinate clause, as in this sentence. The two sentences should stand in a logical or contrasting relationship to each other, and ideally they should employ the same grammatical construction for maximum effect. Here are just two further examples:

> When he arrived in Berlin, he bought a flat; when he left, he sold it again.

> Mr Wilson believed that the new extension would cut off a significant amount of daylight from the library; Mr Smith contended that, because it was not a very tall structure, it would do no such thing.

Semicolons in Lists

Semicolons may do the work of commas by marking off items in a list or phrases in a series that themselves contain commas. This is a case of promoting a few commas to semicolons to achieve clarity and avoid ambiguity. Notice how hopelessly confusing this sentence is when commas only are used:

> The people on the guest list included Sarah Wilson, a writer of biography, Andrew Stephenson, one of the country's most distinguished poets, Robert Bronson, an industrialist, art collector and motor racing enthusiast, and the Bishops of Bristol and Bath and Wells.

With semicolons separating the items, everything becomes clear:

> The people on the guest list included Sarah Wilson, a writer of biography; Andrew Stephenson, one of the country's most distinguished poets; Robert Bronson, an industrialist, art collector and motor racing enthusiast; and the Bishops of Bristol, and Bath and Wells.

Semicolons add to the literary quality of this accumulation of infinitives:

To stand firm, even when the world is telling you that you are wrong; to face adversity with a calm spirit; to die for your country, if need be — such are the qualities that I would wish to see in you, my son.

Non-Punctuational Uses

The chief non-punctuational use of the semicolon is to separate items or categories of item in an inventory, string of bibliographical references, etc.:

Ground Floor: three reception rooms, kitchen and onservatory; First Floor: four bedrooms, bathroom and WC; Outside: garage (with space for two family cars), spacious garden to rear.

V.E. Nash-Williams, 'The Roman goldmines at Dolaucothi', *Bulletin of the Board of Celtic Studies*, xiv (1950), 79–81; G.D.B. Jones, I.J. Blakeley and E.C.F. Mcpherson, ibid. xix, 71–84.

In some dictionaries, the semicolon serves to separate two synonymous or almost synonymous words or phrases in a definition. For example, a definition of the word *doleful* might run:

characterized by grief; sad or sorrowful.

Chapter 4

Colon

Dr Samuel Johnson, in his famous *English Dictionary* of 1755, defines the word colon like this:

> A point used to mark a pause greater than that of a comma and less than that of a period. Its use is not very exactly fixed; nor is it very necessary, being confounded by most with the semicolon. It was used before punctuation was refined, to mark almost any sense less than a period. To apply it properly, we should place it, perhaps, only where the sense is continued without dependence of grammar or construction; ...

If Dr Johnson were alive today, he would probably find that not much has changed regarding the use of the colon, except perhaps that far fewer people employ it nowadays, and of those that do, most have trouble discriminating between it and the semicolon. Indeed, in sentences the two punctuation marks may be made to do substantially the same jobs. Yet there is still an important place for the colon in our punctuation system and an even more important one in the area of non-punctuational uses.

Colon in a Sentence

We can divide the use of the colon within a sentence into two main categories: the true stop or pause mark and the mark of introduction. Of these two categories the second is by far the more important, but in order to preserve some logic and clarity of approach, we shall deal first with the colon as a stop, mainly because this is exactly what it was originally.

History of the Colon

The colon is another of our punctuation marks that has
its beginnings in Greek oratory and rhetoric. It is
interesting that there is an anatomical connection,
although not the one you may be expecting: in ancient
times the Greek word *kolon*, literally meaning 'limb' or
'member' (rather than 'part of the large intestine' − that
sense comes from a different *kolon*), signified a passage
of rhetorical discourse midway in extent between the
periodos, or period (*see* the chapter on Full Point) and the
komma (*see* the chapter on Comma). (A *kolon* also meant
part of a strophe in a choric song or a division in Greek
prosody or versification.) Naturally, the Greeks had a
mark signalling the end of a *kolon*, and that mark, which
was in fact a simple point placed high, became known as
a *kolon* too. The Romans, who borrowed their rhetorical
ideas from the Greeks, gave us our word colon.

The double point : now used for the punctuation mark
that we call the colon has been part of the punctuation
system since the eighth century. It was used to mark off
sections of written text in medieval manuscripts, often in
conjunction with a single point (:.), although its force as a
pause mark was not always consistent. In the sixteenth
century, soon after the age of printing began, the double
point − that is, the colon − became part of the modern
punctuational hierarchy, halfway between the full point,
or period, and the semicolon. In practice, however, the
colon usurped many of the duties of the semicolon,
proving (as Dr Johnson implied) that English punctuation
needed only one pause mark between the full point and
the comma.

The semicolon made a comeback during the eighteenth
century, and by the end of the nineteenth the colon had
been all but restricted to the status of a mark used for
introducing a quotation or list.

1. Colon Between Clauses. This is the area in which confusion can most readily arise between the colon and the semicolon. In certain instances, the colon can function as a strong semicolon even in modern writing. But in general, today's authors have restricted their use of the colon quite severely: it is largely confined to signalling a narrow range of logical connections.

A couple of general points are worth stating. The first thing to note is that colons should generally be used to link only two independent or co-ordinate clauses. And secondly, the clauses may or may not be connected by conjunctions, such as 'and', 'but', 'or', etc.

(a) Balancing Clauses. A sentence that naturally falls into two equal parts contained within a pair of independent clauses may have the break between the clauses signalled by a colon:

> The managing director has only just heard about Jones's report: he demands to see it straight away.

> I'm thirsty: please give me a cup of tea.

(b) Contrasting Clauses. More often than not, balanced sentences contain contrasting or antithetical clauses, one of which is the opposite of the other, as in these well-worn proverbs:

> To err is human: to forgive is divine.

> Man proposes: God disposes.

More practical examples, perhaps, include the following:

> Audiences and critics loved her: her fellow artists despised her.

He may be a good man: he is certainly a foolish one.

(c) The Colon of Promotion. In an involved sentence, in which semicolons have already been used, a colon may be introduced to mark a major break. For example:

Time, as we all know, is a great healer; it worked its miracle for Jane: but who could have known how short-lived that miracle would be?

(d) Explanatory or Interpretive Clauses. In this usage, the colon separates two independent clauses, the second of which serves to explain, amplify, interpret or reveal something connected with the first.

Getting hold of the explosive would be simple: the store room was full of it, and as security officer Evans had the key to the room.

Haydn was a prolific composer: his output included more than 100 symphonies, about 80 string quartets, 50 sonatas, and more than 40 piano trios.

Mission control was becoming anxious: there had been no radio contact with the astronauts for four hours.

Our report is based on the most exhaustive investigations: we have made a detailed analysis of all the data for the first six months of the year and have rigorously cross-checked comparable data for the same period last year.

2. The Colon of Introduction. The examples given under 1 (d) provide the link to the most characteristic use of the colon: namely, its employment as an introductory device. We said that the colon is used to separate two clauses, the second of which is an explanation, interpretation or amplification of the first. The reverse, as it were, is also true. We can regard the first clause as a preface or introduction to the explanation contained in the second:

He gave good reasons for his lateness: signal failure had delayed the arrival of his train at Waterloo, and there was a tube and bus strike that day too.

In a celebrated and much-quoted phrase, H.W. Fowler said that the colon in its introductory use had 'acquired a special function, that of delivering the goods that have been invoiced in the preceding words.' In this and all the punctuational uses that remain to be considered, that is exactly what it does.

(a) Between Phrases and Clauses. Either the first or second element of a sentence containing an introductory colon can be an incomplete clause or even a single word.

Tuesday 11 July: the work was progressing well.

Only one naturally occurring mineral remains to be discussed: diamond.

To sum up: research has shown that, of the nine planets in the solar system, only the Earth currently supports life as we know it.

In written communications such as memos or on public notices and official documents containing admonitions, cautions, etc., the colon may generally be followed by a capital letter:

Warning: Trespassers will be prosecuted.

Attention: No dogs allowed.

To whom it may concern: Any personnel who have not been informed to the contrary by 5.0 p.m. may consider their employment terminated with effect from tomorrow.

(b) Before a List. The colon commonly introduces a list, regardless of whether the items of the list are presented numbered on separate lines or as a continuous string with each item marked off by a comma:

The contents of his briefcase included the following: a copy of *The Times*, a packet of sandwiches, an apple, a paperback novel and several top secret files.

Before 1986 only five moons were known to orbit the planet Uranus. They were the following:

(1) Ariel
(2) Miranda
(3) Oberon
(4) Titania
(5) Umbriel

Note that listed items on separate lines are frequently indented for clarity, as in the previous example.

Words such as *namely*, *viz*, *etc.* may or may not be used before the listed items:

Three minerals have yet to be considered: talc, corundum and diamond.

or

Three minerals have yet to be considered: namely, talc, corundum and diamond.

A colon is never used to interrupt the grammatical logic of a sentence. In these two examples, the colon is wrong and should be deleted:

One mineral that we have yet to consider is: diamond.

His briefcase contained: sandwiches, an apple, a copy of *The Times* and some office files.

However, if the list of items is set out with each one on a separate line, a colon may introduce it, because the grammatical logic has already been disrupted by this method of presenting the list:

Until 1986 the five known moons of Uranus were:
  (1) Ariel
  (2) Miranda
  (3) Oberon
  (4) Titania
  (5) Umbriel

But

Until 1986 the five known moons of Uranus were Ariel, Miranda, Oberon, Titania and Umbriel.

(For the now old-fashioned use of a dash after a colon at the head of a list, *see* the chapter of Dash.)

(c) Before a Summary. In this particular use a capital letter is sometimes employed after the colon, but it should not be:

The company's offer therefore amounted to this: it would pay the agreed salary increase but would not back-date it to the start of the fiscal year.

His whole life could by summed up as follows: he had been the greatest actor in the history of the modern theatre and had used his talent to search for truth.

(d) Before a Direct Quotation. It is easy to overdo this particular instance of the colon by placing it directly after every verb that indicates saying or writing. In these two examples the colon is wrong and should be commuted to a comma or even nothing at all:

Tom said: 'Don't be so silly.'

He rushed in and shouted: 'The Russians are coming!'

A more extended introduction to a quotation, however, in which the verb of saying or writing may be implied or even suppressed, needs to be followed by a colon before the quotation:

Davies began the case for the defence with these words: "Ladies and gentlemen of the jury, imagine if you will the circumstances in which the defendant found himself only two days before the murder of which he is accused."

He had just two words for his unwelcome visitor: "Get out!"

In 1959 Kenneth Tynan wrote of Olivier: "The dark imprint of [his] stage presence is something one forgets only with an effort, but the voice is a lifelong possession of those who have heard it at its best."

If the quotation begins a new paragraph, then a colon invariably precedes it. This is especially true when the quotation carries no inverted commas and is indented in smaller type. Here is the colon in front of quotation marks:

All the while Jones had been listening intently to what his opponent had to say. Now he got up to make his reply and began:

"Friends, I know that much of what Tom has just said is true. But. . . ."

And here is the colon in front of an indented passage:

Kenneth Tynan's admiration of Olivier was considerable, as one of his reviews in the late 1950s made clear:

The dark imprint of Olivier's stage presence is something one forgets only with an effort, but the voice is a lifelong possession of those who have heard it at its best.

(e) Before a Saying or Adage. Allied to the use of the colon before direct quotations is its employment before sayings, as in the examples that follow. (Note that in this instance quotation marks are not used and a capital letter after the colon is permissible.)

My motto is this: Do as you would be done by.

Being a cautious man, my uncle had an old proverb that ruled his every action: Look before you leap.

(f) Before an Example. The practice of placing a colon before a clause or sentence containing or representing an example parallels what was said about the use of 'for example' under the section on the semicolon. In fact, if the connecting words *for example* are used, the colon should be replaced by a semicolon. Note the difference between the following sentences:

Her relatives disliked her intensely: her aunt refused to communicate with her at all.

But

Her relatives disliked her intensely; her aunt, for example, refused to communicate with her at all.

Some dictionaries introduce example sentences or citations with a colon. Here is how one defines the idiom *to break bread*:

to take food or have a meal (with someone): It was his first offer to break bread with me... (Honey Dec 1974)

And it will not have escaped your notice that the punctuation examples throughout this book have been introduced by colons.

Non-Punctuational Uses
Most of the non-punctuational uses of the colon can be thought of as special instances of the introductory colon. In

many cases a larger unit or element precedes (or introduces, if you like) the unit or element that stands next to it in significance. Not all the non-punctuational uses of the colon can be conceived in this way, however, so we shall confine ourselves to the process of merely describing and illustrating each one as we come to it.

1. Business Uses. In the United States, the colon is placed after the salutation at the start of a formal or business letter:

Dear Sir:

Thank you for your inquiry about our product . . .

In letters written to friends or relations, the comma is used instead of the colon:

Dear Jim,

It was great to meet up with you at the baseball game last Saturday . . .

(Note that in many countries outside the United States, notably Great Britain, a comma is used after the opening salutation in all circumstances. *See* the chapter on Comma. It is also worth mentioning that there is an increasing propensity for dispensing with punctuation marks in this situation altogether, because the new paragraph that invariably begins after the salutation makes punctuation unnecessary.)

Office memoranda are frequently headed by a set list of items detailing the author, recipient(s), date, subject, etc., with a colon introducing each piece of information. For example:

INTEROFFICE COMMUNICATION

To: Jerry Smith

From: Tim Jones

Subject: Preparation of Internal Reports

Date: 7 October 1990

2. Biblical References. In citing passages from the Bible, it is customary to separate chapter and verse numbers with a colon:

Job 24:7   2 Corinthians 6:8 or   II Corinthians 6:8

Some publishers use a full point in this situation, but a colon is clearer. Strings of biblical references should be separated by semicolons, whereas two verses cited from the same chapter should be separated by a comma without repetition of the chapter number. An en rule (short dash) separates the first and last verse numbers in a passage from one chapter and the first and last chapters in a section from the same book. The following examples illustrate all eventualities:

Matthew 21   (Chapter 21 of the Gospel according to St Matthew)

Job 24:7   (Verse 7 of Chapter 24 of the Book of Job)

2 Chronicles 10:6—11   (Verses 6 to 11 of Chapter 10 of the second Book of Chronicles)

Ezra 7:1,6   (Verses 1 and 6 of Chapter 7 of the Book of Ezra)

Genesis 1—4   (Chapters 1 to 4 of the Book of Genesis)

1 Kings 17:1—2 Kings 2:11 (Verse 1 of Chapter 17 of the first Book of Kings to Verse 11 of Chapter 2 of the second Book of Kings)

We may string these references together, using correct Bible order, by means of semicolons:

Genesis 1–4; 1 Kings 17:1 – 2 Kings 2:11; 2 Chronicles 10:6-11; Ezra 7:1,6; Job 24:7; Matthew 21.

3. Bibliographical Use. A colon is sometimes used for the following purposes:

(a) Between a title and a subtitle. Note that the subtitle may begin with an initial capital letter:

Cyrus Gordon, *Forgotten Scripts: The Story of their Decipherment*, 1968.

(b) After the place of publication. This is not a common use:

London: Harrap, 1987

Cambridge, Mass.: 1992

(c) Between the volume and page number of a periodical or the volume and page number of a large-scale work (an encyclopaedia, for instance). The volume number may be in Roman or Arabic numerals:

Antiquity XXXII:227 (1958)

Encyclopaedia Britannica (1986) 27:103

A colon is sometimes used between the act and scene numbers in a play, especially a play by Shakespeare:

Macbeth IV:ii:7   Coriolanus II:2:7

4. Use in Dialogue. A characteristic use of the colon is found in the scripts for plays. A colon is placed after the name of a character and immediately before the lines of dialogue assigned to that character. Note that any stage directions relating to the way the character is meant to deliver his or her lines also precede the colon:

Ursula: John, what on earth are we going to do? If Henry finds out —

John: He won't. Darling, trust me. And never forget that I love you.

Sarah [backing away]: You surely don't mean —

William [*smiling mirthlessly*]: Oh yes. I'm the killer they're all looking for.

5. Date and Time. In American usage, the figures representing the date and time in the all-figure format are normally separated by colons:

6:30 p.m.   18:30   2:27:89

Note that in British usage it is customary to use full points to separate the figures of the time and either full points or slashes (solidi) to separate the figures of the date (*see* the chapter on Full point). Note also that in American practice, as exemplified above, the order is month:day:year. British usage favours the slightly more logical ascending order of day:month:year. Hence, using colons, the above date would be rendered as 27:2:89 in the United Kingdom.

6. Ratios. These are expressed in this way:

5:4 is equal to 80:64, not 64:80.

In some countries women outnumber men in the ratio 3:2.

The scale on the old inch-to-the-mile maps was 1:63,360.

For more information on punctuation relating to numbers, *see* the chapter on Numbers.

Chapter 5

Parentheses

In the section on the comma, we described various types of
parenthetical material. A piece of parenthetical material,
which we may from now on refer to as a parenthesis, is a
word or group of words that stand outside the main
grammatical structure of a sentence. A parenthesis can be a
single word, a phrase, a clause, or even a whole sentence.
The word parenthesis, plural parentheses, is Greek in origin
and means literally 'an insertion beside'. The notion of a
parenthesis being a kind of insertion is a very helpful one; in
fact, a parenthesis is an insertion that disrupts but does not
break the logic of a sentence. You could remove a parenthesis
and the sentence would remain basically intact.

We have so far seen how a parenthesis can be marked off
by using commas. Here and in the next chapter, on the Dash,
we shall describe the role of other punctuation marks in
carrying out this task.

Symbols of Parenthesis
What we are primarily discussing here is a set of symbols that
are usually found in pairs, one sign being the mirror image of
the other:

$$( ) \qquad [\ ] \qquad < >$$

The brace too comes as one of a mirror-image pair { }, but its
use is rather different from the other signs. We shall return to
it later.

Before we get down to details, we need to sort out some confusion in assigning names to the first two of the above symbols. In the United States and among printers and publishers generally, the first pair ( ) are known as parentheses, a term obviously linking them with the parenthesis that we have just been discussing. The second pair [ ] are referred to as brackets. In Britain, parentheses ( ) are known as brackets or, where a distinction seems necessary, round brackets, whereas brackets proper [ ] are usually called square brackets. The other symbols { } and < > are respectively and universally known as curly, or hooked, brackets and angle brackets. For the sake of clarity, and in view of the popular conception in Britain of what brackets are, we shall compromise. We shall talk of parentheses ( ) and square brackets [ ], curly brackets { } and angle brackets < >.

Note for Typists. Old typewriters are generally not able to produce the full range of signs discussed in this section, but virtually all electronic typewriters and word processors include them on their keyboards. If your machine cannot produce at least square brackets in addition to parentheses, you ought to consider upgrading it. Correctly used and correctly produced square brackets can make a typescript look like a quality production.

Parentheses

The parentheses ( ) were part of the punctuation scene by the start of the sixteenth century. In 1566 Aldus Manutius the Younger, who was one of the earliest people to advocate a syntactical approach to punctuation, wrote of them in his *Orthographiae Ratio* (Spelling Method) as follows:

Those words ought to be enclosed in a parenthesis,* which
are not a part of the sentence, and do not depend upon any
word either preceding or following: words whose absence
causes no loss to the sentence.

Manutius' sensible point seems incredibly modern, even if his
punctuation is not.

Parentheses should be reserved for enclosing anything that
is not immediately relevant to the argument of a sentence.
Pieces of text in parentheses can either be contained within
the sentence or stand outside to form sentences of their own.
(*See* later under 'Punctuation in Connection with
Parentheses'.)

Parentheses function as a shorthand for such a phrase as
'by the way'. Note the following examples:

Julie is bringing John (whom she met in Corfu last
summer) to our party next week.

The meeting took place without the presence of Mr West
(his wife was due to have her first baby that afternoon) and
passed the resolution that you see before you.

Parentheses enclose material that can be classified as one of
the following: an afterthought, a comment, an explanation or
a reference. We shall give a couple of examples of each.

Afterthought:

The scent of jasmine pervaded the air (it always does at
this time of year), and the crickets chirruped loudly.

I didn't usually see him on Wednesday (or any other day,
for that matter).

---

*What we would now refer to as a pair of parentheses.

Comment:

Sharon from the typing pool (a very tasty little blonde) sat on the opposite side of the room from Andy.

He is a top academic (though you wouldn't think it by looking at him) and has gained a number of distinctions and honours.

Explanation:

The Earth is a huge sphere (ball) covered with water, rock and soil, and surrounded by air.

Mr Kurosawa (who is the head of our Japanese client company) is in Britain for a few days and will be visiting our factory here in Swansea.

Reference:

I have already taken up this point in a previous chapter (see p. 81, n. 3).

In the famous shield passage (Aeneid, VIII, 626–728), Virgil reviews the panoramic history of Rome as though it were a dazzling prophecy.

Life dates, dates of composition and translations of foreign titles of books, plays, paintings, etc., are also placed within parentheses:

The French writer Stendhal (1783–1842) is famous for his novel *Le rouge et le noir* (The Red and the Black), written in 1830.

Stendhal's most famous novel was *Le rouge et le noir* (1830).

Parentheses have a particular use with abbreviations. They may either enclose the full form following the abbreviation or they may enclose the abbreviation following the full form. This usually happens when the name of an organization, etc., is first mentioned in a piece of text, the abbreviation being used thereafter:

The strike at the BBC (British Broadcasting Corporation) threatened the coverage of this year's Wimbledon tennis championships. In the event, however, BBC staff did not disrupt the screening of Wimbledon after all.

The British Broadcasting Corporation (BBC) originally offered their staff a 7 per cent pay increase in 1989.

Parentheses serve to indicate an alternative option within a word:

Police are anxious to track down the person(s) who dug up the twelfth green on Beckenham golf course.

Strong (wo)men required to help set up the staging for Saturday's performance at the Church Hall.

Care should be taken over what constitutes the optional element in the word concerned. This next example is wrong because the optional elements are not properly bracketed off:

We have a vacancy for a barman(maid).

A slash or solidus should be used here. The advertisement should read:

We have a vacancy for a barman/barmaid (or a barman/maid).

In the report of a speech, especially a parliamentary one, parentheses enclose interruptions by the audience:

Mr Speaker, I am happy to tell the House that the siege in Kensington is over and all the hostages are safe. (Loud cheers.)

Parentheses should not be overused, and it is a good rule to use them as little as possible. Their primary purpose is to set off material that really is of purely marginal significance and should be reserved for that use. Thus we prefer to write:

Mrs Thatcher, Britain's prime minister, visited Paris in July.

because Mrs Thatcher's post as prime minister is of great material significance to her going to Paris. If we were to write:

Mrs Thatcher (Britain's prime minister) visited Paris in July.

that would imply that Mrs Thatcher's post was of purely academic interest and had very little to do with her being in Paris.

However, there is some merit in using parentheses to avoid a clutter of commas. In the next two examples, (b) is preferable to (a):

(a) Mary, whose shopping basket, a vast portmanteau full of fruit, tinned food, packets of cereal, and all sorts of other groceries, was obviously too heavy for her, struggled unaided out of the supermarket and into the car park.

(b) Mary, whose shopping basket (a vast portmanteau full of fruit, tinned food, packets of cereal, and all sorts of other groceries) was obviously too heavy for her, struggled unaided out of the supermarket and into the car park.

There may be no potential ambiguity in sentence (a), but sentence (b) is preferable largely because it is neater and clearer.

At all costs the text within parentheses must not be too long. In the following example, the reader is kept waiting for ages before the main verb appears without any inkling as to what it is likely to be:

> Closer co-operation between university science departments and local industry (the co-opting of local industrial magnates onto university boards and similar arrangements under which scientific academics representing university departments may become directors of local companies have already proved successful in other countries) will obviously assist in the revitalization of the manufacturing sector in the national economy.

This thoroughly bad sentence is not only a discourtesy to the reader; it is an affront to good English and should be completely recast. Try this:

> Closer co-operation between university science departments and local industry is likely to prove invaluable to the national economy. The co-opting of local industrial magnates onto university boards and similar arrangements under which scientific academics representing university departments may become directors of local companies have already proved successful in other countries. Such co-operation here will obviously assist in the revitalization of the manufacturing sector.

More words perhaps, but better English and a much clearer message more quickly communicated to the reader.

There is no excuse either for this sentence, quoted in Gowers' *Complete Plain Words*, in which the writer, as well as the reader, gets hopelessly lost:

> ... Owing to a shortage of a spare pair of wires to the underground cable (a pair of wires leading from the point near your house back to the local exchange, and thus a pair of wires essential to the provision of a telephone service for you) is lacking ...

Only this part of the sentence is quoted, but it may be that we can put it right by inserting 'the fact that' after 'Owing to'. It iss still a bad sentence, though — too many references to 'pairs of wires'.

Punctuation and Parentheses

The placing of punctuation marks in relation to parentheses is governed by whether the marks belong to the text enclosed in the parentheses or not. The rule is that the only punctuation allowed inside the parentheses is the punctuation that goes with the text there.

In practice, the only stop likely to cause difficulty is the full point. If the text within parentheses is inside the sentence, there is no full point inside the parentheses, even when the parenthetical text is syntactically a whole sentence itself or actually ends the sentence in which it is contained:

> The main course consisted of roast duck à l'orange (I love roast duck) and two vegetables.

> I have already mentioned this point in an earlier chapter (pp. 81–2).

If the parenthetical text lies right outside the sentence and forms another sentence entirely in parentheses, the full point goes inside the parentheses:

> I have already discussed this matter at length. (*See* Transactions, pp. 81–2.)

When parentheses take the place of commas, never put in the commas as well as the parentheses:

> Curare (which South American Indians have long used to poison their arrows for hunting) is now well established as a medicament.

Not

> Curare, (which South American Indians have long used to poison their arrows for hunting), is now well established as a medicament.

But if text in parentheses comes at the end of a passage already set off by a pair of commas, both those commas remain:

> Jean, who was deep in conversation with Francisco (a handsome Spaniard who was just her type), hardly noticed Tom's departure.

Colons and semicolons generally stand outside parentheses:

> Elijah prophesies drought in these terms (1 Kings 17:1): 'As the Lord God of Israel liveth, before whom I stand, there shall not be dew nor rain these years, but according to my word.'

> To err is human (this we know as a fact); to forgive is divine (this some of us hope and believe).

Question marks and exclamation marks forming part of the text inside parentheses will be included inside the parentheses:

> Jones (the idiot!) then proceeded to kick the ball into his own goalmouth.

> Then the youngest of the Smiths (how many are there, for goodness' sake?) trooped up to collect their prizes as well.

Spaces and Parentheses. Some inexperienced typists put spaces on each side of each of pair of parentheses. These spaces after an open parentheses sign (and before a close parentheses sign) are wrong, In text produced on a word processor, they can generate some very odd effects, the most notable being the lonely sight of a close parentheses sign at

80

the start of a line. If that happens to be the last line of a paragraph, the effect is ludicrous.

If you type text on a word processor (as many people do), do not put spaces on both sides of your parentheses signs (it can look very silly, as this example will surely show).

So the rule is: include (as part of the first word and) as part of the last, provided that there is no full point. If there is, the) comes straight after it.

Square Brackets

Parentheses (round brackets) deal with material added to a sentence by the author of that sentence. Frequently, some of us (especially editors of books seeking to make things clear for the reader) may add things to sentences written by somebody else. This latter type of addition, a phrase or sentence not included in the original author's text, is enclosed within square brackets []. Square brackets are generally most often encountered with direct quotations and serve to introduce an editorial comment, explanation, correction, or other interpolation:

> John Bunyan's *Pilgrim's Progress* begins: 'As I walked through the wilderness of this world, I lighted on a certain place, where was a den [Bedford jail, where Bunyan was imprisoned for 12 years]; and I laid me down in that place to sleep ...'

> '... and on the other side, what sighs and groans brast [i.e., burst] from Christian's heart.' Thus Bunyan writes of the fight between Christian and Apollyon.

Similarly they may occur in indented quotations:

> On the question of soccer violence, AP of Beckenham writes:

Sir — I feel that the unemployed louts who habitually cause trouble on the terraces [many of the most serious offenders are in fact holding down highly paid jobs in the city] should receive stiff prison sentences, not fines ...

Editors of classical texts or books of inscriptions use square brackets to enclose letters that are thought to be present in the text or inscription but are now illegible. Angle brackets may perform a similar function. This is a very specialized use of square brackets that the ordinary writer is perhaps unlikely to encounter. *See* the chapter on Ellipsis.

A particular use of square brackets that crops up rather more frequently is in enclosing the Latin word *sic*, meaning 'thus', to draw attention to the fact that an old, unusual or incorrect spelling, date, etc., is reproduced exactly as it appears in the original author's work. It amounts to an editorial comment that says 'Yes, the original author really did write that.' The word sic is set as here, in italics. This device should not be overused but should be reserved for cases where sense or clarity might be in momentary jeopardy:

Campbell's London Tradesman (1747) complains bitterly about the type of person setting up in the music selling trade at that time:
The Masters of Musick shops ... can scarce hum a tune in proper time, but if they new [sic] a little more before they set up the trade, ... they would have a better chance to thrive.

Note that the spelling 'Musick' is accepted as an ancient one that crops up all the time. It is therefore not deemed incorrect, and so we do not have to insert [sic] after it.

Square brackets are also occasionally put around an editorial or critical question mark. The query may concern the soundness of the original author's text or the content of that text. Many readers do not like this device: some consider it a vulgar intrusion, while others think that it oversteps the bounds of editorial interference. In any event it is ambiguous.

> Jones writes: 'Science fiction is more ancient than one might think. As long ago as about AD 180 [?], the Greek satirist Lucian wrote a story about a trip to the moon. ....'

In this example, what is the basis of the editor's or reviewer's query? Does he or she disbelieve the date, or is the writer's assertion about the beginnings of science fiction such a surprise? Square brackets around question marks are best avoided.

A special use of square brackets is found in linguistics, in which they are conventionally used to enclose a so-called narrow phonetic transcription. Some dictionaries that provide pronunciations often enclose them in square brackets:

> knight [nait], *n*., a mounted soldier in the army of a feudal superior ...

Other Types of Brackets

Curly brackets { } and angle brackets < > have a number of specialized uses that ordinary writers and editors rarely encounter. These uses are to do with the preparation of classical texts or books of ancient inscriptions for publication.

Curly brackets enclose letters that are superfluous to the text. Angle brackets enclose letters that should have been in the text but were left out or written down wrongly by the scribe who copied the text. Sometimes the conventions for using square, curly and angle brackets are different from those set out here. They may also call for the use of double square brackets, e.g. for indicating letters that are thought to have been present but were later rubbed out. The way in which these different types of brackets are used is normally explained in the book in which they appear.

Brackets within Brackets

These should be avoided if possible, but if they cannot be, one may use either square brackets or parentheses within parentheses. For example:

> Twenty Thousand Leagues Under the Sea (a novel by Jules Verne [1828–1905]) is one of the best early science fiction novels in the genre.

There are two alternative ways of setting down this sentence:

(a) *Twenty Thousand Leagues under the Sea* (a novel by Jules Verne (1828–1905)). ...

(b) *Twenty Thousand Leagues under the Sea* (a novel by Jules Verne, 1828–1905). ...

Sentence (b), using commas, is preferable here, but where the parenthesis with a parenthesis is longer, one of the other methods should be used.

Non-Punctuational Uses

There are several non-punctuational uses of parentheses ().

1. In Lists. Parentheses are used purely as a convention to enclose numbers or letters against each item in the list. The items may be written out continuously or on separate lines:

> His writings may be grouped under the following headings:
> (a) philosophy; (b) satire; (c) history; (d) pornography.

or

> His writings may be grouped under the following headings:
> (a) philosophy
> (b) satire
> (c) history
> (d) pornography

Half-parentheses like this) may be employed in lists of this nature:

Subjects under review include the following:
1) Student grants
2) Accommodation
3) Staffing provisions

2. In Mathematics. Elements in mathematical expressions that must be taken together in order for their calculations to be carried out before the solution of the whole expression are placed within parentheses:

$$(x^2 - xy - 6y^2) \times (2x^2 + 4xy + y)$$

For 'brackets within brackets' in mathematical expressions, the parentheses may contain either square brackets or another set of parentheses. (*See* above.)

Half-angle brackets (either < or >) are used in mathematics as signs of inequality. The < implies that the preceding quantity is less than the one following; the > implies that the preceding quantity is greater than the one following.

3. In linguistics. The signs < and > indicate the direction of derivation. As a shorthand used in etymologies given in dictionaries, the sign pointing left < indicates that what follows is the origin of the word or idiom being defined:

iridium, *n.*, a precious metallic chemical element ... (< New Latin < Latin *iris*, rainbow; named from its iridescence when found in solution)

Braces
The brace is a large version of the curly bracket. Its use is to link related items in a list, especially when they are in a table. It is also used in mathematics and music. But its primary use is to show that one item is comprised of or equivalent to two or more others. These examples show it in action. Mark well the direction in which the kink or hook should face:

chemistry
physics
botany ⎫
zoology ⎭ biology ⎫
              ⎬ natural science

Celtic ⎧ Brythonic ⎧ Welsh
                ⎨ Cornish
                ⎩ Breton
     ⎩ Goedelic ⎧ Irish
                ⎨ Scots Gaelic
                ⎩ Manx

Chapter 6

Dash

The dash formally joined the English punctuation scene during the seventeenth century. As a symbol, it is distinguished in being a truly elastic mark of punctuation, both in handwriting and in printing. It does indeed come in different lengths. Printers and editors speak not of the dash as such but of various lengths of rule: the en rule (–), the em rule (—) and the double em rule (——). These ens and ems are printer's measurements (an em is the square of the body of a given size of type; an en is half an em). The length of an em or en rule therefore depends on the type size that the printer is using. To a typist, however, and to you and me as readers or authors with little interest in typographical niceties, all lines that are longer than a hyphen can be regarded as dashes.

In typing, we usually represent the dash as a single hyphen with spaces on each side of it (-). Journalists, working quickly and aware of the realities of editing and typesetting, often represent a dash as a double hyphen with no spaces each side (--). Copy-editors distinguish between an en and an em rule by writing *n* or *N* or *EN* over one type of spaced hyphen and *m* or *M* or *EM* over another. In certain of the usages listed below, a typist can make no practical distinction between a hyphen and a dash, whereas a typesetter would probably make the distinction between a hyphen and an en rule without being told to. In our discussion, we shall try to make such distinctions clear.

Parenthetical Dashes

The most notable function of a dash is to mark off parenthetical material within a sentence. As we have seen, commas and brackets can perform the same function, but the dash does the job with more panache, more flamboyance or sensationalism, and in an altogether more disruptive way:

> The tenor soloist — one wondered at times whether he was actually performing the same piece as the other forces on the platform — sang with such a wayward technique and such a disregard for the conductor's tempi that I felt genuine relief as each of his contributions came to an end.

> When, as an actor, one is selected for a role in a classic play, one simply goes along to the nearest bookshop — Richmond & Page is my local — and buys a copy of it.

Parenthetical dashes come in pairs, as do parentheses and parenthetical commas. As in the case of text enclosed in parentheses, one should be able to take the words between the dashes out of the sentence altogether without damaging the grammatical wholeness of the sentence.

A 'dashed' parenthetical phrase placed at the end of a sentence takes only the first or introductory dash; the second dash coalesces with the full point:

> The title of his book, *The Greening of the Desert*, was powerful — one might almost say dramatic.

A parenthetical sentence between dashes does not end in a full point but can take a question mark or exclamation mark:

> He is — how can I put it? — a raving lunatic.

> Then Nigel — what an idiot he is sometimes! — spilt the whole bottle of wine down my dress.

It is extremely easy to overdo the use of the dash in marking off parentheses. Some journalists employ it at almost every opportunity, mainly because of its impact. Unfortunately, overuse has inevitably led to a weakening of the effect of the dash, so that all too often it is used where a pair of commas would be quite adequate. Note this example:

Jones — the owner of the car — was surprised at how dirty it was.

The dashes here represent overkill. The information concerning Jones's ownership of the car is not a major digression, as the dashes would naturally imply, but a rather relevant point. This is, admittedly, an extreme example, but it is useful in pointing to a trend that should be discouraged. Dashes should be reserved for barely related digressions, not as a lazy alternative to commas or parentheses. It all comes down to thinking about what one is trying to communicate.

Dashes and Commas. In an extended parenthesis that contains words or phrases linked by commas, it can often be clearer to mark the beginning and end of the parenthesis by dashes. We noted a similar use of round brackets (parentheses) earlier on.

Even here, however, care should be taken to avoid overdoing the dashes. This example shows how effective dashes can be when used in this way:

A mountain of debris — smashed furniture, papers and books thrown all over the floor, and ornaments shattered to smithereens — was the disheartening sight that greeted him.

It is worth noting, as we did when discussing parentheses, that we do not combine dashes and commas in the same positions in the sentence.

Compound punctuation marks made up of dashes and

other stops were used at one time and are described at length by Eric Partridge (*You have a Point There*, pp. 86–8). They are virtually a vanished breed now. But see the reference to the colon and dash before a list in the next part of this chapter.

The Single Dash

1. Before Lists and Summaries. A single dash can take the place of a colon in introducing a list, summary or conclusion:

All the member nations of NATO were represented – Belgium, Canada, Denmark, France, West Germany, Greece, Iceland, Italy, Luxemburg, the Netherlands, Norway, Portugal, Spain, Turkey, the United Kingdom, and the United States.

Booze, women, gambling – his life was one long round of debauchery.

At one time, it was common practice to introduce a list with a combined colon and dash (:–). Typists used to render it as a colon and hyphen. This practice was particularly used for lists in which the items were set out on separate lines, with each item indented, as in this example:

The items stolen included the following: –
A half-hunter watch
Jewellery valued at £3,000
A set of Meissen figures, value £10,000

This style is now largely obsolete; a colon is sufficient.

2. Introducing the Attribution of a Quotation. This may be used with a direct quotation enclosed in quotation marks:

'History is bunk.' – Henry Ford.

or on a separate line, usually ranged right, after an indented quotation not marked off by quotation marks:

> My heart leaps up when I behold
> A rainbow in the sky ...

> — William Wordsworth

3. Introducing an Afterthought or Break in Continuity. The informality and disruptive character of the dash make it an ideal mark for setting off an afterthought — especially an ironic one — at the end of the sentence and for signalling an abrupt change of subject or other break in the flow of a sentence:

> The last time Tom had seen Sam, he looked as if he were at death's door — obviously, death hadn't been at home that day.

> John, I've poured you a gin and — oh, I forgot, you only drink orange juice, don't you?

4. Signalling Breaks and Hesitations in Speech. A dash or a number of dashes may be used in writing dialogue to signal hesitancy:

> 'Mr Henderson, I — ' Lewis broke off as Henderson's secretary entered the office with a tray of coffees.

> 'I — er — that is — I — don't know who you mean,' stammered Jones.

For the use of an ellipsis in simulating halting speech, *see* the chapter on Ellipsis.

5. Indicating a Change of Speaker. A dash is used to indicate a change of speaker when the text of a conversation is set continuously, like this:

> Jones met Smith in the corridor: 'Smith, where have you been?' — 'Don't panic, Jones. I got held up, that's all.'

This is perhaps an old-fashioned use of the dash. In most cases of quoted dialogue, each character's words start on a fresh line. *See* the chapter on Quotation Marks.

6. The Equivalent Use of the Dash. This is a rather informal use, in which the dash does duty for the word 'equals':

+ – plus

× – multiplied by

7. In Informal Notetaking. This is chiefly a special use of the dash in handwriting, found for example in lecture notes:

1856 – Treaty of Paris ends Crimean War...

This is not a disciplined use of the dash. Like many informalities of handwriting, it may or may not be a trait peculiar to certain people.

En Rule

1. To Distinguish Compounds that are Not Hyphenated Compounds. This is best explained by example:

The blue-green sea (Hyphen)

He suffers from red – green colour blindness (En rule)

2. To Mark off Words where the First Element is not a Modifier of the Second. For example:

The former Liberal – SDP Alliance (En rule)

The Tyson – Bruno fight (En rule)

3. In Date Ranges, Page References, and Linked Places. The en rule is typically used as shown in the following examples:

The 1914 – 18 war

The German composer and organist J.S. Bach (1685 – 1750)

Typographical Note on the Choice of Em and En Rules

The uses of the dash so far discussed can all be represented in typing by a spaced hyphen (-). Typesetters are, however, faced with a choice between two basic alternatives: either they can use an em rule closed up to each of the words on each side—as in this sentence—or they can use an en rule – like this – with a space on each side. The unspaced em rule is the older form, but among modern editors and designers a preference is growing for the spaced en rule. The latter probably has a more up-to-date look, and the choice may also be governed by the size and style of type involved. But in the end it does not much matter which rule is used for the dash, as long as the choice is consistently followed throughout.

In the next section of this discussion, however, the use of en and em rules is more restricted. We shall group our usages in accordance with which rules are to be used, with a note on how they should be represented in a typescript. We shall also mention double em rules as we need to.

(*See* pp. 8 – 9, 11 – 13 and 61 – 2.)

The Gatwick – Malaga flight has been delayed for two hours.

The Chinese – Soviet border

The following sentences wrongly use the en rule:

From 1946 – 71 she was a lecturer in French at a provincial university. (Write 'From 1946 to 1971 ...'.)

We should like to use a second colour in the section of the book between pages 65 – 80. (Write '. . . between pages 65 and 80'.)

En rules meaning 'and' or 'to' do not usually have spaces each side. But there are times when spaces help clarity of reading:

Friday 21 July – Saturday 16 September
c. 1494 – c. 1520

However, be careful not to cause confusion with parenthetic dashes if you are using spaced en rules for these.

4. Denoting Negative Numbers or Quantities. An en rule immediately followed by a number may be used to denote a negative quantity.

– 4.6   – 273°C

However, it should be noted that most typesetters have a minus sign that is intermediate between an en and an em rule. A typesetter would probably use this automatically for scientific work.

Note for Typists

A typist can represent en rules by hyphens with or without spaces each side. If the typescript is intended to be printed and published, an accompanying typographical specification will say whether parenthetical dashes should be en or em rules. Other dashes will have to be marked up by a copy-editor, especially closed-up hyphens that should be en rules.

Em Rule
1. To Mark Omission. An em rule (or a double em rule, if the

em rule is being used for the parenthetic dash) is used to
denote a partly or wholly suppressed name or swear word:

> Last summer, she had an affair with Lord —.

> I travelled to the small hilltop village of P—, where I
> stayed the night at a pleasant inn.

> Keep your —ing nose out of my affairs.

2. In Indexes and Bibliographies. Em rules or double em rules
are used, often as an alternative to indention, to indicate a
repeated entry heading in an index or a repeated author's
name in a bibliography:

> Dickinson, A.E.F., 'The Legacy of Vaughan Williams: A
> Retrospect', *Music Review* XIX (1958), pp. 290–304

> ——, 'Toward the Unknown Region', *Music Review* IX
> (1948), pp. 275 ff

> ——, *Vaughan Williams*, Faber & Faber (1963)

3. In Tables. Em rules are sometimes used in the columns of
a table to indicate a lack of available data or an inapplicable
item.

4. To Introduce a Quotation in a Foreign Language. This is
encountered in languages such as French:

> *—Comment allez-vous, M Dubois, dit Marie.*

Note for Typists

For the uses of the em rule that we have specified, the
double hyphen (--) is preferred, with a suitable
explanation to the typesetter if you are preparing a
manuscript for the press. Do remember, however, that if
you are using an em rule to represent a parenthetical dash,
you can type this as a spaced hyphen. The copy-editor
should mark it up as an em rule if need be.

Chapter 7

Ellipsis

The Greek word *elleipsis*, a noun taken from the verb *elleipein*, 'to leave behind, leave out, omit', is the origin of our English word ellipsis, the act or an instance of omitting part of a word, sentence or passage, especially in quoted material. A succession of full points, written as ... or .... separated by regular spacing, is the signal for an ellipsis. In some languages, such as French, the ellipsis may be set as a single character (...) and is often referred to as 'points of suspension'.

Ellipsis in Quotations
The chief use of an ellipsis is to mark the gap in a quotation resulting from the omission of a word or words from that quotation.

1. Non-Scholarly Use. Three or four dots are normally used for the ordinary ellipsis in non-scholarly usage. Strictly, the typographical form preferred in Britain is three dots, usually with spaces each side, although sometimes American practice is to close up these spaces. A three-dot ellipsis is used to mark an omission of words within a sentence.

Four dots are used when the portion of the quotation just before the omission itself ends with a full point. In such a case, the first dot in a four-dot ellipsis is in fact that full point and is closed up to the end of the preceding word. A four-dot ellipsis is also often used when the final words of a quotation are omitted but what remains makes complete sense.

The following examples illustrate the use of the three- and four-dot ellipsis. They are based on the following source quotation:

It is of course as a composer that we know Rakhmaninov best today, an artist still speaking to us directly in a musical language that was growing old when he was still young. For Rakhmaninov was the last of the 19th-century Russians, never more at his best than when presenting his listener with a long, flowing melody imbued with what Michael Kennedy has called 'a resigned melancholy'.

The three-dot ellipsis indicates omission within a sentence:

It is ... as a composer that we know Rakhmaninov best today, an artist still speaking ... in a musical language that was growing old when he was still young. For Rakhmaninov was the last of the 19th-century Russians, never more at his best than when presenting ... a long, flowing melody imbued with what Michael Kennedy has called 'a resigned melancholy'. .

The three-dot ellipsis is also used to mark off a quotation broken off without making complete sense:

It is of course as a composer that we know Rakhmaninov best today, an artist still speaking to us directly in a musical language that was growing old when he was still young. For Rakhmaninov was the last of the 19th-century ...

A three-dot ellipsis may also introduce a quotation when it starts in the middle of a sentence, whether the resulting extract makes complete sense or not:

> ... an artist still speaking to us directly in a musical
> language that was growing old when he was still young.
> For Rakhmaninov was the last of the 19th-century ...

The four-dot ellipsis is used when the part of the quotation immediately before the omission is a sentence ending in a full point:

> It is of course as a composer that we know Rakhmaninov
> best today, an artist still speaking to us directly in a
> musical language that was growing old when he was still
> young .... the last of the 19th-century Russians, never
> more at his best than when presenting his listener with a
> long, flowing melody imbued with what Michael Kennedy
> has called 'a resigned melancholy'.

The four-dot ellipsis is also often used to mark a quotation broken off at the end but leaving a remnant that makes complete sense:

> It is of course as a composer that we know Rakhmaninov
> best today, an artist still speaking to us directly in a
> musical language that was growing old when he was still
> young. For Rakhmaninov was the last of the 19th-century
> Russians ....

It should be noted that this last usage is intended to signal the fact that the quotation has been broken off in mid-sentence. If we had stopped the quotation after 'young', there would have been no need to use an ellipsis at all.

The ellipsis is used whether the quotation is enclosed within quotation marks or set off separately or in smaller type. When quotation marks are used, the introductory ellipsis may be dispensed with if the quotation is made to form part of the syntax of the sentence; if, however, the quotation follows a colon, the introductory ellipsis is used within the quotation marks. Compare these two examples:

We learn that Rakhmaninov was 'an artist still speaking to us directly in a musical language that was growing old when he was still young.'

But:

> As a composer, Rakhmaninov owed much to the 19th century. This is how a noted music critic has recently described him: '. . . an artist still speaking to us directly in a musical language that was growing old when he was still young.'

2. Scholarly Use. The number of dots (that is, full points) used to signal an ellipsis can vary in scholarly editing. In critical editions of classical texts or historical documents, illegible parts of words are represented by dots, one for each letter that cannot be read or is assumed to be missing. Three dots signal the omission of whole words or passages that are unreadable or missing from the source, while a line of dots stands for a more significant gap. Missing lines of poetry may also be signalled by a row of dots that can run the length of the average line. Dots representing large gaps are normally widely spaced apart. Dots of omission may be used in conjunction with square brackets to clarify the text, as in this example:

> Catherine's diary for August 1889 revealed her feelings. The entry for 7 May ran:
> J..n [John] v...t.d me at B..u...on [Broughton]. He promised at l.st that he wd ... [? marry me] next yr.

Critical editions using dots in this way are of scholarly interest only. More practical editions for the general reader may use square brackets only. Thus the diary entry might be rendered:

J[oh]n v[isi]t[e]d me at B[ro]u[ght]on. He promised at l[a]st that he w[oul]d [? marry me] next y[ea]r.

Other Uses of Ellipsis

The three-dot ellipsis (any more than three is looked on by most sensible readers and writers as an extravagance or a piece of vulgar sensationalism) is used in fiction to indicate a number of effects.

1. Halting dialogue. For example:

The wounded soldier spoke with difficulty: 'Doc, you ... you've got to ... promise me you'll ... look after Myra.'

2. Tailing off. An ellipsis marks a trailing away at the end of a sentence. It represents a much less abrupt break than a dash. For example:

'The trouble is,' she said, 'I love you and I just can't live without you and ...'

He stood on the outer limits of the town and gazed at the road before him. Beyond the town lay the savannah, and beyond that lay the mountains, and beyond those ... what?

3. To Close an Incomplete List or Endless Series. This is both a general and technical use. The general use may be thought of as rather informal. Here are examples of both:

A typical geometric progression is this one: 1, 2, 4, 8, 16, 32, 64, 128, ...

Eggs, butter, washing powder, ... Her shopping list had all the usual household items.

4. In mathematical expressions. An ellipsis marks an omission of terms in a series before the *n*th term. For example:

In the sequence of terms, the index r takes on the successive values of 0, 1, 2, 3, ..., n.

5. *The Ellipsis with Exclamation and Question Marks.* When required, exclamations or questions may end in an ellipsis. In this case, the exclamation mark or question mark follows the ellipsis. For example:

How I detest his haughtiness, his patronizing attitude, his self-righteousness ...!

Who is going to tell him? John? Alison? Tom ...?

Chapter 8

Quotation Marks

The translators of the Authorized Version of the Bible, which was published in 1611, knew nothing about quotation marks:

> ... and He asked them, saying, Whom say the people that I am? They answering said, John the Baptist; but some say, Elias, and others say, that one of the old prophets is risen again. He said, But whom say ye that I am? Peter answering said, The Christ of God.
>
> – Luke 9:18–20

By the eighteenth century, however, English writers had discovered quotation marks, and punctuation pundits are glad they did, for there is still much to argue about in the use of these marks, not least whether they should be single or double. (*See* the remarks on single and double quotation marks below.)

In typewritten documents, reports or other manuscripts, and also in some pieces of handwritten material, quotation marks are represented either as ' ' or as " ". In printed books and the output from some word processors or desktop publishing equipment, as well as in carefully handwritten manuscripts, the symbols are differentiated, being set down as either ' ' or " ".These latter symbols are what are called inverted commas (or speech marks) in Britain. The term 'inverted commas' has been a generally accepted synonym for 'quotation marks' for a long time, even though only the opening marks are true inverted commas (the closing ones

being ordinary commas placed above the level of the letters).
In this account, we shall use the more descriptive term
'quotation marks, as we have done elsewhere. We shall also
note that they are often called quote marks or quotes for
short.

Quotation Marks in a Sentence

The main function of quotation marks is to enclose the actual
words said or written by somebody. These words generally
have to be introduced, interrupted or otherwise accompanied
by a clause or phrase that places them in the context in which
they are being quoted — e.g., 'she said' or 'Tom replied'.
Such a clause or phrase, not being part of the quotation, goes
outside the quotation marks. Some people refer to it as a
'reporting' clause; for convenience, so shall we:

> 'You, sir,' shouted Colonel Napier, 'are a scoundrel!'

> Turning towards him, she said calmly, 'I think that you
> had better leave.'

> Smith tried to keep the emotion out of his voice: 'We have
> to face it — the spaceship has disappeared.'

> 'Emma Woodhouse, handsome, clever, and rich, with a
> comfortable home and happy disposition, seemed to unite
> some of the best blessings of existence; and had lived
> nearly twenty-one years in the world with very little to
> distress or vex her.' So begins Jane Austen's novel *Emma*.

Reporting clauses and Commas. Reporting clauses are
regarded as parenthetic phrases and as such are set off from
the part of the sentence that forms the quotation by commas
like this:

> Jean said, 'Jim, I love you.'

> 'Jim,' said Jean, 'I love you.'

> 'Jim, I love you,' said Jean.

In these examples, a comma in the original quotation is preserved throughout. But note that in the last example the full point ending the quotation is replaced by a comma. This is because any pause in the quotation coming directly before the reporting clause is conventionally replaced by a comma. This comma is suppressed by a concluding question mark or exclamation mark. (*See* below.)

Note the position of the comma in this sentence:

> 'You', he thundered, 'will repay every penny you have ever borrowed from my family.'

Because there is no comma in the original quotation ('You will repay every penny ...'), a true parenthetical comma placed outside the quotation marks sets off the reporting clause from the rest of the sentence.

Note that in American usage, the comma always goes inside the quotation marks, even in the example above:

> 'You,' he thundered, 'will repay every penny you have ever borrowed from my family.'

When Commas are Absent. Commas can be omitted after verbs of saying when the quotation is an exclamation functioning as the direct object of the verb concerned or when it is suppressed by an exclamation or question mark in a preceding quote:

> He rang the bell and shouted 'Fire!'

> 'Look out!' he yelled. 'The wall's collapsing!'

> 'Didn't you hear me?' said the old man. 'I said "Look out!"'

(For the use of double quotation marks in the last example, see the part of this chapter devoted to double and single quotes.)

Note that when the object of the reporting clause's verb is yes or no, quotation marks are in certain circumstances not used:

Tom and Jane were asked if they would come but they said no.

Asked if he would like a cup of coffee, John smiled and said, 'Yes, please, I'd love one.'

Quotation Marks in Dialogue. Sections of dialogue in a novel may dispense with reporting clauses, provided that there is no doubt about which person is speaking. Usually, as in the following example, the words assigned to each speaker in a piece of quoted dialogue begin on a new line every time.

... a man and woman were speaking. He listened for a moment to their conversation.

'Come on, Sally, love. Just one.'
'Fred, I told you. I'm not that sort of girl.'
'Well, look — can I take you out tomorrow night?'
'I'm washing my hair tomorrow.'

Quotation Marks and Paragraphs. In long discursive writing, often in translations of Greek or Roman speeches, it is necessary to set out the quoted speech in a series of paragraphs. The convention is to introduce the speech with an 'open-quotation' mark and to repeat this mark at the start of each new paragraph within the speech. The only time that the 'close quotation' mark is used is right at the end of the final paragraph of the speech. The following example illustrates the procedure, although in practice the paragraphs are generally much longer:

There was applause as he rose to speak. Gesturing for silence, he began:

'My friends, I have asked you here today for two main reasons, which I shall be glad to explain to you.

'Firstly, I have been fortunate enough to attain my eightieth birthday and wanted you to help me celebrate it. Some of you I haven't seen for ten years or more.

'And secondly, I'd like to find out which one of you is trying to murder me.'

Double or Single Quotes. H.W. Fowler was the most eminent advocate of the use of single quotations marks for normal use and double ones to enclose quotes within quotes. British publishers have generally followed this practice, but publishers in the United States and elsewhere have stuck to the use of double quotes for ordinary direct speech and singles for quotes within quotes. In a letter or business report, it does not much matter which order is adopted as long as the writer follows a consistent policy. On the whole, it would seem best to use double quotation marks as standard and only use single ones for quotes within quotes, as the Americans do. Authors of books are generally told what to do by their editors. The likely confusion between a single 'close-quote' symbol and an apostrophe is possible, but is perhaps overemphasized. *See* the chapter on Apostrophe.

Quotes within Quotes. Quotations can be nested one inside the other, rather like Russian dolls. We signal the different 'levels' of quotation by alternating between single and double quotation marks (or doubles and singles, if you prefer). Thus a main quotation is marked off by, say, single quotation marks, the quotation within the quotation is marked off by doubles, the quotation within that is marked off by singles, and so on. For example:

The police inspector referred to his notes: 'When arrested the prisoner said, "All right, I confess." He then asked "Can I please make a phone call?" '

'I remember', said Bert, 'my old dad telling me, "Son, your grandfather had a motto. 'Do as you would be done by,' he used to say, and I've never forgotten those words to this day. Nor should you." And, do you know, I never have.'

Lawson asked, 'Am I right in thinking that Capt. Smith said "I heard the sentry shout 'Halt!' "?'

It is generally impractical to go further than a quote within a quote within a quote. Rather than involve yourself in such complications, you ought to consider using reported speech.

Direct and Reported Speech

Although this book is not a grammar, it is worthwhile mentioning at this point the distinction between direct and reported speech. Direct speech is the verbatim reproduction, enclosed within quotation marks, of what somebody actually said. Any of the earlier examples in this section illustrate it.

Reported speech, by contrast, is a restatement by the writer of the meaning of what someone said. In reported speech, which is also called indirect speech or indirect discourse, the reporting clause introduces or otherwise accompanies a sentence not en-closed in quotation marks. When the reporting clause precedes such a sentence, the two are often linked by the word 'that'. The restated sentence of reported speech, unlike the verbatim quotation of direct speech, agrees in tense with the reporting clause, being removed one step back into the past from the tense of the original words upon which it is based.

It is beyond our province here to go too deeply into the recasting of direct speech into reported speech. These two labelled examples must suffice:

Tom said, 'I will be glad to come to see you on Friday. Are you still living where you were last year?' (Direct)

Tom said that he would be glad to go to see her on Friday. He asked if she was still living where she had been the previous year.(Reported)

Thoughts are often expressed as direct quotations without quotation marks. The tense of the part of the sentence expressing the thought may or may not be the same as that of the verb of thinking, and question marks may or may not be retained. Some flexibility is allowed, as these examples illustrate:

(a) Where, he wondered, would he find a hotel in this deserted place? He could see that this job was going to be more difficult than he had realized.

(b) Where, he wondered, am I going to find a hotel in this deserted place? I can see that this job is going to be more difficult than I realized.

(c) He wondered where he was going to find a hotel in this deserted place. He could see ... (The sentence continues as for (a))

(d) Where was he going to find a hotel in this deserted place, he wondered. He could see ...

(e) Where am I going to find a hotel in this deserted place, He wondered. He could see... (Continue as in (a) − or) I can see ... (Continue as in (b))

Other possibilities may be allowed. *See also* the chapters on the Full Point and Question Mark.

The 'That' Trap. Avoid using quotation marks in a that-clause. Quotes are only to be used for the actual words said or written. The following example is wrong:

Bill said that 'he wasn't going to take that lying down'.

What Bill actually said was: 'I am not going to take that lying down.' To make the sentence correct and still keep the flavour of the quotation, we can move the quotation marks on a bit:

Bill said that he wasn't going to 'take that lying down'.

But using quotation marks in a that-clause is a style of writing prone to error, and it should be avoided.

Other Uses of Quotation Marks

Quotation marks are used in several ways that do not directly relate to verbatim transcriptions of things said or written. They are conventionally used to enclose the following:

(a) Words or phrases used ironically, sarcastically, technically or in some other way than normal:

Some people who think of themselves as 'fashionable' are just plain vulgar.

The decision worried him, but he knew that he had 'burned his boats'.

(Note that well-known idioms such as the one in the second example are not usually enclosed in quotation marks these days.)

(b) Slang words:

Acapulco is a 'glitzy' resort where the rich and beautiful go to have fun.

(c) Words or phrases to which the author wishes to draw attention – what Eric Partridge called 'words named as words':

109

The abstract nouns 'virtue' and 'vice' are complete opposites.

The word means 'to fall over backwards'.

(d) Titles of paintings, poems, short stories, essays, and chapters within a book:

'Sunflowers' is one of Van Gogh's finest paintings.

Have you read Gerard Manley Hopkins? His poem 'Pied Beauty' is one of my favourites.

'Aristophanes and the War Party' is a brilliant lecture by Gilbert Murray. It was written and delivered in 1928 and included in Murray's Humanist Essays.

(Note that the titles of books, magazines and newspapers are rarely given between quotation marks in printed matter nowadays except when an italic form of a given typeface is unavailable. *See* the chapter on Italics.)

Quotation Marks and Other Punctuation Marks

This is one of the most hotly contested issues in punctuation. In practice, the question boils down to this: should the comma, the full point, and so on, be placed inside or outside the quotation marks? We have already briefly gone over the ground in earlier sections. Here we shall restate some basic principles and provide some further examples.

The underlying rule is that generally stops, exclamation marks and question marks go inside the quotation marks if they belong to the quotation and outside if they do not. Exclamation marks and question marks are relatively uncomplicated in this regard. For example:

He rang the bell and shouted 'Fire!'

'Help!' she screamed. 'Let me out!'

'Where are you, William?' she called. 'Where have you gone?'

Did he say 'Titan' or 'Triton'?

Did I hear you shout 'Fire!'?

To think that you could be so tactless and ask me 'What is love?'!

How stupid you were to shout 'Fire!'!

Did Pilate really ask Christ, 'What is truth?'?

In the last two examples, some authorities recommend that one or the other of the two exclamation marks and question marks should be dropped.

Parentheses and square brackets can go inside quotation marks and quotation marks can go inside parentheses and square brackets. Here is an interesting example of the latter, in which punctuation marks seem to pile up:

I attach copies of the relevant sections (with which, incidentally, Mr Jones said he could 'find no fault'!).

Dashes need to be handled with a little care. If the original quotation contains a phrase between parenthetic dashes, it is wise to break the quote if you must before the first dash and include that dash in the second part of the quote. In this pair of examples, the first is recommended usage:

'I bought a pair of jeans,' he said, ' – blue ones they were – in a shop in Croydon.'

'I bought a pair of jeans – ' he said, 'blue ones they were – in a shop in Croydon.'

The first sentence avoids confusion as to whether the text has been abruptly broken off rather than being just interrupted. The second example leaves room for doubt.

Commas, semicolons, colons and full stops at the break point in an original quotation are all represented by a comma inside the quotation marks when the quotation is contained within a sentence. If the comma is replacing a full point, semicolon or colon, then the reporting clause (the 'he said' clause) ends with the full point, semicolon or colon as appropriate.

'To err is human,' she said; 'to forgive is divine.'

'Man proposes,' says the proverb: 'God disposes.'

'Come in,' she said. 'Would you like a cup of coffee?'

The Comma, the Full Point and Quotation Marks. The placing of the comma with respect to quotation marks has already been discussed in the parts of this chapter headed 'Reporting Clauses and Commas' and 'When Commas are Absent'. There is no more to add on the positioning of commas, except to repeat that Americans always place the comma inside the quotation marks under all circumstances. The full point is also placed within quotation marks on all occasions by American writers. But in Britain it is not. The full point goes inside quotation marks only if it marks the end of the quotation, and the end of that quotation coincides with the end of the sentence containing it.

Eric said, 'You have a point there.'

Logic would say that the full point inside the quotation marks ends the quotation only and would demand that another one be placed outside the quotation marks to end the containing sentence. That second full point is, however, suppressed.

The full point goes inside the quotation marks in a sentence that is taken up entirely by a quotation. For example, in dialogue:

She spoke quietly to John: 'How can I make you see the foolishness of all this?'

'You'll never convince me that it is foolishness, Jane.'

'But it is, darling. In fact, it's complete lunacy.'

On the other hand, if the containing sentence ends with only a phrase from the quotation or a portion of it that does not make complete sense, the full point is generally placed outside the quotation marks:

Under no circumstances can this invention be regarded as 'modern and up-to-date'.

He said that he would not 'take this lying down'.

General Use of Quotation Marks

Quotation marks should be used as little as possible in ordinary writing. The ironic, sarcastic or technical uses of them should in particular be controlled to avoid an irritating 'peppering' of quote marks on a page. It is worth noting that once you have given the first mention of a technical or slang word in quotation marks, subsequent mentions need not also be in quotes.

Chapter 9

Apostrophe

The apostrophe, taken in from the Greek language, joined
the English system of punctuation in the seventeenth century.
It is symbolized by ' (a superior comma) and therefore
appears to be identical with the mark that closes a quotation.
This resemblance has led a few authorities to disown the
system of using single quotation marks as standard on the
grounds of potential, if not actual, confusion. For example:

'Aristophanes' plays were popular with Athens' citizens.'

One has to accept that the lobby against the use of single
quotation marks undoubtedly has a case. Unfortunately,
British publishers have taken single quotes to their hearts and
would be reluctant to make a change to double quote marks
as part of their house styles. There is of course nothing to
stop writers of letters, company reports, memos, and the like
from using double quotes if they wish, and that is something
we have already recommended. British authors, however,
usually have to be to be guided by their editors on this point.
To be practical and honest, the case of those opposed to
single quotes is overstressed. Good writers and editors will
recast such a sentence as the above if actual confusion is
likely:

'The plays of Aristophanes were popular with the citizens
of Athens.'

History of the Apostrophe

The Greek word *apostrophos*, meaning 'a turning away', is the origin of the English word *apostrophe* as applied to the ' symbol. As such it provides a very good guide to the basic use of the apostrophe both by the Greeks and by ourselves. In Greek manuscripts of medieval times it was written as part of a word in order to show that letters had been 'turned away' — that is, omitted, or (more technically) elided — from that word. When the English took it over in the seventeenth century, they began by using it for the same purpose — that is, to mark omissions.

Poets welcomed it to show the dropping of unstressed syllables in lines that would not otherwise scan properly. The dropping of v in *e'en* (for even), *e'er* (for ever) and *o'er* (for over) is a literary survival that we readily recognize today, and published editions of Shakespeare often contain such forms as *in't* (for in it) and *th'* (for the).

Even when the apostrophe is used to denote possession or an analogous relationship, it is really the extension of the symbol's use as a mark of omission. In the early sixteenth century, early Modern English still retained certain inflexions or word endings from its previous Old and Middle stages similar to those still found in German today. One was the use of *-es* to mark the genitive, or possessive, case in certain masculine and neuter nouns. In dropping the *-e-* of the genitive ending, writers of the seventeenth century began to signal its absence with an apostrophe. The resulting *'s* was then gradually extended to words that had never had the *-es* ending in the genitive. The general possessive *'s* became standard practice in the eighteenth century.

And what happens when the double-quoter needs to use single quotation marks for an internal quotation? For example:

> John said, "My professor began his lecture like this: 'Aristophanes' plays were popular with Athens' citizens.'"

Sadly, argument is ultimately fruitless.

For convenience we now divide the uses of the apostrophe into three main groups: the possessive use, the use in marking omissions and the plural use.

The Possessive Use

1. The possessive form is shown by *'s* (apostrophe + *s*) in the case of the following four groups of nouns, whether they are in the singular or in the plural:

(a) Nouns that have the same form in both singular and plural:

sheep   deer   wildebeest   salmon

A wolf in sheep's clothing.

These salmon's spawning areas are in the rivers of Yorkshire.

(b) Nouns in which the vowels and perhaps the way of showing some consonants change:

mouse—mice   man—men   woman—women
goose—geese   tooth—teeth   foot—feet

The mouse's hole — the mice's tails.

The man's house — the men's room.

(c) Nouns with irregular plurals, some of which are archaic or obsolete:

child—children   die—dice   penny—pence
brother—brethren

The child's chair—the children's playground.

My brother's car—thy brethren's love.

(d) Nouns forming foreign plurals:

nebula—nebulae   phenomenon—phenomena
stigma—stigmata

The nebula's shape resembles that of a horse's head.

The precise extent of these phenomena's effects is not known.

The *'s* is also used to show the possessive in the case of all singular nouns that form their plurals by adding *-s*.

The boy's bike   The girl's coat   The horse's head

Maurice's boutique

So far we have no problems. Unfortunately, with the remaining groups of nouns we enter a more difficult area.

We continue to use the *'s* (apostrophe + *s*) to signal possession in the following cases:

(i) With most common and proper nouns whose singular forms end in *-s*:

James's reign   Charles's kingdom
William Morris's art   John Williams's guitar
Keats's poetry.

There are now fewer exceptions to this rule than there used to be. Some authorities have recommended that words ending in *-s* having more than one syllable should take only an apostrophe to indicate possession. Thus, we ought to write of

117

John Williams' guitar. This procedure, however, is no longer sustainable in the face of current usage.

(ii) With nouns ending in *-ess* or *-ness*. This is a special case of *-s* above, but is worth picking out because some writers have legislated against the use of *'s*, again flying in the face of modern usage:

The princess's crown   The lioness's cubs

2. *The possessive* is shown by means of the apostrophe alone in the following cases:

(a) The plural form of all nouns whose plurals end in *-s* or in *-es*:

The boys' jackets   The horses' tails   The buses' tyres.

Those girls' bikinis are very revealing.

(b) Most classical and biblical names ending in *-s*:

Euripides' plays   Hercules' strength   Tacitus' Annals
Moses' law   Jesus' miracles.

Thucydides' *History* is an unbiased account of the Peloponnesian War.

Note that this principle extends to people such as St Thomas Aquinas and Paracelsus also:

Paracelsus' theories paved the way for modern medicine.

(c) Many other foreign names ending in *-s* or *-z*:

Cervantes' stories   Boaz' wife

(But note that in the latter case 'Boaz's wife' is becoming increasingly common. Note also that the simple apostrophe for signalling the possessive form of French names ending in an unpronounced *-s* or *-x* - e.g. King Louis' reign − is on the way out. Hart's *Rules* did not support it in the 1960s and 1970s, and we have no reason to do so now; thus we prefer 'King Louis's reign'.

(c) Certain nouns ending in *-nce*, especially in set phrases:

appearance' sake   conscience' sake

(Note also in this context the phrase 'for goodness' sake'.)

The examples under 2(c) are heavily influenced by pronunciation, which is a reasonable guide when it comes to common collocations such as 'for goodness' sake'. But how can one distinguish between 'Charles Dickens' novels', which is the way some people say it, and 'Charles Dickens's novels', which reflects 'other people's habits'. In such a case, apostrophe + *s* is always preferable to apostrophe alone because it follows a general pattern.)

3. Multi-word possessives in which the noun concerned is a tightly bound phrase or involves two or more people acting together, add *'s* or *'* to the last word of the phrase or list

William and Mary's reign

Her Majesty the Queen of England's only daughter

Where the people or things on the list are considered as separate, the *'s* or *'* is attached to each person or thing:

John and Mary's family (The family belong to both John and Mary.)

But:

John's and Mary's family (The family of John and the family of Mary — two separate families.)

4. The possessive use of the apostrophe + *s* (that is, *'s*) is found in many place names and addresses:

St John's, Newfoundland   St John's Wood
St Michael's Mount   Land's End   Lord's Cricket
Ground.

But it is also excluded from many such names in modern usage:

Earls Court   Golders Green   St Albans
Bury St Edmunds

Johns Hopkins University.

5. *We use* 's *informally* to designate familiar addresses and locations:

I have an appointment at the hairdresser's.

We can meet at Angela's after the concert.

I shop at Woolworth's.

Note that in the last of these examples the apostrophe is increasingly falling out of use in British English; 'I shop at Woolworths' is almost standard usage.

6. *Possessive Before Gerund.* A purely grammatical use involves whether or not one should employ a possessive before a gerund (a verbal noun ending in *-ing*). In practice what this means is: Which of these sentences is right?

(i)   John singing really annoys me.

       John's singing really annoys me.

(ii)   I hope you don't mind Tom being here.

       I hope you don't mind Tom's being here.

(iii) John came without Sally knowing about it.

       John came without Sally's knowing about it.

(iv) He wouldn't hear of me paying back any of the money.

He wouldn't hear of my paying back any of the money.

Which is right? They all are; only the first reads a little awkwardly. The use of the 's or ' form or of the possessive pronoun is more formal and literary. The other* is more likely to be heard in speech. A report might look more polished and less colloquial if the possessive + gerund form is used. But beware of pomposity:

Owing to our department's having been reorganized recently, your original requisition form has been mislaid.

Use in Marking Omissions
1. *The apostrophe* is regularly used to indicate the omission of a letter or letters in a word or phrase. For example:

'Fraid I haven't seen him. Can't tell you where he is (I am afraid I have not seen him. I cannot tell you where he is.)

This use of the apostrophe is more or less confined to the most informal writing. The most typical instances are:

don't, won't	do not, will not
shan't, can't	shall not, cannot
aren't, isn't	are not, is not
hasn't, haven't	has not, have not

The verb 'to be' has the following apostrophe forms for colloquial usage:

I'm, you're, he's	I am, you are, he is
she's, we're, they're	she is, we are, they are

---

*Strictly speaking, in the non-apostrophe form, the -ing word is a present participle.

Note also these:

I've, you've, he's	I have, you have, he has
she's, we've, they've	she has, we have, they have
I'll, you'll, he'll	I shall/will, you shall/will he shall/will
she'll, we'll, they'll	she shall/will, we shall/will. they shall/will

And finally these:

I'd, you'd, he'd,	I had, should or would, you
she'd, we'd, they'd	had, should or would, etc.

It's and Its. This continues to be a major problem for some writers, even though the distinction is very easy.

The form *it's* is a shortening of *it is* or *it has*:

It's a nice day.

It's been fun working with you, John.

This is an informal use.

The form *its* is a possessive pronoun parallel with *his* and *her*. For example:

Its leaves have withered.

The museum presents its exhibits to the public in an imaginative way.

This is a standard, non-colloquial use.

The forms *it'll* (= it shall/will) and *it'd* (= it had, or it should/would) are also encountered.

Note that there is no apostrophe in *his*, *hers*, *ours*, *theirs*, and *yours*:

This is an old dress of my mother's

This is an old dress of hers.

122

But note also that the possessive of the pronoun *one* is *one's*, with an apostrophe:

It is difficult to keep one's hair clean in a grimy city.

Finally, please do not confuse *their*, *there* and *they're*. Try this sentence as a mnemonic:

They have left their luggage there and they're coming back for it.

2. *In names and stock phrases.* The prefix *O* in Irish names is conventionally (though wrongly) capitalized and followed by an apostrophe in Anglicized Irish names, presumably on the analogy of *o'* (of) in such phrases as will-o'-the-wisp (*see* below). (In Irish, there is no apostrophe, and the form is lower-case *o* followed by a space (*o* means 'descendant of').) Examples of the accepted Anglicized procedure are:

    O'Connell   O'Casey

In some names of Scottish origin beginning with *Mac* or *Mc*, an apostrophe is occasionally encountered:

    M'Dougal   M'Quillian

Other names in which apostrophes represent missing letters include:

    D'Cruz   D'Arcy

The apostrophe of omission is found in many stock phrases. For example *o'* replaces *of* in:

John o'Groats (a place name)   cat-o'-nine-tails
will-o'-the-wisp   o'clock (of the clock)

3. *Contracted Words.* These include many nautical terms and represent spellings that reflect pronunciations.

Fo'c's'le   bo's'n

Note that the forms *forecastle* and *boatswain* are preferred in non-nautical usage.

We no longer write 'flu for flu (influenza), 'cello for cello (violoncello) or 'plane for plane (aeroplane or airplane). There are a few publishers who would probably like to restore these apostrophe spellings, but they are in a dwindling minority.

4. Contracted Numbers. This usage applies primarily to years and again is an informal use:

I was born in '47 (. . . in 1947)

The class of '89 (. . . of 1989)

The book is a brilliant portrayal of life in the '50s (. . . the 1950s)

The Plural Use

The apostrophe is commonly used before the -*s* that serves to form the plural of letters and words used (often in italics) as letters and words, not as units of meaningful discourse:

Mind your p's and q's.

There are five and's in that sentence.

This practice is justifiable in avoiding confusion between *as*, *is* and *us* on the one hand and *a*'s, *i*'s, and *u*'s on the other. To keep consistency all letters should be treated the same — that is, they should all take apostrophes.

However, the use of the apostrophe is on the wane as a signal of the plural. The sentence 'Mind your *ps* and *qs*' is not hard to understand, especially if the letters are placed in italics and the pluralizing -*s* is left in Roman type. In the second sentence, ands works just as well as and's.

Eric Partridge, however, cites a very good use of the pluralizing apostrophe:

The class includes three Louis's and two Lewises.

Plural Numbers. There is no longer any justification for retaining the apostrophe in 1920s, mid-70s, and similar phrases. It represents needless clutter and looks old-fashioned:

We are getting ready for the new single Europe of the 1990s.

Tomorrow's temperatures will be in the low 30s Celsius.

Somehow these sentences would not look so up to date with apostrophes.

Possessive and Plural Abbreviations

Abbreviations and sets of initials retain their full points − if they have them − when used in the possessive or cited in the plural. A plain -s is used to indicate the plural; the apostrophe + s is used to indicate possession when the abbreviation is single; and the s + apostrophe is used to indicate possession with abbreviations in the plural. Although the apostrophe + s has been used to show plurals of abbreviations in the past, there is really no point in perpetuating this waste of charcters.

These examples must suffice to illustrate the usage:

The BBC's revenue comes mainly from licence fees.

Throughout the 1960s Smith & Co.'s profits went up each year by about 2 per cent.

There are four Ph.D.s teaching at this institute.

Yesterday Parliament debated MPs' salaries.

General Point

Several commentators have noted that the apostrophe has been or is being dropped in many areas. Printers often set singular and plural possessives without it. Paradoxically, greengrocers and market-stall owners put it on signs where it either should not be or may be rather unexpected. References to *cox's*, *tom's* and *pot's* (or *potato's*) are actually not wrong because the apostrophe signals omission of letters; references to *lettuce's* and *cabbage's* are wrong, however, and should be avoided. And anybody who writes the word *baby's* for *babies* cannot spell.

Chapter 10

Question Mark and Exclamation Mark

The question mark and the exclamation mark are, strictly speaking, not stops, or pause marks, but are in fact marks of expression or tone. An important fact about their function, however, is that they replace the full point at the end of sentences that are interrogative or exclamatory. To this extent at least, they deserve to be classed as punctuation marks. And since they share the nature of being expression marks – rather like crescendo and diminuendo marks in music – they may be conveniently treated together in one chapter of our punctuation survey.

Question Mark in a Sentence

In its most usual employment as a punctuation mark, the question mark (also known as the interrogation mark, the interrogation point, the point or mark of interrogation, or – especially among journalists – the query) replaces the full point in the sentences in which it occurs. However, since it is a tone mark, it may be, and often is, employed in mid-sentence. Its most frequently encountered uses are the following:

1. At the End of a Direct Question. A direct question is a straight, ordinary question. The question may be either real, expecting and getting an answer, or rhetorical, expecting no actual answer but often implying a negative one. For example:

History of Question and Exclamation Marks

The question mark, for which ? is the symbol in English and certain other European languages, was the first of these two tone marks to appear in the punctuation system. Scribes introduced an early form of the question mark, known as the *punctus interrogativus*, into their Latin manuscripts in the ninth century AD. Some experts now believe that the *punctus interrogativus* was borrowed from a very early form of musical notation. According to an alternative theory, the ? is a corrupt or stylized form of the first and last letters of the Latin word *quaestio*, 'a question', or its related verb *quaero*, 'I question', the *q* being represented by the top part of the symbol, with the *o* having been reduced to a dot.

The exclamation mark, for which the symbol ! is used, did not appear until the seventeenth century, by which time nearly all the other punctuation marks were in place. It too is said to have had its origins in a Latin word, in this case the interjection *io*, an expression of joy equivalent to 'hurray'. The letter *i* may be seen as being represented by the vertical stroke, with the *o* again reduced to a dot.

Do you take sugar?

Is there life on Mars?

Can anyone doubt our leader's sincerity?

All direct questions introduced by the interrogatives *how*, *what*, *where*, *when*, *which*, *who* or *why* also end in question marks:

What's the time?

To whom do you wish to speak, please?

How do you like your eggs done?

Where will it all end?

Interjections introduced by 'How dare ...' may appear to be questions but are regularly treated as exclamations and marked accordingly. *See* below.

. *Questions Framed as Statements.* Sentences having the word order of a statement may nonetheless be questions, and this is indicated by means of a question mark. The presence of such a word as 'surely' may also indicate that the sentence is a question. However, 'surely' is also often found in exclamations (*see* below). Examples of statement-questions are:

You mean you bought that house after all?

You're surely not serious?

Questions framed as statements but containing an interrogative also take a question mark:

You've done what?

She sings in which choir?

3. *Elliptical Questions.* Partial sentences functioning as questions end in a question mark. The interrogatives used alone come into this category (*What? Where? When? How? Who?* (or *Whom?*), *Which?* etc.), and so do the following examples:

Coffee, tea or orange juice?

What for?

Anybody there?

Mr Jones? — Yes?

4. Tag Questions. A question mark is used at the end of sentences in which the writer seeks to confirm the truth of a statement or assertion by tagging a question on the end of it which expects the answer that he needs in order to make that confirmation. In fact, tag questions expect the answer 'yes' or 'no'. For example:

Sounds complicated, doesn't it?

Here are a few other examples:

You come from Wales, don't you?

He wasn't in the car, was he?

She has a great love of music, does she not?

(Note that the last example is rather formal.)

5. Indirect Questions and Polite or Formal Requests
We have already covered these topics under the chapter on the Full Point. We said there that an indirect question was a statement with a question embedded in it and that a polite or formal request was a weak command. In neither case is the question mark used. A few further examples here should make the point clear. First, an indirect question:

I want to know who you are and what you want here.

Note that a direct question would have the word order turned in this way:

Who are you and what do you want here?

Note also that in indirect questions the tense of the question agrees with the tense of the main verb of asking:

Where is my wife?

He asked where his wife was.

Under the section on the Full Point, we noted that the following sentence does not generally take a question mark at the end:

What would he be like, she wondered.

However, we did show an alternative, namely:

What would he be like? she wondered.

Some writers dislike placing the question mark in the middle of the sentence in this way. But there are those who feel that, even though the question is 'reported' in the past tense (the same tense as 'wondered'), the question mark makes it more vivid.

Some writers follow the rule that if the verb of thinking or wondering is present, and the thought/question is in the present or future, then a question mark may be placed at the end of the sentence:

What will he be like, I wonder?

Why is she so charming, I ask myself?

If, however, both verbs are in the past tense, then no question mark is used anywhere:

What would he be like, I wondered.

Why was she so charming, I asked myself.

If the tenses are mixed, though, a question mark is justified in mid-sentence on the grounds that the thought/question is virtually a verbatim quotation:

What will he be like? I wondered.

Why is she so charming? I asked myself.

The unturned indirect question is a kind of sentence in which the embedded question has not been cast into its usual indirect form. In this kind of sentence, we have to use our judgement. The question mark is a genuine rhetorical device rather than a grammatical one. If in an unturned indirect question the embedded question somehow takes precedence over the sentence as a whole, so that the verb of asking or wondering is virtually parenthetical to it, the question mark should undoubtedly be used. But otherwise it should not be used. Compare these two examples:

This book attempts to teach us what are the most important points regarding parliamentary procedure. (No question mark.)

If you know, sir, tell me where is my beloved husband? (Question mark.)

A polite or formal request is generally framed like this:

Could you please send me ten extra copies of your report.

Would all passengers please refrain from putting their feet on the seats?

Such requests are commands, instructions or imperatives cloaked in the garb of questions. But they are not true questions. Compare the use of a question mark with a straight request or inquiry:

Could I have another piece of cake, please?

May I go to the pictures with Debby tonight please, mum?

Question Marks and Quotation Marks
The question mark is placed inside quotation marks if it belongs to the quotation. Otherwise it is placed outside:

'Where are you going?' he asked.

Why did he use the word 'poison'?

If the quotation ends in a question mark and comes at the end of a sentence, the full point ending the sentence is omitted:

'John,' she asked petulantly, 'where are you going now?'

Note that these two sentences mean the same:

The question 'Is there life on Mars?' remains unresolved.

The question of whether there is life on Mars is unresolved.

The omission of quotation marks from sentences such as the first in this pair of examples is also common:

The question Is there life on Mars? remains unresolved.

The use of quotes is clearer and less offensive to those who hate question marks in the middle of sentences.

Non-Punctuational Uses
The chief non-punctuational use of the question mark is to signal doubt.

1. In Life-dates. The question mark, usually placed in front of a year of birth or death, signals the author's uncertainty as to whether this is the correct year:

Hieronymus Bosch (?1450–1516)

Where there is absolutely no clue as to the year concerned, a question mark only may be used:

The Welsh harpist John Parry (?-1782)

Many publishers, however, prefer this form:

. . . John Parry (died 1782)

There is (theoretically, at least) a distinction to be made between the use of a question mark and the use of *circa* or *c*.

The word *circa* means 'about' and denotes an informed guess about the accuracy of the year mentioned. The question mark, by contrast, expresses doubt as to whether the year is actually correct. In practice this distinction seems to be rarely made: most authors and publishers use either one or the other but not both in the same book or article. Note that in

Hieronymus Bosch (?1450–1516)

doubt is being expressed only about the first date.

2. Surprise or Irony. In this context, the question mark may stand in mid-sentence and is usually enclosed in parentheses or square brackets:

Tell me about the advantages (?) of living in Docklands.

He paid just £10,000 (?) for that cottage.

Careful authors fight shy of this use of a punctuation mark sent to do the job that words should do, and authorities on written style loathe it. Some call it vulgar. On the whole, the practice is best avoided.
Above all, do avoid multiplying question marks:

With you as a friend (??), I don't need any enemies.

3. In Chess Notation. A special use of the question mark as a signal of doubt and surprise is found in the written records of chess games. It is a shorthand way of saying that the move concerned is a mistake. A double question mark signifies a blunder:

Q × B ?   R × P ??

(For the use of square brackets with a question mark, *see* the chapter on Parentheses.)

134

Exclamation Mark

This was once called a mark or point of admiration and is now generally known in the United States as an exclamation point. Journalists often call it a bang, largely perhaps because it is regularly used after onomatopoeic words such as Bang! and Crash!

Like the question mark, the exclamation mark replaces the full point at the end of a sentence that is described as exclamatory. The description 'exclamatory' is necessarily a loose one, since it can cover anything from an expression of astonishment to a peremptory command.

While the cases in which we can use a question mark are fairly restricted and easy to define, those covering the exclamation mark are not; we need to be much more discriminating about the way we use this latter mark. Its overuse is frowned on as vulgar, and despite what one sees in print, multiple exclamation marks, such as the pair at the end of this sentence, stand for deplorable sensationalism and ought to be banned!!

It is rare, if not unlikely, that the writer of a business report or an academic paper on anything other than a literary subject will ever need to use an exclamation mark at all. The mark has virtually no place in technical prose, quality journalism or a sober essay. For poets and writers of fiction, however, it may prove a useful adjunct to their list of punctuation symbols. And the tabloid reporter, who regards the exclamation mark as part of his or her stock in trade, would surely be lost without it.

It would be easy enough to recommend complete avoidance of the exclamation mark were it not for the fact that, sensitively placed and properly employed, it can liven up an otherwise dull piece of writing. Although it must be said that no writer should rely upon punctuation to perform a task that choice of language and good prose style ought to perform, we have to acknowledge that the odd exclamation mark will add welcome spice.

1. The Exclamation Mark after Words or Phrases. The most characteristic way in which exclamation marks may be used with reasonable impunity is after interjections or after words that represent a loud, sharp noise.

(a) With Words Representing Sounds. These are also known as onomatopoeic words and include the following:

Splash!   Boom!   Thud!

Crash! went the window

His business has gone phut!

(Note that in the second example the exclamation mark is located in mid-sentence. This is normal when exclamation marks are used with onomatopoeic words.)

We may add to the onomatopoeics a number of 'comic strip' words such as these:

Pow!   Zap!   Splat!

(b) With interjections. Interjections expressing a range of emotions (alarm, anxiety, pain, relief, joy, surprise, amazement, anger, despair, etc.) may be followed by an exclamation mark. We list a few here in the order of the emotions just specified:

Hey! Look out!   Oh! Ow! (or Ouch!)
Ah!   Hurray!
Good heavens!   By Jove!   Bah!   Alas!

(The use of 'Alas!' is of course archaic or self-consciously pompous. 'Ah me!', another expression of despair, is also archaic.)

(d) Sharp Commands or Imperatives. Typical of these are the following:

Halt!   Stop!   Attention!   Quick march!
Present arms!

(e) With Oaths, Obscenities and Expletives. These include not only swearwords but also miscellaneous intensifying expressions. Typical are:

Damn!   Christ!   Well, I'll be blowed!
Gracious me!   So there!   Right you are!

(f) With Insults. These include name-calling and insults that function grammatically as imperatives and subjunctive phrases:

Idiot!   Liar!   You bastard!   Go to hell!
God damn you!

2. Exclamation Marks at the End of Sentences. This is where the greatest caution needs to be exercised. Certain forms of short sentence expressing any of the emotions or feelings mentioned in the previous section regularly take an exclamation mark, but only when an urgent or dramatic effect is present or is being sought.

The following series of examples will suffice to illustrate legitimate use of the exclamation mark in ordinary sentences:

God, I've lost my key!

Hell, I'll be late!

I can smell gas!

Hello! Is anybody there?

I wish I hadn't eaten those green apples!

Just because a writer feels that a statement or interjection is arresting or full of powerful impact, however, there is no need to assume that it should be followed automatically by an exclamation mark. Take this example:

Gentlemen, we are at war.

3. *Traditional Exclamatory Sentences*. The exclamation mark is used, almost by custom or common consent, at the end of certain sentences and phrases following one of a number of set patterns. The patterns, with examples, are as follows:

(a) Non-interrogative Sentences Introduced by 'How' or 'What'. These may be full or elliptical sentences:

How nice!

How kind you are!

How dare you! (How dare he say that! How dare they!)

What an idiot!

What lovely big eyes you have!

(b) Exclamatory Questions. These are rhetorical questions requiring no real answer and said with a tone of surprise, satisfaction, despair, etc.:

Isn't she strong!

Wasn't that a marvellous film!

Will I never have any peace!

(c) Phrases introduced by 'That' or 'To think that'. For example:

To think that I nearly got a job with that firm!

Oh, that I should have lived to see this country go to the dogs with such eagerness!

(d) Expressions of Surprise in the Form of Negative Conditional Clauses Introduced by 'If', 'Well, if', or 'Why, if'. For example:

Well, if that doesn't take the biscuit!

Why, if it isn't my old friend John Clark!

(e) Wishes Introduced by 'If only'. For example:

If only I'd known!

If only she could love me as I love her!

(f) Wishes Expressed in a Clause with a Subjunctive Verb. For example:

Long live the Queen!

God forbid!

God help us!

(g) Blessings or Curses Introduced by 'May'. For example:

May God have mercy on your soul!

May he be boiled in oil!

May good fortune shine upon you!

(h) Urgent Warnings. For example:

Take care!

Mind my foot!

(j) Urgent or Brusque Commands. For example:

Pick up this mess!

Get up to bed at once!

139

Exclamation Marks and Quotation Marks

The exclamation mark goes inside the quotation marks if it belongs to the quotation. If the end of the quotation coincides with the end of the sentence, the full point is omitted. The following examples illustrate all cases:

How I love Gainsborough's painting of 'The Blue Boy'!

'Help!' he shouted. 'I can't swim!'

Non-Punctuational Uses

The exclamation mark in parentheses, expressing surprise, is one of the most frequent non-punctuational uses. For example:

Somebody paid him £500(!) for his bashed-up old Peugeot. I wouldn't have given him even half that.

The same strictures that were set forth concerning the 'parenthetical' question mark apply here also. Most careful writers avoid the exclamation mark in parentheses as an overdone gimmick.

In chess notation, the exclamation mark indicates that a move is very good. A doubled exclamation mark (!!) indicates an excellent or inspired move:

White: P × Q !!   Black resigns

It is worth noting that chess reports also make use of different combinations of ? and ! P × Q !? indicates an interesting move that may be dangerous. P × Q ?! indicates a seemingly poor move that may prove to be clever in the long run.

In mathematics, the exclamation mark placed after a whole number represents the factorial of that number, the result obtained by multiplying the number by all the whole numbers below it. Thus:

$$5! = 5 \times 4 \times 3 \times 2 \times 1 = 120$$

Chapter 11

Capital Letters

We are so used to seeing a mixture of capital letters and
'small' letters, with capitals at the start of each new sentence
and at the start of certain words within a sentence, that
anything different has major impact because it is so
unexpected. The American poet Edward Estlin Cummings
provided many instances of this in his work, from which
capitals were deliberately excluded. He is better known as e.e.
cummings, shunning capital letters even in the preferred
orthographical representation of his name (he contended that
only God merited a capital).

Printers and editors regularly refer to capital letters as
'upper-case' letters and 'small' letters as 'lower-case' letters.
This terminology derives from the days of printing with metal
type, which was stored in a divided tray. The two sections of
the tray were called cases, the capitals being located in the
upper case, with the 'small' letters being in the lower one.
Even in the days of word processing and computer
typesetting, printers continue to use the old terminology.

Uses of Capital Letters

There is only one genuine punctuational use of capital letters,
given as (1) in the list below. The other uses are largely a
matter of orthographic convention, and in some cases writers
and editors can choose whether to use a capital or not, as
long as they follow a consistent policy on the matter.

History of the Capital Letter

Modern English capital letters are of Roman origin. The even, upright letter forms found on such ancient Roman monuments as Trajan's column, erected between AD 106 and 113, were echoed in the so-called majuscule letters of classical and early medieval manuscripts. The majuscules were less angular than the stone-cut letters but still had an even appearance.

With the introduction of minuscule (that is, 'small') letters in the eighth century by the Anglo-Saxon monk Alcuin, Charlemagne's educational adviser, manuscripts lost their even look but gained in legibility. Majuscules, or capitals, now took on a different role. In enlarged and illuminated form they stood at the beginnings of chapters and paragraphs as the first letter of the first word. In the course of time they began to be used within the paragraph, to distinguish the first letter of the first word of each new sentence. Thus, before the age of printing began in the late fifteenth century, the capital letter had already evolved the function for which it is primarily used even today.

Avoid Unnecessary Capitals. In general, if there is a choice, most authorities recommend the use of lower-case ('small') letters rather than capitals. The reason is that words with an initial capital letter stand out from the majority of words, which take a lower-case initial. There are times when this can be helpful to a reader, showing him or her that words are being used in a unique or specific way. Overuse of capitals vitiates this useful distinction. Therefore avoid capitals if you do not need them.

1. A the Start of Sentences and Paragraphs. For the sake of emphasis the first letter of every paragraph and of every sentence beginning after a full point is a capital letter. This is true whether or not the sentence is in quotation marks. For example:

> The old man said, 'The day war broke out my wife and I got married.' He gazed tearfully at her photograph as he spoke.

New sentences following questions or exclamations also begin with a capital:

> What can this rising new company do for you? A whole array of tasks from manning the phones to emptying the wastepaper baskets.

In certain circumstances a capital letter may follow a colon:

> My father had an old saying: Do as you would be done by.

(*See also* the chapter on Colon for the instances in which capitals are allowed.)

2. At the Start of Each Line in a Poem. Traditionally, the first letter of each line in a piece of verse is a capital:

> If all the good people were clever,
> And all clever people were good,
> The world would be nicer than ever
> We thought that it possibly could

> – Elizabeth Wordsworth

3. The Names of People and Places. All proper names (place names and personal names) in English begin with a capital letter:

Terry Wogan   Birmingham   France   South Africa

This category includes street names and the names of public houses, cinemas, theatres, national buildings and institutions, and places of public interest:

Oxford Street   The Red Lion   The Odeon
The Comedy Theatre   The British Museum
Hyde Park   Times Square

Adjectives and nouns directly derived from proper names also take an initial capital:

France–French   Jung–Jungian   Marx–Marxism

Names of objects, scientific units, etc., derived from personal or place names are not always written with an initial capital, especially when they have become firmly established in the language:

balaclava   watt   wellingtons   joule

Adjectives derived from personal or place names are not written with an initial capital when their association with the proper name from which they are derived becomes distant:

french windows   french horn   brussels sprouts

Most verbs derived from proper names are not written with a capital:

frenchify   bowdlerize   pasteurize

4. *Foreign Languages.* The names of all languages are treated as proper names in English:

English   Welsh   French   German

5. *Brand Names, Trademarks, etc.* All brand names, trademarks, company names, and the objects to which they may refer are written with initial capitals:

144

Go out and buy me a packet of Persil.

I own some shares in British Gas plc.

When a brand name or trademark stands for a particular type of object in regular use, write it with a lower-case initial:

Would you mind running the hoover over the drawing-room carpet?

I have to go to the launderette (or laundromat).

6. *Modes of Address, Titles, etc.* These should in general take an initial cap only when used in front of a personal name:

Professor Jones   Professor Michael Jones

But:

Michael Jones is professor of linguistics.

Other examples are:

Sir Peter Smith   Good morning, Sir Peter.

But:

Good morning, sir.

The prizes were presented by His Grace the First Duke of Exton. Following this ceremony, the duke made a fine speech to the whole school.

All the normal modes of address take initial capitals: Mr, Mrs, Ms and Miss.

7. *Official Posts.* The same rules apply as for (6) above. When the post is given as a title forming part of the name, it takes an initial capital. But otherwise not:

Prime Minister Margaret Thatcher visited Washington for talks with President Bush.

The British prime minister met the US president.

King Charles I reigned from 1625 to 1649.

Charles I was the first king of England to be executed.

Full official titles should be written with initial capitals:

The President of the United States addressed the whole nation from the Oval Office of the White House last night.

8. Unique Things. Initial capitals should be used for such things as the following:

The Statue of Liberty   The British Telecom Tower

The Crown Jewels   The Oval Office   The White House

This category includes certain specific references, as opposed to general ones. For example, the (British) Government is often given a capital, while the lower-case letter is used when the reference is to any legislative body in general:

The Government has announced ...

No government is completely perfect.

Note that official bodies take an initial capital when the names are used in full but not when the names are shortened, as in the following example:

The Department of Health is to be wholly reorganized. Mr C—, the minister responsible for running the department, explained the changes.

9. Initials and Acronyms. These are generally written, typed or set as capital letters, usually without full points:

BBC   CBS   MP   RSC (Royal Shakespeare Company)

UNESCO   USA   USSR

It is good practice to provide the name of the organization, institution, etc., in full at the start of an article, report, etc., with the initials in parentheses, and then to use the initials for all subsequent references. For further information on initials, *see* the chapter on the Full Point. *See also* the chapter on Parentheses.

10. Principal Words in Headings and Titles. The first word and all the main nouns and verbs in the title of a book, play, essay, poem or report, and also in a heading or subheading, are traditionally written with initial capital letters. Pronouns, conjunctions, prepositions, the definite and indefinite articles, and parts of the verb 'to be' are generally written with lower-case initials:

> *The Corn is Green*   *How Green was my Valley*
>
> *The Mill on the Floss*   *Men and Machines*

A style that is gaining ground, especially in the preparation of bibliographies, is the writing of titles and headings with an initial capital for the first word and thereafter only for words that would take a capital in ordinary usage. Thus we would have, for example:

> *The corn is green*   *Men and machines*
>
> *The fall of the house of Usher*

This new system has much to recommend it; in particular it parallels many other languages (e.g. French) in which titles and headings are presented in this way. The more traditional use of capitals in titles and headings is still the more prevalent, however.

For further information on titles, *see* the next section on Boldface and Italics and the section on Paragraphs.

11. Miscellaneous Uses. The following are conventional uses of initial capital letters:

(a) The First Person Singular Pronoun, *I*. Example:

I think, therefore I am.

(b) All pronouns referring to God or Jesus Christ. For instance:

God so loved the world that He gave His only begotten son . . .

With all due respect to e.e. cummings, this is a use that is declining. The Revised Standard Version of the Bible, in the edition known as *The Common Bible* (1973), uses lower-case initials for these pronouns, and perhaps we should too.

(c) Days of the Week, Months of the Year and Geological or Historical Periods. For example:

Clocks go back on the third Saturday in October.

He is an expert on the Pleistocene epoch.

Oliver Cromwell ruled England during the Protectorate.

Capitals and Small Capitals

Writing, typing or printing whole words, phrases or sentences in capitals is fine for titles or chapter headings, to which the reader's attention must be drawn. In ordinary text this practice certainly attracts attention too. Warnings can be especially effective if treated in this way:

. . . you are trying to observe. WARNING: YOU MUST NEVER POINT A TELESCOPE DIRECTLY AT THE SUN. You should always observe the sun by projecting it onto a screen or piece of card . . . .

However, the use of capitals in the middle of plain text is regarded by many as garish.

Much more discreet but still reasonably emphatic is the use of small capitals. These are characters whose shapes are the same as those of full capitals but whose heights are equivalent to those of lower-case letters.

Small capitals are used for certain abbreviations (AD, BC), for initials and acronyms when full capitals are deemed to be too emphatic (BBC, UHT), and often (with an initial full capital) for the first word or two in the chapter of a book — for example:

WHEN WE are very young, we regard the ability to ride a bicycle as one of the most highly prized skills ...

In many modern dictionaries, small caps are used to pick out a word, e.g., in an etymology, where further information can be found:

waistcoat ... [from WAIST + COAT]

Capitals and Alphabetical Order

The traditional method of ordering an alphabetical list when two items are identically spelled but one has an initial capital letter is to put the lower-case form first:

eye (organ of the body)

Eye (place in Suffolk)

However, many encyclopaedia publishers (*Encyclopedia Britannica*, for example) use the order Person — Place — Thing, which would make capital forms precede lower-case ones. Placing capitals before lower-case forms is also the order that most computers use in generating alphabetic lists. Computers can be programmed to place lower-case forms first, but left to themselves they usually compile the list on the basis of numerical values assigned to letters on the basis of the American Standard Code on Information Interchange

149

(ASCII). It happens that the ASCII codes for capitals come before those for lower-case letters.

Modes of Address within the Family
Finally, capitals are used in sentences such as these:

Where's my coat, Mum?

Yes, Father, I understand.

Hello, Uncle John.

I'm staying with my Uncle John.

This is my uncle. His name is John Smith.

Chapter 12

Boldface

Boldface and italic type are typographical terms and used to apply only to typeset or printed material. Nowadays, the dot-matrix or daisywheel printers set up to work with most word processors can produce a passable dark type similar in function to the printer's boldface and a rightward-sloping version of roman that can pass for italic. We shall come to italic in the next chapter.

Boldface, or bold type, is a heavier version of the roman type belonging to a particular fount or typeface normally used for text. It is possible to have a bold italic in some modern typefaces, but generally the most widely available style of bold is a roman one. Small capitals are generally not available in boldface.

Authors who write for publication should indicate boldface not by printing it as such on their word processors or typewriters but by typing ordinary text and underscoring it with a wavy line.

Newton's Early Life. Newton was born at Woolsthorpe, Lincolnshire . . .

Uses of Boldface
Boldface is used exclusively for emphasis or contrast. Its main use is in headings and subheadings. Usually such headings are the same point size as the text face or a point or two larger. But boldface may also be used in a much bigger point size for display headings, book or chapter titles, etc. The chapter titles and main headings in this book are in bold.

Boldface may be used in the middle of ordinary (roman) text to pick out specific words.

I must have **all** your forms in by the end of this week.

This usage is often found in reference-books, dictionaries, encyclopaedias, etc. A dictionary definition may, for example, use different strengths of bold type:

harmless adj. not causing or likely to cause harm or hurt —**harmlessly** adv.—**harmlessness** n.

(Usually this means that the stronger or primary bold type is a point larger than the secondary, which in its turn is the same size as the text face.)

Use in Indexes and Bibliographies. Page references in an index may be set in bold when they point to the most substantial or significant treatment of the indexed item in the book concerned. For example:

Tiglath-Pileser III, 274, **276−80**, 285, 315, 316

(In the above citation, the bold type indicates that the major reference to Tiglath-Pileser III is to be found on pp. 276−80.)

In bibliographies in scientific books, where dates of publication, volume numbers, page numbers and column numbers may cause confusion, the page numbers are frequently in boldface:

Heller, H. & Lederis, K. 1958. Paper chromatography of small amounts of vasopressin and oxytocin. *Nature*, London, **182**, 1231−2

(The above example is quoted in Judith Butcher, *Copy-editing: The Cambridge Handbook*.)

In Mathematical Books. Vector and tensor quantities are set in boldface italics:

$$(s + t)a = sa + ta$$

(Needless to say, this is a very specialized use.)

Punctuation and Boldface

Any punctuation directly following a bold title, heading or word in text is usually included in the boldface. Note the appropriate examples above and this one:

balalaika: A triangular stringed musical instrument popular in Russia . . . .

Chapter 13

Italics

Italic type (italic, or italics, for short) is an elegant, light, almost cursive, rightward-sloping style of type used for various forms of emphasis. It is the typographical equivalent of underlining a word or words in a piece of handwritten text, and indeed authors and editors preparing typescripts for the press signal italicized words and passages to the printer by putting a straight line underneath them.

Most typefaces that one encounters in books, newspapers and magazines have an italic form, and the dot-matrix printer forming part of virtually every office's word-processing equipment these days can produce a sloping version of its standard roman fount that provides sufficient contrast to function as a passable italic type.

Francesco Griffo cut the very first italic typeface in 1500 for the great Venetian printer Aldus Manutius the Elder. It was based on an informal kind of handwriting used in the papal chanceries during that period. This compact, humanistic style of type was at first used as a main text face – Griffo used it for the Aldine edition of the poems of Virgil in 1501. It can still be attractive as a text face even today, but it is more commonly encountered in the emphatic uses described here.

Uses of Italics
We use italics in the following ways:

1. Emphasis. For example:

You *must* ensure that all the necessary arrangements are completed by Friday.

We shall *under no circumstances* be responsible for property lost or damaged in transit.

Careful writers avoid excessive italicization for emphasis.

2. Chapter Headings and Subheadings. In this respect italic type is used in a similar way to boldface. Two illustrations will suffice:

> *The Solar System*
> Nine planets orbit the Sun along with meteoroids, asteroids and comets, to make up ...

> *Newton's Discoveries.* Newton's scientific work spanned the fields of optics, mechanics, ...

3. Drawing Attention to a Letter, Word or Phrase for its own Sake. Another instance of 'naming a word as a word'. We met a similar use under the section on quotation marks:

> I cannot stand people who use the constructions *different to* or *different than*. The correct phrase is *different from*.

> *Catherine* has nine letters.

> There are two *l*s in artillery.

In the last example, note that the letter *l* is in italics but the pluralizing *-s* is in roman.

4. Foreign Phrases. Italics are used for words or phrases that do not yet seem to have become fully naturalized in the English language:

> In 1820 Schubert wrote a one-act opera that achieved a modest *sucès d'estime*.

The Soviet orchestra's tour had been made possible by the new climate of *glasnost*.

But italics are not used for words and phrases that are naturalized:

She offered him a canapé as they continued to talk.

The general's coup d'état took place at dawn on Thursday.

5. *Names of Ships, Aircraft and Other Vehicles*. For example:

We went to America on the *QE2*.

The first victim of the German ship *Bismarck* was HMS *Hood*.

The *Bluebird*'s design was revolutionary.

Note in the last example the fact that *Bluebird* is in italics but the possessive *'s* is in roman.

6. *Titles of Books, Plays and Long Poems*. The titles appear in italics for self-contained publications (full-length novels, plays, long poems, non-fiction works, etc.). Chapters, articles, essays or short poems that form part of larger collections are left in roman between quotation marks:

Have you read *War and Peace*, by Leo Tolstoy?

Last night we saw Tom Stoppard's play *Professional Foul*.

D.B. Fry, 'Speech Reception and Perception', *New Horizons in Linguistics*, edited by John Lyons. Penguin, 1970.

T.S. Eliot wrote *The Wasteland* and a short poem called 'Gerontion'.

To these may be added musical plays and films:

Oklahoma and *South Pacific* are still among the best musicals that Rodgers and Hammerstein ever wrote.

Dustin Hoffman is outstanding in *Rain Man*.

7. *Musical Compositions* (Symphonies, Operas, Ballets, etc.). Named musical compositions (especially those on a large scale) are generally placed in italics:

Handel's oratorio *Israel in Egypt*.

Beethoven's *Pastoral Symphony*.

Compositions that are identified merely by a genre and a number are left in roman.

Beethoven's Symphony No. 6.

Prokofiev's Piano Sonata No. 7.

8. *Magazines, Newspapers and Periodicals*. The word *The* is only included in the italic title if it appears on the publication's mast-head:

I read it in *The Daily Telegraph*.

I saw the story in the *Daily Mail*.

However, whether it stands as part of the italicized title or not, the definite article can be missed out when necessary:

Have you seen this morning's *Daily Telegraph*?

9. *Latin Genus and Species Names of Plants or Animals*. Note that (a) genus names begin with an initial capital letter and species names never do, even when they are derived from proper names, (b) if a genus name needs to be repeated only the italic form of its initial capital letter is given, followed by a full point, and (c) all divisions above that of genus are written in roman:

The dog (*Canis familiaris*) and the wolf (*C. lupus*) both belong to the family Canidae.

The garden contained two fine buddleias, one a specimen of *Buddleia davidii*, the other of *B. globosa*.

10. Mathematics. Most variables in mathematics are set in italics by printers.

$$x^2 + 2x + y^2$$

11. Italics as Punctuation. In a piece of text the mere change from roman (or normal) type to italics may under certain circumstances obviate the need for any other punctuation. For example:

... From Late Latin *incarnare* to make flesh, from Latin IN^2 + *caro* flesh

In the above example, taken from an etymology in a dictionary, we might have expected commas after *incarnare* and *caro*. The use of italics allows the commas to be omitted.

12. Italics within Italics? Emphasis by means of italics when the typeface is already italic is clearly impossible. In such cases it is legitimate to use quotation marks. Compare these:

He wrote a brilliant assessment of *Pilgrim's Progress*.

His book was called *An Assessment of 'Pilgrim's Progress'*.

Another conventional device is to set in roman those words that would normally be italicized when the main text is in italic (such as a caption):

This illustration shows a fine example of Buddleia davidii *and its usual congregation of butterflies.*

Chapter 14

Numbers in Text

Numbers are of two main types: arabic numerals (popularly
called 'figures', especially by printers) and Roman numerals
(often called just 'numerals' by printers). In typed or printed
matter arabic numerals may either be 'lining' (that is, aligned
with each other) or 'non-lining' (that is, with the six and eight
extending above the average height of the other figures and
three, four, five, seven and nine extending below it. Non-
lining figures are a little old-fashioned these days, and most
modern typefaces have lining figures. There is no problem
about this, except that if you are referring to lines in a poem
it may be best to write 'lines 11 – 13' rather than 'll. 11 – 13'.

Arabic Numerals
1. Figures or Words? In ordinary text it is safest to use words
for small numbers (that is, below 10 or below 11) and figures
for the rest. The only real exception occurs in text that is
typeset in narrow measure: that is, a book where the length
of the lines of type is relatively short. Many publishers have a
rule about numbers below 10 or 11 enshrined in their house
style. If a range or series of numbers is involved, do not mix
words and figures. The following examples illustrate the
customary practice.

He held a teaching post for seven or eight years.

The encyclopaedia caters for readers between the ages of 7
and 30.

(*See also* the discussion on ranges of numbers below.)

Round numbers may also be expressed in words (twenty, thirty, forty, ... a hundred, two hundred, ... a thousand, two thousand, etc.). With round numbers above a million, the most prevalent style is to use a figure or figures followed by the words 'million' or 'billion': e.g. population, 3 million; £320 billion; $7 billion (or 7 billion dollars).

It is a rule that numerals should not be used at the start of a sentence. In these examples, therefore, (a) is preferred to (b):

(a) Forty-four people were killed in yesterday's air disaster ....

Not:

(b) 44 people were killed ....

Billion or Thousand Million? The British billion (that is, a million million, or 1,000,000,000,000) is virtually a thing of the past. All the British press, everyone working in the City of London, and even British schoolchildren have so completely accepted the American billion (that is, a thousand million, or 1,000,000,000) that there seems little point in drawing attention to the distinction any longer. Those who wish to stand by the British billion, however, are welcome to do so.

2. Four and More Figures and the Decimal Point. Writers have a choice in the ways in which they represent numbers consisting of four or more digits.

(a) To comma off from the right (starting at the immediate left of the implied or actual decimal point) all numbers greater than 999.99 ... :

   2,759   21,796.75   234,853.625   13,089,654.875

(b) To write four-figure numbers without commas and to comma off from the right all numbers above 9999.99 ... :

   2759   21,796.75   (*See* the remaining numbers in (a).)

(c) To write four-figure numbers without commas and to use standard or thin spaces instead of commas in numbers above 9999.99 ... (this is now common usage in scientific journals such as *Nature* and *New Scientist*, and is also found in many science textbooks):

   2759   21 796.75   234 853.625   13 089 654.875

(d) To write all numbers out continuously with no spaces or commas and no breaks other than the decimal point, as in most books on mathematics:

   2759   21796.75   234853.625   13089654.875

In the last two cases (using spaces or using no breaks at all), a decimal point may be represented by a comma in accordance with practice on the continent of Europe:

   21796,75   234 853,625   13 089 654,875

In normal British usage, the decimal point is either a full point (.) or a centred dot ($\cdot$).

Figures following the decimal point are generally written out as a continuous string:

   The value of pi (to nine decimal places) is 3.141592654

3. Percentages. In ordinary writing percentages are usually given in figures followed by the word 'per cent' (or 'percent' in normal American usage). There is no full point after 'per cent'.

   5 per cent   8.8 per cent   23.9 per cent

You can also use the sign % in ordinary text:

161

Wheat accounted for 18% of the country's gross national product.

And you should always use the % sign in tables, often in the heading to one of the columns (e.g. a column might be entitled 'Proportion of Population under 18', and underneath would be written '(%)').

4. Number Ranges. If you use the 'x to y' or 'between x and y' constructions when quoting number ranges, page references, date ranges, etc., you must include the whole of the numbers involved:

From 1956 to 1987 he taught in a Roman Catholic seminary in West Africa.

You will find a table of English monarchs and their reign dates between pp. 254 and 257.

The other way of expressing ranges of numbers is by separating the numbers with an en rule (*see* the chapter on the Dash). When using this style remember that the second number (the one to the right of the en rule) is often not given in full. Part of it is omitted, or elided. Authors may find that publishers' preferences vary as to whether the last one or the last two digits are retained in the elided number. Retaining the last two is on the whole clearer, even if it does entail one more keystroke. The following examples illustrate the recommended procedure:

See pp. 5−7, 9−11, 11−18, 20−23, 31−34, 45−51, 96−102, 113−16, 118−23, 134−36, 211−16, 244−47, 256−61, 291−307, 1014−16, 1025−26, 1078−81, 1098−1105.

Fred Smith (1896−1961) had a son called John Smith (1918−87). Fred fought in the 1914−18 war. John was a

prisoner of war in World War II during the period
1941–45.

The rule is to elide as much as possible without destroying
clarity. Some publishers require the last digit to be retained
except in the 'teens' of any hundred, where two are kept. For
example, 112–14, but 141–6. This is obviously a workable
system, but the one illustrated above is less ambiguous and
easier to remember.

Date Ranges BC. Note that in dates between the tenth and
first centuries BC, all the figures should be repeated for
clarity.

Pericles (495–429 BC)   Socrates (470–399 BC)

Julius Caesar (100–44 BC)

To be crystal clear, we should properly repeat the 'BC' after
both dates:

Julius Caesar (100 BC – 44 BC)

Some writers also extend this 'all the figures' rule to dates
between AD 1 and AD 1000, although there is no need to
repeat AD before each date:

Offa was king of Mercia during the period AD 757–796.

5. *Dates*. Exact dates should be shown in the following form:

Wednesday 6 September 1989

There is no need for any commas in this formula, except
when the date is followed by another number:

On Wednesday 6 September 1989 I completed my book on
punctuation.

On Friday 2 September 1939, 21 people died in a German
air raid on Warsaw, Poland.

This method of showing the date is logical and reflects general British practice, following an ascending order from day to year. An older method, showing month-day-year, is also widely used, especially in the United States. It requires commas:

On Wednesday, September 6, 1989, I finished my latest book.

or:

On Wednesday, September 6th, 1989, I finished my latest book.

The first method (day-month-year) gives a more up-to-date and less cluttered appearance.

All-figure Formats for Dates. The figures representing the date in this abbreviated form of representation are separated by full points, colons or slashes (solidi). Remember that the British and American formats differ. In this example we note the main British and American ways of showing the date 6 September 1989:

| British | 6/9/89 | 6.9.89 | 6:9:89 |
| American | 9/6/89 | 9:6:89 | 9.6.89 |

The forms 06:09:89 (UK) and 09:06:89 (USA) are also encountered.

Years. All years consisting of four figures are written without commas. Five-figure years take commas.

AD 1066   1500 BC   13,000 BC

Note that, as in the examples given here and earlier, AD precedes the year, while BC follows it. Even though we may popularly refer to 1066 AD, careful writers always render that year as AD 1066.

6. Time. Ways of showing the time of day have been discussed in the chapters on the Full Point and the Colon. The best way of showing times in races, astronomical events, etc., is exemplified in this illustration:

Smith's time of 2h 12m 14.2s shattered the previous record of 2:13:06.3, set last year by Bert Jones.

7. Measurements. In quoting most measurements, especially ones containing decimal quantities, it is clearer with a space between the number and the unit of measurement:

208.6 cm   300 kg

Some publishers, however, insist on:

208.6cm   300kg

A thin space should be used by printers in setting temperatures, but typists and those who write by hand can ignore such refinements.

Do not elide measurement ranges, e.g. temperature ranges, to avoid confusion between ascending and descending scales:

Tomorrow's temperatures will be in the range 21−23°C

8. Catalogue Numbers, Telephone Numbers, etc. There are many variations in usage in this area, but some items in this category − for example, the international standard book number at the front of this volume − have a standardized format within an internationally accepted system. The same applies to American Library of Congress catalog numbers. In quoting an ISBN, do use spaces between the groups of digits, not hyphens.

British Telecom recommends that telephone numbers should be shown in one of the forms below:

London numbers   01–234 5678
Other cities, e.g. Birmingham   021–234 5678
Other UK codes, e.g. Aylesbury, Bucks.   (0296) 81234

Other telephone networks, e.g. Mercury, may have recommended methods of showing their telephone numbers that differ from the above.

When British Telecom changes the numbering system, the above formulas may alter. For example, from May 1990, London will be divided into 071 and 081 areas. A number in central London might therefore read 071–287 0214.

International numbers vary, but American numbers usually follow this pattern:

(010 312) 245–1234 (for a number in Chicago)

Postcodes follow an established system in Britain, consisting of two groups of letters and numbers separated by a space. They are not written as a continuous string. US ZIP (Zoning Improvement Plan) codes consist of continuous strings of figures.

BR3 3LJ (a UK postcode)   60653 (A US ZIP code)

9. Numbers in Lists. Numbers introducing items in a list may be plain, may be followed by a full point or a single closing bracket, or may be enclosed in brackets (parentheses). *See also* the chapters on the Full point and on Parentheses.

Roman Numerals
Roman numerals may be shown as upper- or lower-case letters or small capital letters.

Full capitals are used for titles such as Queen Elizabeth II or Pope John XXIII.

In biblical usage, LXX (in full capitals) signifies the Septuagint.

Small capitals (if they are present in the particular fount being used) are employed for all other purposes, chiefly for volume numbers in bibliographies:

Antiquity XXXII:226 (1958)

(Note that small capitals do not look attractive with lining figures; they look better with non-aligning figures.)

Lower-case numerals are used to number the preliminary pages of a book, and are sometimes employed in act-and-scene references to Shakespeare's plays:

Macbeth, Act 2, scene ii, lines 13–14

Using lower-case roman numerals for the month in all-figure dates is a practice that is still occasionally encountered:

27.ii.47

But this is rather old-fashioned nowadays.

Chapter 15

Accents, Diacritics and Textual Symbols

This section is a mixed bag of signs and symbols, some of which apply to foreign languages. The contents are necessarily selective, partly because space is limited and partly because our purpose is to concentrate on conventional symbols in English, not to provide a typographer's textbook on foreign language setting.

Diacritics, or diacritical marks, are signs written above or below characters or letters to show that they have a different sound quality from that which is normal or is expected, or that they are pronounced with a special stress or intonation. Accents are a specific type of diacritic written above a vowel (*a, e, i, o, u*) or a letter functioning as a vowel, such as *w* or *y* in Welsh. Most European languages have a considerable array of diacritics, but English is exceptional in having virtually none. Consequently, most mechanical typewriters have never been designed to print such symbols and cannot reproduce them, although some electronic typewriters, word processors and typesetting machines can.

Because of such deficiencies, the use of appropriate accents on foreign words in English has become relatively uncommon during this century. Even as links with Europe continue to be strengthened during the 1990s, it seems likely that the avoidance of accents will continue. Long-established foreign phrases generally lack their accents anyway. However, there are some words that tenaciously retain their accents, and foreign names, especially in a literary context, should be spelled with the appropriate diacritics.

Textual symbols — for the purposes of this discussion — include such items as footnote symbols (asterisks, daggers, superior figures, etc.), the ampersand, currency symbols, and foreign language punctuation marks, where these are likely to be encountered.

We shall deal with the items in this section in alphabetical order, saying what each one is and providing short remarks and examples where necessary.

Acute Accent (´)

This accent mark distinguishes a certain vowel quality in French and is used for stress on other languages such as Spanish and Italian. In English it marks the strong syllables in poetry:

I wándered lónely ás a clóud

The acute accent is retained on foreign imports largely to aid correct pronunciation:

attaché; blasé; cliché; communiqué; éclat; élan; emegré; fiancé (and fiancée); passé; protégé; touché.

Ampersand (&)

Originally 'and per se and', meaning the sign for 'and' itself, the ampersand is a textual symbol used as a shorthand for the word 'and'. The sign probably arose as a scribal contraction of the Latin word *et* ('and'). It was much used in early printed books, as was the symbolic abbreviation *&c* (for 'etc.'). These uses are now gone. Its usual modern use is in quoting the names of commercial companies and firms: Marks & Spencer, Sears & Roebuck.

Asterisk (*)

This textual symbol, which is not called an *asterix* - that is the name of a French comic-strip hero — has a variety of uses.

It serves as a symbol indicating a footnote. It follows a word in text on which a footnote gives further information. If an asterisk covers a whole sentence, it follows the full point closing the sentence.

Text: Anthony Brown* has suggested a possible solution to this difficult problem. ...

Note: *Philosophical Transactions, xii (1945), pp. 2325.

The asterisk is the first of a series of footnote symbols that are used in turn on each page. The sequence is * † ‡ § || ¶.

In mathematics and computer work, the asterisk is used as a multiplication symbol. In linguistics it designates a hypothetical linguistic form, sentence, etc., or one not attested in the written record:

*John elapses books.

Dot [from ME *dot, from OE dott, head of a boil]

When placed before a date, an asterisk indicates that it is a birthdate:

Bach, Johann Sebastian *1685 †1750.

Breathings
The rough and smooth breathings (*spiritus asper* ' and *spiritus lenis'*) are accents placed over initial vowels and the letter *rho* in writing and setting classical Greek texts. They resemble, but are not the same as, the 'open-quotation' (rough) and 'close-quotation' (smooth) marks. Similar-looking accents are used over Arabic or Hebrew vowels.

Breve (˘)
This curved accent written over vowels (*a, e, i, o*) indicates

that they are metrically or phonetically 'short'. It is used primarily as a linguistics and classical scansion symbol.

Cedilla (̧)

This is a diacritic written beneath the letter *c* (appearing as ç) before *a*, *o*, or *u* in French and Spanish to indicate that it is to be pronounced as an *s*. In English it may be omitted from *facade* (originally *façade*), but is retained in *soupçon*. It also appears in such phrases as *comme ci*, *comme ça*, occasionally used in fictional dialogue.

Circumflex (̂)

This accent is retained on such French words as these (some of which may also be italicized):

bête noire; coup de grâce; crêpe-suzette; papier mâché; pâté (pâté de foie gras); raison-d'être; tête-à-tête.

It is also required in certain Welsh terms as Meibion Glyn Dŵr, a Welsh nationalist organization.

Currency Symbols

In most cases, the amount follows the sign for the currency involved, e.g. £300 or $300. The most common currency symbols are:

Cent	¢
Dollar	$
Florin	*f*
Franc	Fr
Peseta	P$_s$
Pound	£
Yen	¥

The international currency symbol # is also occasionally encountered.

Dagger (†)

This is a textual symbol used as a footnote indicator just as the asterisk is. It comes second in the footnote system outlined under the earlier paragraph on the Asterisk.

The dagger is also used in linguistics to signal an obsolete form:

The word *broad* comes from an earlier †*brad*.

The dagger also signals a deathdate:

Bach, Johann Sebastian, *1685 †1750.

The double dagger (‡) is used only as a text indicator and corresponding footnote symbol.

Diaeresis (¨)

This accent, called a dieresis in the United States, is used in ancient Greek, and by extension in French and other languages, to mark the fact that two vowels which would normally have coalesced to form a diphthong are to be pronounced separately. The same sign does duty for the German umlaut, which 'modifies' *ä*, *ö*, and *ü*. It is generally not preserved for Greek and French borrowings, except in the mythological-astronomical name Boötes and the French word noël used as a name (i.e., Noël), when it is placed over the scond vowel of the pair. It is usually omitted in naive (originally naïve or naïve). The German umlaut is preserved in many names, but in some, such as *Schönberg*, it is can be correctly rendered by leaving out the umlaut and adding an *e* to the vowel, giving *Schoenberg*. The diaeresis, once used in such words as *coöperate*, *coördinate*, etc., proved only a temporary trend and is no longer normally encountered in these words.

Foreign Language Symbols

In French, German and Spanish, special symbols exist for showing quotation marks.

In French, special signs called guillemets (« ») are used to signal ordinary or isolated quotations:

Qu'est-ce que vous dites, «franglais?»

Dialogue is shown by means of a double em rule preceding each character's speech:

——*Bonjour, M Dubois, dit Marie.*

——Bonjour, Marie. dit M Dubois.

In German, two main methods exist for displaying verbatim speech in quotation.

(1) To enclose the speech within double commas, the second pair being inverted or turned:

,,Wie geht es Dir, Hans?" fragte Rudolf.

(2) To enclose the speech between inward-pointing guillemets:

»Wie geht es Dir, Hans?« fragte Rudolf.

It is also worth noting that in German *all* nouns (not merely proper nouns) are capitalized.

In Greek, the question mark is identical with the English semicolon (;), while the colon is represented by a superior full point (·). Note also that Greek uses the acute, circumflex and grave accents, even in its modern form. The breathings, however, are used only in classical Greek.

In Spanish, the same method of showing quotations is used as that for French. But note that all questions are prefaced by a turned question mark (¿) and followed by a normal question mark (?), and all exclamations are prefaced by a turned exclamation mark (¡) and followed by a normal one (!).

Grave Accent (`)

This accent is retained for reasons of pronunciation in the following French words:

> *à la* (in such phrases as à la carte, à la king); crème de la crème; *père* (as in Alexandre Dumas *père*); pied-à-terre.

Hacek (�‚)

The hacek, an angular symbol, not curved like the breve, is used in modifying certain consonants and vowels in Czech names. In ordinary use it is often omitted from Dvorák, which is a well-established name in English, but is still used for such people as Leos Janáček (which also takes an acute accent).

Inferior Numerals

These are figures set in smaller type below the level of the line of printed text ($_1$, $_2$, $_3$, etc.). They have a variety of scientific uses, the best-known of which is perhaps to be found in chemical formulae such as H_2O. *See* the later paragraphs on Superior Numerals.

Macron (¯)

This accent, placed over vowels (a, e, ı, o, u), indicates that the vowel concerned is phonetically or metrically long. It is the counterpart of the breve, for example *kōlon*.

Mathematics and Science

Variables (*a*, *b*, *c*, *x*, *y*, *z*) are generally in italic. Chemical formulae are set in roman. The mathematical operators + (plus), − (minus), × (multiplied by) and ÷ or / (divided by), together with parentheses, brackets and braces, are only part of the great panoply of signs and symbols that the typing or setting of mathematics requires. Greek letters and symbols, including a large sigma (Σ) used in integration, as well as a long strokeless f ($\int$), also used in integration, all form part of the mathematician's fearsome armoury. Set theory is also replete with unusual signs, such as ∪ (indicating the union between two sets).

This is a highly specialized area. Editors as well as authors who work in these fields regularly are usually qualified mathematicians and scientists. There is, however, a publication to which the experts and novices can refer: Chapter 13 of Judith Butcher's *Copy-editing: The Cambridge Handbook*, CUP (1981, 2nd edition) gives an invaluable rundown of everything science and maths authors and editors need to be aware of.

Paragraph Marker (¶)
The paragraph marker (also known as a pilcrow) is used to introduce a paragraph that in some way needs to be isolated from the main text, usually because it contains additional information of marginal rather than primary signficance or indeed because it needs to be emphasized. For example, a dictionary editor might use a ¶ to set off a note on usage from the rest of the definition or etymology.

In addition to this basic use, the paragraph marker is also employed in the footnote system along with the asterisk and dagger (*see* earlier).

Per Cent Sign (%)
This is typed or printed close up to the figure concerned. The same also applies to the less common per thousand ‰ symbol:

23.6%   18.5‰

Section Marker (§)
This is a textual symbol that is used primarily to divide up a chapter into main sections. It precedes a figure or figures and is usually accompanied by a section heading.

§3: Medieval Punctuation

The section marker is also used in the asterisk-dagger footnote system. *See* the earlier paragraph on the Asterisk.

Superior Numerals

These are figures in small type written above the line of the text (^{1}, ^{2}, etc.). They are used as text and footnote indicators as an alternative to the asterisk, dagger, etc. In mathematics superior figures are used to show that a number or variable has been raised to a power specified by the figure (it is an exponent).

Superior numerals are used in chemistry and atomic physics to denote isotopes (where the numeral is the mass number):

$$^{90}\text{Sr} \qquad ^{238}\text{U} \qquad ^{238}\text{Pu}$$

although Sr-90, U-238 and Pu-239 are accepted and easier to typeset.

Note also that superior letters can be used in a similar way to figures. For further information on the functions of superior and inferior figures and letters, see Judith Butcher, op. cit.

Superior Ring

This accent occurs on top of å in Danish and is also found in Czech in names such as Martinů. In the Danish name Ångstrøm, we can also see the use of the 'stroked o'. The modifications produced by these changed letters give the name a pronunciation something like [ONG *strurm*].

Tilde (˜)

This accent marks the fact that an ñ in Spanish is to be pronounced *ny*. It also indicates that certain sounds in Portuguese are pronounced with a nasal quality. The tilde is retained in such words as these:

mañana; piña (as in piña cloth); señor; sertão (the countryside of northern Brazil).

The tilde is used in phonetics to indicate the nasalization of a vowel. An enlarged, centrally placed tilde, also known as a swung dash (~), has a number of applications, e.g. in lexicographical work.

Chapter 16

Paragraphs, Indention and Headings

Everything we write concerns a subject or theme. It does not matter whether the piece of writing is a letter about one's holiday, a business report, an article for a women's magazine or the chapters of a book on fly-fishing. There may be only one subject or theme in it or there may be several different ones. Even if there is only one, it will almost inevitably be divided into different topics or aspects, each looking at the whole subject from a different angle or explaining or introducing different parts of it. We show the division of a subject or theme into topics or aspects by arranging the sentences dealing with these topics or aspects into paragraphs.

The importance of the paragraph is easy to overlook. It is in fact part and parcel of good communication. In 1905 T.F. and M.F.A. Husband, writing in *Punctuation: Its Principles and Practice*, said:

> ... the paragraph, while itself only part of a larger whole, is the expression of continuous and unified thought; ... there is running through it a central nerve of thought which dominates the secondary systems; and ... these secondary systems or groups of ideas are set forth sentence by sentence, according to the character of each and its relation to the whole, some of them taking short sentences as their fittest form, others long.

The writer's duty is to make sure that the 'central nerve of thought' is crystal clear to his or her reader.

Paragraphs may be long or short, consist of one sentence or many, or contain a single topic or a set of closely related ones. The writer must choose the arrangement that best suits the material or information that he or she is trying to put across and the medium — newspaper, book, magazine — through which he or she is communicating with the reader. For instance, short one-sentence paragraphs in a newspaper or advertisement are not just there for the ignorant masses with short attention spans, despite what G.V. Carey and other pundits might say. Even busy readers of *The Times* and *The Guardian* strap-hanging their way into work appreciate the one-sentence paragraphs in the front-page stories that allow them to assimilate the data quickly. In a serious novel or a work of non-fiction, however, short paragraphs might have a breathless effect that may be out of place. In general, a mixture of different lengths of paragraph is usually best.

Although the need for paragraphs as so far described is a rhetorical one (that is, we need paragraphs, for example, to make clear the steps in an argument or the important points in a piece of narrative), careful writers also take account of the visual appearance of the printed page. There is nothing more intimidating than a page with no paragraphs on it.

A comprehensive book on the use of English — Eric Partridge's *Usage and Abusage*, for instance — will tell readers more about paragraphs than we are able to do in this book. Our main concern here is to explain a little about how to treat them in writing or on the printed page.

Layout of Paragraphs

The Greeks signalled a change of topic in a piece of writing by drawing a line next to the text at the point where the new topic began. This was called a *paragraphos* ('a line drawn beside'). The Romans accomplished the same task by starting the line of text in which the new topic began with a large capital letter that jutted out into the left-hand margin. In medieval times this capital became further enlarged and beautifully illuminated. Since the illumination was done last, the scribe copying the manuscript would leave room for it by commencing the rest of the first line of the paragraph some way in from the left-hand margin.

The business of taking a bite out of paragraphs in this way is called indention (a word derived from the Latin word *dens*, 'a tooth'), and we say that the first line of each paragraph is indented. Paragraph indention was carried over into printing and applied even to paragraphs that were not to be illuminated. From the seventeenth century it became standard and continues to be the prevailing practice today, although typists and typesetters also practise the art of not indenting paragraphs but setting them flush with the left-hand margin and with a line or half-line of space between them:

This is an example of the non-indention of paragraphs. Note that a half-line space between these paragraphs can look attractive.

The effect works very well for letters, press releases, pamphlets and technical manuals, where a fast intake of information is needed. It can also have a racy feel to it, which suits some types of fiction.

In serious novels or non-fiction books, where the reader is considered to have time to digest what he or she reads, this form of paragraph layout is less appropriate. Some would say that it gives the book a cheap and cheerful effect.

How big a bite should a writer, typist or printer take when indenting the first line of a paragraph? There are some fairly sensible guidelines on this point, but to explain them we need to remind you about ems and ens. In the chapter on the Dash we met em and en rules, long and short horizontal lines. Here we meet ems and ens of space, usually represented for the benefit of the printer as rectangular boxes. In fact em spaces only are shown like this, and in practice we need only concern ourselves with em spaces.

With short lines of type, known to a typesetter or printer as narrow measure, such as that encountered in a newspaper column or a certain type of dictionary, it is sufficient to set the normal paragraph indention to one em space. Often this amount of indention is also sufficient for books. But if the lines of type are long, the first lines of paragraphs should generally be indented two ems space.

Other Forms of Indention

We normally set off long quotations in a book, article or report by indenting them. In this way we make a clear distinction between the quotations and the rest of the text. Typists usually use a different line spacing for such indented text. The main text may be double-spaced, while the indented text may be one-and-a-half-spaced or even single-spaced. Printers also use different line spacing and also use a smaller size of type, usually one point smaller than the main text. We shall explain more about points in the section on the space.

All the examples in this book are indented, so that you can readily see that they are examples. This one shows indention within indention:

Regarding the question of indention, Horace Hart makes the following pronouncement:

Indention of first lines of paragraphs to be generally one em for full measures. Sub-indention [that is, indention within indention] should be proportionate: the rule for all indention is not to drive too far in.

This rule about not driving too far in is often broken by trendy printers who think nothing of indenting 8 picas in lines that are only 19 picas long. The waste of space is colossal and the effect, when the last line of the previous paragraph is short, is ludicrous.

You can see just how ludicrous this can be by looking at this example of a line indented by 7 picas, just under half the length of a line in this book!

Indention within indention finds its most beneficial use in indexes, where complexity can be lessened by this device.

Hanging Indention. A typographical device often employed in reading lists, tables, and so on, is hanging indention, in which the first line of an entry is set full out (that is, flush left), while the turnover lines (the remaining lines resulting from the fact that not all the information can be accommodated on a single line) are indented. The amount of indention is again one or two ems of space, depending upon the measure involved:

> *Places of Interest in Lincolnshire*
> Boston is famous for The Stump, a church tower over 80 metres high from which visitors have excellent views of the surrounding area.
> Grantham, the birthplace of Margaret Thatcher, Britain's first woman prime minister, has a good museum and a fine church housing a chained library. . . .

Quotation Marks and Paragraphs
In a quoted conversation, the speech assigned to each character taking part is given a fresh paragraph each time:

'The trouble with today's youth, Mr Jones,' said Mrs Lampton, 'is that most of them have got too much money and time on their hands and haven't the least idea how to make use of that time and money.'

'Surely the problem is that their energies are not being properly channelled,' said Jones. 'Kids need guidance — '

'Kids need discipline,' Mrs Lampton interrupted. 'They loaf around without a thought for anybody else. They vandalize property and get away with it — '

In a quotation that extends over several paragraphs an 'open-quotation' mark introduces each separate paragraph, but the corresponding 'close-quotation' mark appears only once, at the end of the last paragraph of the quote. (For an example of this, see the chapter on Quotation Marks.)

Headings and Subheadings

In book chapters, articles or reports, headings can prove a useful aid in guiding the reader through the various topics of the author's argument. These should, however, be used in moderation.

Headings can be of three main types: centred headings, or cross heads, printed at the top of a chapter, article or major section; side headings, or shoulder headings, printed above a paragraph; and run-on side headings, which actually form the start of a paragraph and may be indented if style requires it.

Centred headings and shoulder headings can be printed in bold or italic type, in capitals or small capitals. Run-on side headings usually appear in bold or italic, but are rarely printed wholly in capitals. Run-on side headings can be followed by a full point to help set them off more clearly from the text that follows, but they may also form part of the first sentence of the paragraph.

Neither centred headings nor shoulder headings, which lie outside the paragraph, should be followed by full points. For the use of capitals in headings, which should be the same as that in titles, see the chapter on Capital Letters.

We shall conclude this section with a few examples of headings:

Centred Heading:

Newton's Discoveries

Newton was compelled by an outbreak of plague to leave Cambridge in . . .

Shoulder Heading:

Nature's Medicine Cupboard
Alkaloids, extracted from many plants throughout the world, are among the most powerful poisons we know; yet in small enough doses their effects can be made to work minor medical miracles. . . .

Run-on Headings

Triton. The largest of Neptune's eight satellites, Triton was revealed by the *Voyager 2* probe to be a beautiful blue and red world full of the activity of what can only be described as ice volcanoes. . . .

Chapter 17

Space

People who write by hand and never have anything to do with a typewriter, word processor or typesetting machine may wonder why there is a chapter on Space in this survey. The fact is that, while a handwriter starts wherever he or she likes on the page, and picks up the pen between words leaving a little gap each time, a typist has to remember to position the paper properly and press the space bar or the carriage return to achieve the same effects. Word spaces for the typist or keyboard operator are as much characters as are the letters, numerals and punctuation marks.

For the traditional printer, space was anything but a matter to be taken for granted. In letterpress printing, only the raised letters carried on pieces of type were inked and made marks on the paper. But they had to be secured in a special frame called a chase by pieces of flat metal that surrounded the type and were lower than the printing surface. The spaces between the words were not empty gaps either, otherwise individual letters would have moved or fallen out. Rectangular flat pieces of metal of various sizes, which were also below the level of the printing surface, marked the word spaces and held the type tight. All these bits of metal were known as quads, or quadrats. Large quads (called quotations) filled up the last lines of paragraphs and the indention of the first lines. Long thin pieces of metal called leading could be inserted between the lines of type to provide space between the lines of text on the page. The leading, quads and quotations, including the metal surrounding the type area (giving the finished page its margins), were all referred to as 'furniture'.

We still put spaces between the lines of text we print or type as an aid to readability, and in typesetting we still refer to such spacing as leading. Mechanical typewriters have special mechanisms that allow the carriage return lever to rotate the platen by differing preset amounts corresponding to half-line, single-line, one-and-a-half, double- and even triple-line spacing. Electronic typewriters, word processors and modern typesetting machines have an electronic equivalent of this mechanism written into their software.

If you are an author, you may have heard your editor say (for example) that a book is to be set in 9 on 10-point, or in 9-point, 1-point leaded (or even 9-point, with 1-point leading). All this is printer's jargon and refers to the size of the type to be used for the main text (in this example 9 point) and the amount of space to be left between each line (1 point). This section includes an account of points and picas, the printer's measuring units. But the reader must bear in mind that this book is not intended to be exhaustive on matters of pure typography, and further information should be sought from a more specialized book.

Ems, Ens and Thins

Both the pica and point are absolute units of measurement, corresponding to an agreed standard. Our old friends the em and en are not. Originally pieces of metal below type height, they were used for spaces in letterpress work. The em is equal to the square of the point size of the type concerned and is thus different in each type size. An en is half an em. They are still type-size sensitive, even in their more modern role of determining the lengths of rules and spaces.

Ems and ens function therefore as relative measuring units.

Points and Picas

European and American printers differ on the actual size
of units involved, but the terms point and pica remain
universal, even in spite of the sweeping changes to metric
measures that are going on. Both points and picas are
units of length. Often in typesetting, points are used for
vertical measurement, and picas are units of horizontal
measurement.

The point in both the United States and Britain equals
0.351 millimetres, and there are about 72 points in one
inch. The size of a piece of type (the vertical dimension of
the type body) is given in points. In the case of a piece of
9-point type, for example, this is 3.16 mm (about an
eighth of an inch).

The pica, equal to 12 points, is used to work out the
horizontal extent of lines of type across the page. Printers
call this figure the *measure* to which the type has been set.

A smaller horizontal unit called a thin, also originaly used for
spacing, equals a fifth of an em. (Other old terms for spaces
include a nut, equal to half an em; a thick, equal to a third;
and a mid, equal to a quarter.)

Old-fashioned printers varied the use of ems, ens, thicks,
thins, nuts and quotations to achieve proportional spacing,
line centring, paragraph indention, and justification (an even
appearance on both right and left of the lines of text). The
work must have been laborious. Computerized setting has
removed the drudgery, but some of the old names remain.

White Space

The amount of empty space at the top and bottom and
around the sides of a page help to focus our attention upon

the text area. But the text area itself often benefits from having some empty space (white space) within it — below chapter titles, above subheadings, between lines in display headings, etc. It is not our province to go into the aesthetics of the printed page, but the author or report writer would be wise to acquire some knowledge on the subject as an aid to learning good presentation.

All the vertical spacing mentioned in the previous paragraph is measured in points, as when an editor or designer writes 'Insert 3 pts space' above a heading.

Spaces between Words

Word separation by spaces was invented in the eighth century by Anglo-Saxon, German and Irish monks. It evolved gradually among a clerical population for whom Latin was a foreign language. Short words, such as prepositions, remained tacked on to other longer words even after spacing was introduced, but by about the end of the fourteenth century the full use of the space was standard.

There is no need to exemplify word-spacing, because you can see it in every page of this book. We should say something, however, about spacing between sentences. Normal typing practice is to tap the space bar twice after the full point ending a sentence, and this should be followed. It should be noted, though, that some publishers ask their authors to type each line to a specified character count, and they may also tell the authors to key only one space between sentences. This is especially likely when the measure is narrow — i.e., when the lines are short. And do not forget that word spaces should be included in such a character count.

Letter-spacing. In certain circumstances very thin spaces are inserted between the letters of a word. This is now rare in

English, but is occasionally encountered in German, especially in books set in the older style of German type. It is used for emphasis, much as italic type is used in English. Here is an example:

Du wirst es n i e m a l s verstehen.

Spaces in Indention. We have already explained that these are measured in ems. For further information on this subject, *see* the section on *Paragraphs*, *Indention* and *Headings*.

Ligatures. Certain letter combinations used by printers in the English language were once cast on one piece of type. They include *ff*, *fi*, *ffl*, and *fl*. Other ligatures represented certain sounds in Old English, such as æ and œ. These latter ligatures and some others are occasionally encountered in linguistics or phonetics. They should not be used to render the diphthongs *ae* and *oe* in Latin words such as *Caesar* or *coeli*.

One Word or Two

Pairings such as *blood stream/bloodstream*, *cabinet maker/cabinetmaker*, and *post horn/posthorn* illustrate the problem of whether certain compounds should be spelled as one word or two. With normal British usage continuing to abandon the hyphen, these are often the only choices. Busy writers may take the line of least resistance on such compounds and spell them solid (that is, as one word). However, words such as *posthorn*, *tophat* and *swamphen*, give rise to letter combinations that at first sight are misleading. Consequently, these should be spelled as two words to avoid ambiguity.

There are no guidelines to give here, except these: make a choice and stick to it, try to be aware of possible ambiguities and avoid them, and if you have any doubts, let a good modern dictionary be your guide.

Chapter 18

Slash, Solidus, Oblique or Virgule

This mark, shown by the / symbol, is known by all the above names and a few more besides, such as the diagonal, slant, slash mark or shilling stroke. The names slash (mark), slant and oblique are predominantly British; the names virgule and diagonal are American. When reading out loud, people often register its presence by calling it simply a stroke, especially in legal or official usage. Thus 'Form PN/13' will be referred to in speech as 'Form PN stroke 13'.

History of the Slash

The slash preceded the invention of printing by a century or two and was originally used as a light pause mark. In writing, it degenerated into a short curved stroke written next to the bottom of the preceding letter and eventually became our modern comma. However, other uses of the slash arose in the course of time − e.g., as a currency symbol. The Italian monetary system of *libri*, *solidi* and *denarii* gave Roman pre-decimal sterling the signs for its units, one of which was the / symbol − hence the name solidus.

The slash today has a variety of conventional uses that we can broadly divide into the ordinary and the technical.

Ordinary Uses

1. Signalling Alternatives. The slash between one word and another means that what is being said in the sentence applies equally to either word. Thus the slash signifies a straight-forward option or alternative:

Each student attending the lecture is asked to bring his/her own writing materials.

And/or. In the special case of and/or, a three-way choice is signified:

There is space under the dashboard for fitting a stereo radio and/or cassette recorder.

In the last example, the space can accommodate a radio only, a stereo cassette recorder only or both a radio and a recorder.

To signal a choice between words that have letters in common, the slash can be used in the middle of a word:

Bookshop manager/ess required. Apply within.

Everyone must do what s/he considers appropriate.

This use of the slash has become widespread as a method of avoiding sexist language and of complying with legislation on equal opportunities.

2. Expressions of Date. When an event or process takes place over successive years, seasons, months, or days, the appropriate time units are separated by a slash.

Our interview with stuntman Fred Smith will appear in the August/September issue of *Heroes of Sport*.

The 1988/9 soccer season was marred by the tragedy of Hillsborough.

Gower and Botham missed the 1989/90 tour to the West Indies.

On the night of 15/16 October, a great storm ravaged England.

(A purely historical use results from the fact that before 1752 Britain and America used the Old Style Julian calendar and started the year on 25 March. A few historians still acknowledge this fact by using a formula such as 4 February 1621/2. People's life dates may also appear as 1629/30 – 1687, for example. The use of the slash in this way is, however, a technicality and many writers avoid it.)

The date is informally shown in an abbreviated all-figure format with slashes separating the figures. Note that British usage requires the day-month-year sequence, whereas American writers employ the order month-day-year.

3/9/90 means 3 September 1990 in Britain and 9 March 1990 in the United States.

See the chapters on Full Point and Numbers.

3. Fractions and Ratios. The slash is often used as the visual representation of a division sign in mathematics and is consequently used to represent fractions, especially when these are not available on a typewriter. Certain typefaces also make use of the slash, separating a superscript figure for the numerator from a subscript figure for the denominator:

A half may be represented by 1/2 or ½

Awkward fractions may be treated in this way:

$^{8}/_{13}$ $^{255}/_{256}$

(Note that the % symbol makes use of the solidus, as does the less common 'per thousand' sign ‰).

4. Sections and Subsections. In legal or official usage, a slash may often be used between the main section of a document and a subsection or paragraph.

'*See* Section B/13*a*' is an instruction to see Paragraph 13*a* of Section B.

5. Abbreviational Use. The slash appears in abbreviations such as c/o ((in the) care of) and a/c (bank or financial account of):

To: Fred Smith, c/o Mrs R. Peterson, 'Sunnyview', ...

a/c R.T. Parkinson

6. In Lines of Verse. When lines of poetry are written out in a continuous format to save space, the line breaks are signified by slashes:

Mid pleasures and palaces though we may roam, / Be it ever so humble, there's no place like home.

— John Howard Payne

Technical Uses

The following are generally restricted to technical contexts.

1. Replacement of 'per'. A special use of the slash used as a division sign is found in scientific writing, as in the following examples:

The Earth's escape velocity is in excess of 40,000 km/h. The acceleration due to gravity is 9.80665 m/s^2, and the atmospheric pressure at sea level is about 1.03 kg/cm^2.

(The previous sentence means that the Earth's escape velocity exceeds 40,000 kilometres per hour, its free-fall acceleration is 9.80665 metres per second per second, and its sea level atmospheric pressure is 1.03 kilograms per square centimetre.)

2. Linguistic Use. The technical linguistic use, found in journals and academic papers on the subject and also in a

193

few general dictionaries, is to enclose a broad phonetic transcription within a pair of slashes:

thyme / taim /, *n*. a plant belonging to the mint family and constituting the genus *Thymus* ...

Chapter 19

Hyphen

The hyphen (-) fulfils a triple role in writing and printing. Its purely punctuational use is of minor importance and causes few problems. Its other functions are apparently paradoxical and are fraught with difficulty in terms of their applications. These uses may be classified under the headings of 'Joining and Compounding' and 'End-of-Line Division'.

Life (for a writer) would be much easier if there were no such thing as the hyphen. The unwillingness of writers of English — British ones especially — to adopt a consistent approach to this troublesome little symbol has led to an inability on the part of any authority to come up with a rational system of guidelines for its use. Broad principles have been worked out, mainly by lexicographers, who have to make consistent decisions about the forms of words, but exceptions to these principles abound.

Any discussion of the hyphen has to start from the acceptance that, although we can make any number of 'rules', usage does not have to abide by them. This seems especially true of the hyphen, and many writers find it such a nuisance that they avoid it. American writers use the hyphen far less often than their British counterparts in similar contexts, and a continuing process of abandoning the hyphen has been going on even in Britain since the 1950s.

Punctuational Uses

We shall clear the decks for more serious discussion by quickly disposing of four uses of the hyphen in the sentence.

The History of the Hyphen

The word *hyphen* is Greek; its derivation — from the words *hypo*, 'under' and *hen*, 'one', hence meaning something like 'under one (word or meaning)' — reveals its primary function in joining or combining parts of words. Aristophanes of Byzantium, the early second-century BC librarian at Alexandria who was the first to devise a punctuation system for Greek, used a curving mark to do the job of a hyphen, but it did not catch on.

Towards the end of the tenth century AD, scribes began using a special sign to mark the point where a word had to be divided at the end of a line because there was not enough space to fit it all in. The rest of the word began the next line. This sign was the — and from the fourteenth to the eighteenth centuries it was frequently doubled, =. Proofreaders, especially in the United States, still use the = to signify the instruction to insert a hyphen. In due course the end-of-line hyphen was joined by the compounding hyphen to perform the task originally intended by Aristophanes' curve.

(It is interesting to note that some publishers, e.g. J.M. Dent & Sons, Ltd., were using the tilde, or 'swung dash' (~) as an end-of-line hyphen in certain of their books well into the twentieth century.)

---

1. With Stems, Endings and Affixes of Words. This is a technical usage mostly encountered in linguistics textbooks:

Nouns whose plurals end in *-s* or *-es* are very numerous in English.

The prefixes *ante-*, *pre-* and *post-* are of Latin origin.

2. To Represent Speech Impediments or Nervousness in Quotations. The hyphen conventionally signals stammering in quoted speech:

> 'I d-d-don't know w-what you m-m-mean,' stammered Trevor. 'I've n-not s-s-seen her s-s-since F-F-Friday.'

(Compare the use of dashes to represent hesitation.)

3. In Linking. Typists especially use the hyphen to link years, places, and other things:

The 1939-45 War

The London-New York flight

The Spurs-Aston Villa match

Printers use the en rule in this context, and if what you are writing is to be printed and published, you should see to it that all such uses of the typed hyphen as this one are marked up as en rules. *See* the chapter on the Dash.

4. The suspended hyphen. A hyphen followed by a space is used in lists of words that have certain letters (stems, prefixes, etc.) in common. The hyphen isolates the parts that are different:

The car is available as three-, four- and five-door models.

The medical unit is equipped to deal with all ante-, peri- and postnatal problems. (Some writers prefer 'antenatal, perinatal, and postnatal'.)

Joining Uses

The use of the hyphen as a joining symbol consists in helping to form compound words, usually adjectives, nouns or verbs. These can be temporary compounds, formed for one use and probably never to be used again — rather like Dylan

Thomas's 'fishingboat-bobbing sea', or they can be permanent, such as the words T-shirt or cure-all.

It used to be said that newly coined compound nouns consisting of two words ought to be spelled as two separate words at their birth. As they grew to be more accepted they would pass first through the stage of being hyphenated (that is, written with a hyphen) and then, after full acceptance, they would become solid (that is, written as one word). For example, *blood stream* would have first become *blood-stream* and finally *bloodstream*.

The reality today is that authors, editors and publishers, who cannot be bothered with the hyphen, either spell a compound noun as one word or two, depending on their own predilections or on which dictionary they use for their house style. Not for them the pedantic justification of *walking-stick* by the Fowlers, who said that the hyphen was essential to prevent the reader from interpreting 'walking stick' as 'a stick that walks'. Today's publishers might at a pinch accept *walkingstick* one day (many Americans already do), but for the majority 'walking-stick' is out, and 'walking stick' is in.

Having said all that, however, we must acknowledge that hyphens are not a completely useless adjunct to our compound-formation process. The following list of cases illustrates usual modern practice, although (as we have already said) exceptions are rife.

1. Hyphen of Readability. Certain prefixes, such as *anti-, co-, micro-, pre-, pro-, semi-*, etc., are usually hyphenated when they are followed by words or word elements that begin with the same vowel as that with which the prefix ends:

anti-imperialism	pre-eminent
co-opt	pre-oestrus
micro-organism	semi-industrial

Otherwise words introduced by these prefixes are solid. Note also that *co-ordinate/coordinate* and *co-operate/cooperate*, and their derivatives, nowadays tend to drop the hyphen.

These remarks are also true of the prolific prefix *re-*. Note such words as *re-entry, re-estimate*, but *rearrange, reinforce, reorder*, and *reunite*.

When a tripled consonant appears in the middle of a word, a hyphen should be included at the affix boundary purely on grounds of readability:

The ordinary garden slug is almost shell-less.

His home is in what used to be called the county of Inverness-shire.

The daffodil has a bell-like flower.

Words such as *de-icer* and *de-mister* also take a hyphen of readability to preserve correct pronunciation.

2. Hyphen for Removing Doubt. Use a hyphen to remove all ambiguity, however fleeting, from the reader's mind:

There are only three pound tickets left. (= three tickets at a pound each.)

There are only three-pound tickets left. (= an unspecified number of tickets, each costing three pounds.)

The hyphen distinguishes between certain compounds introduced by the prefix *re-*. Thus we write *recover* (to regain one's health, composure, etc.), but *re-cover* (to furnish with a new cover) and recreation (relaxation), but *re-creation* (creation anew or for a second time). Other pairs distinguished by hyphens include:

199

reform (change)	re-form (form again)
react (register an effect)	re-act (act again)

3. *Hyphen Before Capitals.* All prefixes or combining forms occurring before a capital letter take a hyphen:

pre-Christian   anti-Nazi   Pan-Hellenic   pro-Iranian un-American

4. *Non- Words.* Up to the end of the 1970s, it could fairly be said that, whereas American writers spelled such words as *nonindustrial, nonliterary, noneconomic*, etc., without a hyphen, British writers spelled them with one: *non-industrial, non-literary, non-economic*, etc. The only exception, as far as British authors and editors were concerned, was *nonconformist* (often *Nonconformist* in its specialized religious meaning), which did not take a hyphen. At the end of the 1980s we can discern the erosion of the hyphen in words beginning with *non-*. Few people are now shocked to see words such as *nonindustrial* in print, even in a British textbook. This is yet another nail in the coffin of the hyphen. Having said that, however, we would advise British writers to use the form *non-profit-making*, for the American term *nonprofit*.

5. *The Hyphen in Word-plus-Word Compounds.* In this part of the discussion, we shall deal not with prefixes but with free words in combination.

(a) Compound Nouns. Hyphens should be generally avoided in favour of one word or two and a modern dictionary should be consulted in case of doubt, except in the following categories:

(i) Spelled-out numbers between 21 and 99, excluding multiples of ten:

She is thirty-two years old

The number is eight hundred and twenty-three

Spelled out fractions:

two-thirds   three-fifths

forty-one sixty-fourths

Three-quarters of those voting were women. (British use. Americans prefer 'Three fourths' ...)

The reaction lasted twenty-one six-hundredths of a second.

(ii) Noun + noun compounds. These are often spelled with an en rule in print, but typists may use a hyphen:

Sir Henry Irving was a great actor-manager.

Athens and Sparta were rival city-states in Greece.

(iii) Onomatopoeic (sound-effect) words. These 'reduplicated' formations take a hyphen not only as nouns but also as verbs, adjectives and adverbs:

He heard the clip-clop of the horse's hooves fading into the distance.

The horse and its rider clip-clopped along the road.

The horse's hooves made a lively clip-clop sound.

The horse went clip-clop along the road.

(iv) Compounds containing a possessive. Among these are words such as *bull's-eye* and several plant names:

The garden is full of mare's-tails.

Venus's-hair is a delicate tropical fern.

(v) Fixed phrases. These also include many popular plant names:

You and I must have a heart-to-heart, my dear.

We're having a get-together at my house on Thursday.

The forget-me-nots look lovely in the spring.

Love-lies-bleeding is a most attractive sight in the British countryside.

Also included in this category are such phrasal nouns as *go-as-you-please, give-and-take* and the slightly old-fashioned *n'ere-do-well*.

(vi) Military ranks and other terms. These are still generally hyphenated and include combinations ending in *-general* and *-major*, especially when used as titles. The term *court-martial*, either as a noun or verb, is also hyphenated. Its plural is courts-martial:

Brigadier-General Sheringham-Smythe is visiting the barracks today.

He was a regimental sergeant-major during the last war.

(vii) Family relationships. These include all the *great-* and *-in-law* connections, but those beginning with *grand* are solid:

Mother-in-law	father-in-law	son-in-law
daughter-in-law	brother-in-law	sister-in-law
Great-grandmother	great-grandfather	
great-granddaughter	great-grandson	great-aunt
great-uncle.		

(viii) Noun + gerund of a transitive verb. These have generally been hyphenated in the past, and quite a few still are, but under American influence some of these are moving to solid or two-word compounds:

... famous for steel-making, wood-engraving, and lager-brewing.

But:

woodworking   metalworking   bricklaying

The agent-nouns associated with these formations — wood-engraver, woodworker, etc. — are treated in the same way.

(ix) Other verb-based noun compounds. Hyphens are customary in the following:

do-gooder; cure-all; has-been; make-believe; runner-up; passer-by; go-between; hanger-on; flare-up

But there are plenty that are spelled solid, such as *rundown, shutdown, breakthrough, breakup, Passover, flypast, flyby*, ...

(x) Letter + noun. Some writers prefer to drop the hyphen in these, but British and US usage continue to support it:

T-shirt   V-neck   X-rays

(Note that the verb 'to X-ray' must be hyphenated.)

(xi) Scientific and analogous units. These include the following:

kilowatt-hour   foot-pound   man-week

(b) Compound Adjectives. Almost any adjective composed of two or more words can be hyphenated when it precedes the noun:

He walked up the stairs to his third-floor office.

But

His office was on the third floor.

He was an entertaining after-dinner speaker.

But

He gave an entertaining speech after dinner.

The adjectives in the above example are hyphenated when preceding the noun (in attributive position) but not elsewhere. As can these:

The house lay above a thickly-wooded hillside.

The hillside was thickly wooded.

They reached a dried-up river valley.

The riverbed was dried up.

He had an up-to-date car but out-of-date ideas.

His car was up to date but his opinions were out of date.

He carried a worn-out coat over his arm.

The coat he carried was worn out.

The following are hyphenated in all positions:

Adjective + adjective: A red-hot news story; this is red-hot.

Adjective + participle: A foul-smelling plant; this plant is foul-smelling; deep-fried fish; I love my fish deep-fried.

(i) Adjective + noun: A first-class choir; our choir is first-class.

(ii) Adjective + noun + *-ed*. She was a big-boned woman; she was big-boned.

(iii) Noun + adjective: A country-wide reputation; news of his escape was now country-wide. (Note that some of the compounds in this class are often written solid: *foolproof, worldwide, waterproof*.)

(iv) Compound adjectives involving numbers and units. These are hyphenated:

> A six-foot-tall man.   A five-metre wall.
>
> A 30-kilometre journey (or a 30-km journey).

Note that the following are also hyphenated in all positions:

> air-cooled   devil-may-care   far-flung   far-reaching
> lantern-jawed   life-giving   long-awaited   never-ending
> poverty-stricken   quick-acting   quick-fire   sure-fire

Some hyphenated compound adjectives rarely if ever occur anywhere in the sentence other than in attributive position:

> real-time − A computer's real-time clock.
>
> sabre-toothed − A sabre-toothed tiger (or sabretoothed tiger).

In some cases, a hyphenated form means something different from an unhyphenated form:

> Her cat was black and white.
>
> Her television was black-and-white.

Note the absence of hyphens in these examples:

> A Foreign Office spokesman.
>
> The United States Ambassador.
>
> A House of Lords debate.
>
> An Old Testament prophecy.
>
> A Friends of the Earth representative.

(v) *Better-, best- ill-, little-, well-, worse-* and *worst-* compounds. These are usually hyphenated in attributive positions but not elsewhere:

A well-known journalist   A little-known journalist

His plan was ill advised   His plan was well thought out.

An ill-advised decision   A well-thought-out scheme.

The worst-paid workers   Few workers were worse paid.

An attributive adjective preceded by an adverb ending in *-ly* is not hyphenated to the adverb.

A richly deserved reward.Her reward was richly deserved.

(c) Compound Verbs. Common hyphenated forms include:

dry-clean   French-polish   cold-shoulder

cold-hammer   bad-mouth   goose-step

sweet-talk   power-lift   stir-fry

(d) Compound Adverbs. These include the following:

big-headedly   hard-heartedly   half-heartedly

They crashed head-on.

He learned his lines parrot-fashion.

(e) Miscellaneous Compounds. Hyphens are customary in the following situations:

(i) Words ending in *-elect*: *President-elect*, but prefer *Vice President elect* (as in American usage).

(ii) *by-blow, by-law, by-election, by-form.* But *byname, byword.*

(iii) Words beginning with *ex-*: *ex-wife, ex-president.* But *ex prime minister.*

(iv) Words beginning with *off*: *off-licence*, *off-chance*, *off-drive*, *off-putting*. But *offset*, *offshoot*, *offspring*.

(v) Among words beginning with *on*, prefer *on-drive*, but write all other words solid: *oncoming*, *ongoing*, *onset*.

(vi) Most adjectives, but not verbs or nouns, beginning with *over-*: *over-proud*, *over-dignified*. But *overbearing*.

(vii) Words beginning with *self-*. All these are hyphenated apart from *selfsame*, *selfconscious*.

(viii) Words beginning with *un-*. Do not hyphenate directly after un-. But do write *unco-operative*, *unco-ordinated*.

(ix) Words ending with *-like*. All these are written solid, except when the first element is a proper name or ends in double *l*: catlike, fatherlike. But *bell-like*, A *California-like* climate.

(x) Virtually all Latin- and Greek-based prefixes are unhyphenated with only a few exceptions, especially where the last consonant or vowel of the prefix is the same as the first consonant or vowel of the rest of the word, although even here the cases are few. Note also the following:

counterculture	counter-revolution
infra-red	infrastructure
quasi-judicial	quasi scholar (USA)
ultra-ancient	ultraviolet (despite infra-red)
ultra-right-wing party	(but on the ultra-right wing of the party)
vice-president	Vice President of the United States
vice-chairman	viceroy (and viceregent)

End-of-Line Hyphenation

The principles of end-of-line hyphenation are in process of change in Britain, from a traditional system based on etymology to a more rational system practised in the United States, which is based on pronunciation and the shape of the word.

End-of-line hyphens should be avoided if possible, because they are obviously not an aid to readability. Most printers do not break words when the setting is unjustified (has a ragged appearance on the right-hand side), especially in narrow measure. End-of-line division should not be completely avoided in unjustified setting, though. A total absence of it reduces the number of words that can be set and can cause some extremely ugly 'gappy' effects on the right-hand side.

The principles of end-of-line hyphenation that we have followed in preparing the word list in the rest of this book are as follows:

1. Words are broken at natural syllable boundaries according to pronunciation: *man-age-ment, mana-gerial*.

2. One-syllable words are not to be divided: *asked, bathed*.

3. Words are broken between two or more consonants, usually after the first one: *illus-trate, prob-lem*.

4. But consonants that form one sound are not divided: *warm-est, bro-ther*. Compare *Beet-hoven*.

5. Break words after a prefix or before a suffix: *pre-amble, un-loved, train-er*.

6. Words ending in *-ing* may be broken before the suffix: *shin-ing, bor-ing*.

7. A doubled consonant before *-ing* or (if the word is polysyllabic) before *-ed* may be divided: *run-ning, rot-ted*; but not *drop-ped*.

8. Misleading word-division must be avoided: *re-adjust*, not *read-just*; *thera-pist*, not *the-rapist*; *extrac-tor*, not *ex-tractor*.

Words such as *women, often*, etc., should generally not be broken.

9. Words must not be broken at points where the result would leave one letter at the end of a line or one letter at the beginning of a line. Therefore, do not divide *about, above, baby, rainy*.

10. Word breaks leaving two letters at the end or beginning of a line are also to be avoided, except in the case of a two-letter prefix, such as *un-, de-, re-: un-known, de-moralized, re-vive*.

11. Where a word is already spelled with a hyphen, the word must be broken at that hyphen and not anywhere else: *one-horse* (a *one-horse* town), *has-been*. (*Court-mar-tial* should be avoided.)

12. Ambiguous word breaks must be avoided: Thus we may break *re-creation* and *re-form* at the hyphen, but we should not break recreation, reform (without hyphens). *See also* Principle No. 8, above.

13. American authorities prefer not to break personal names at the ends of lines, but forms such as *Steven-son, Priest-ley*, are more-or-less acceptable in British English. We have, however, excluded names from our list for reasons of space. Nouns and adjectives derived from personal names are subject to end-of-line division: *Marx-ism, Keynes-ian*.

14. A line must not end in the middle of a set of initials: *J. S. Bach* is wrong; you should instead use the form *J.S. Bach*.

15. Figures and units should likewise never be separated. *33 km* is unacceptable. The same applies to dates given with BC or AD and also to the time of day.

Hyphenation Dictionary

aard/vark
ab/ac/ti/nal
aba/cus
aba/lone
aban/don
ab/at/toir
ab/bess
ab/bey
ab/bot
ab/brevi/ate
ab/brevi/ation
ab/di/cate
ab/di/ca/tion
ab/do/men
ab/domi/nal
ab/du/cent
ab/duct
ab/er/rant
ab/er/ra/tion
abey/ance
ab/hor
ab/id/ing
abil/ity
ab/ir/ri/tate
ab/ject
ab/la/tion
ab/lu/tions
ab/ne/gate
ab/nor/mal
ab/nor/mally
ab/nor/mal/ity
ab/norm/ity

ab/ol/ish
ab/ol/ition
ab/om/in/able
ab/or/igi/nal
abor/tion
abort/ive
ab/ra/ca/dab/ra
ab/ra/sion
ab/ras/ive
ab/re/ac/tion
ab/ridge/ment
ab/ro/gate
ab/rupt
ab/ruptly
ab/rupt/ness
ab/scess
ab/scond
ab/sence
ab/sent
ab/sen/tee
ab/sen/tee/ism
ab/sinth
ab/so/lute
ab/so/lutely
ab/so/lu/tion
ab/so/lut/ism
ab/solve
ab/sorb
ab/sorb/ent
ab/sor/ber
ab/sorp/tion
ab/stain

ab/ste/mi/ous
ab/stemi/ous/ness
ab/sten/tion
ab/ster/gent
ab/stin/ence
ab/stract
ab/strac/ted
ab/strac/tion
ab/struse
ab/surd
abun/dance
abun/dant
ab/use
ab/us/ive
abut/ted
abys/mal
abys/sal
aca/cia
aca/demic
acad/emy
acan/thus
ac/cede
ac/cel/er/ate
ac/cel/er/ation
ac/cel/er/ator
ac/cent
ac/cen/tor
ac/cen/tu/ate
ac/cept
ac/cess
ac/cess/ible
ac/ces/sion

211

ac/cess/ory
ac/ci/dent
ac/ci/den/tal
ac/ci/den/tally
ac/cipi/ter
ac/claim
ac/cla/mation
ac/cli/mat/iz/ation
ac/cli/mat/ize
ac/col/ade
ac/com/mo/date
ac/com/mo/dat/ing
ac/com/mo/dation
ac/com/pani/ment
ac/com/pany
ac/com/plice
ac/com/plish
ac/com/plish/ment
ac/cord
ac/cord/ance
ac/cord/ingly
ac/cor/dion
ac/cord/ion/ist
ac/cost
ac/count
ac/count/able
ac/count/ancy
ac/count/ant
ac/coutred
ac/cou/tre/ment
ac/credit
ac/cre/tion
ac/crue
ac/cu/mu/late
ac/cu/mu/lator
ac/cur/acy

ac/cur/ate
ac/cursed
ac/cu/sa/tion
ac/cu/sa/tive
ac/cuse
ac/cu/sing
ac/cus/tom
acerb/ity
acet/ate
acet/one
acet/yl/ene
achieve/ment
Achil/les' heel
ach/ing
ach/ro/matic
acid/u/lous
ac/knowl/edge
ac/knowl/edge/me-
nt
aco/lyte
ac/on/ite
acous/tic
ac/quaint
ac/quaint/ance
ac/qui/esce
ac/quire
ac/qui/sition
ac/quisi/tive
ac/quit
ac/quit/tal
acre/age
ac/rid
ac/ri/mo/ni/ous
acri/mony
ac/ro/bat
ac/ro/batic

ac/ro/po/lis
ac/rylic
act/ing
ac/tion
ac/tion/able
ac/ti/vate
ac/tive
ac/ti/vist
ac/tiv/ity
act/ress
ac/tual
ac/tu/al/ity
ac/tu/ally
ac/tu/ar/ial
ac/tu/ary
ac/tu/ate
acu/ity
acu/men
acu/punc/ture
acute/ness
ada/mant
ad/apt
adap/ta/bility
ad/ap/ta/tion
ad/dax
ad/ded
ad/den/dum
ad/der
ad/dict
ad/dic/ted
add/ing
ad/di/tion
ad/di/tive
ad/dress
ad/dres/see
ad/duce

ad/emp/tion
ad/en/oids
ad/equate
ad/here
ad/her/ence
ad/her/ent
ad/he/sion
ad/he/sive
ad/hibit
ad/ia/batic
adi/pose
ad/ja/cent
ad/jec/ti/val
ad/jec/tive
ad/join
ad/journ
ad/ju/di/cate
ad/ju/di/ca/tion
ad/junct
ad/just
ad/just/able
ad/just/ment
ad/ju/tant
ad/meas/ure
ad/min/is/ter
ad/min/is/tra/tion
ad/min/is/trat/ive
ad/min/is/trator
admir/able
ad/miral
ad/mire
ad/mir/able
ad/mir/ably
ad/mir/ation
ad/mi/rer
ad/mi/ringly

ad/miss/ible
ad/mis/sion
ad/mit
ad/mit/tance
ad/mit/tedly
ad/mix
ad/mix/ture
ad/mon/ish
ad/mon/ition
ado/les/cence
ado/les/cent
adop/tion
ad/ore
ad/or/able
ad/or/ation
ad/orn
ad/orn/ment
ad/ren/alin
adroit/ness
ad/sorb/ent
adu/la/tion
adul/ter/ate
adul/terer
adul/ter/ess
adul/tery
ad/vance
ad/vance/ment
ad/van/tage
ad/van/ta/geous
ad/vent
ad/ven/ti/tious
ad/ven/ture
ad/ven/tur/ous
ad/verb
ad/ver/bial
ad/ver/sary

ad/verse
ad/versely
ad/ver/sity
ad/vert
ad/vert/ence
ad/ver/tise
ad/ver/tise/ment
ad/ver/tiser
ad/ver/tis/ing
ad/vice
ad/vis/able
ad/vise
ad/vis/edly
ad/viser
ad/vis/ory
ad/vo/cacy
ad/vo/cate
ae/gis
aepy/ornis
aer/ial
aero/batic
aer/obic
aero/drome
aero/dy/nam/ics
aero/foil
aero/naut/ical
aero/naut/ics
aero/plane
aero/sol
aero/space
aes/thete
aes/thet/ic
aes/thet/ically
affa/bility
af/fable
af/fably

af/fa/bil/ity
af/fair
af/fect
af/fecta/tion
af/fect/ing
af/fec/tion
af/fec/tion/ate
af/fer/ent
af/fi/da/vit
af/fili/ate
af/fili/ation
af/fin/ity
af/firm
af/firm/ative
af/firm/atively
af/fix
af/flict
af/flic/tion
af/flu/ence
af/flu/ent
af/ford
af/for/est/ation
af/fray
af/fright
af/front
afore/men/tioned
Af/rica
after/care
af/ter/math
after/noon
after/shave
after/thought
after/wards
aga/pan/thus
ag/ate
agen/das

ag/glom/era/tion
ag/grand/ize
ag/gra/vate
ag/gra/vat/ing
ag/gra/vation
ag/gre/gate
ag/gres/sion
ag/gress/ive
ag/gressor
ag/grieved
ag/gro
agil/ity
agit/ate
agi/ta/tion
agit/ator
ag/nostic
ag/on/ized
ag/on/iz/ing
ag/ony
ago/ra/phobia
ag/rar/ian
agree/able
agree/ment
agri/cul/tural
ag/ri/cul/ture
ag/ro/nomic
ail/eron
ail/ing
ail/ment
aim/less
aim/lessly
air/borne
air/brake
air-con/di/tion
air/cooled
air/craft

air/craft/man
air/craft/woman
air/crew
air/field
air host/ess
air/ily
air/lift
air/plane (US)
air/port
air/ship
air/sick
air/sick/ness
air/strip
air/tight
air/worthi/ness
ala/bas/ter
alac/rity
al/ba/core
al/ba/tross
al/bin/ism
al/bino
al/bum
al/bu/men
al/chem/ist
al/chemy
al/co/hol
al/co/holic
al/cove
al/der
Al/ex/an/drian
al/fresco
al/gae
al/ge/bra
al/go/rithm
alien/ate
ali/men/tary

ali/mony
al/kali
al/ka/line
al/lay
al/le/ga/tion
al/lege
al/legedly
al/le/gi/ance
al/leg/or/ical
al/leg/ory
al/ler/gic
al/lergy
al/levi/ate
al/levi/ation
al/ley
al/li/ance
al/lied
al/li/ga/tor
al/lit/er/a/tion
al/loc/ate
al/lo/ca/tion
al/lo/morph
al/lot
al/lot/ment
al/low
allow/able
al/low/ance
al/loy
al/lude
al/lure
al/lur/ing
al/lu/sion
al/lu/vial
al/lu/vium
al/manac
al/mighty

al/mond
al/most
alms/house
along/side
alo/pe/cia
al/pha/bet
al/pha/beti/cal
alp/ine
al/ready
al/sa/tian
al/tar
al/ter
al/ter/ca/tion
al/ter/nate
al/ter/nately
al/ter/na/ting
al/ter/na/tive
al/ter/nator
al/though
al/ti/meter
al/ti/tude
al/to/gether
alu/min/ium
alu/min/um (US)
alum/nus (US)
al/ways
alys/sum
am/al/gam
am/al/gam/ate
am/al/gam/ation
ama/teur
ama/teur/ish
am/aze/ment
amaz/ing
am/bas/sador
am/bas/sa/dress

am/ber
am/ber/gris
am/bi/dex/trous
am/bi/ence
am/bi/guity
am/bigu/ous
am/bi/tion
am/bi/tious
am/biva/lent
am/bler
am/bro/sia
am/bu/lance
am/bush
ameli/or/ate
ameli/or/ation
amen/able
amend/ment
amen/ity
Am/er/ica
ameth/yst
ami/able
ami/ably
am/ic/able
amic/ably
am/meter
ammo/nia
am/mon/ite
am/mu/ni/tion
am/ne/sia
am/nesty
amoe/bas amoe/bae
am/or/ous
amorph/ous
amor/tize
am/père
am/per/sand

215

am/phet/amine
am/phib/ian
am/phib/i/ous
am/phi/theatre
am/phora
amp/li/fi/cation
am/pli/fier
amp/lify
am/poule
am/pu/tate
amuse/ment
amus/ing
ana/chron/ism
ana/chron/istic
an/ae/mia an/e/mia
   (US)
an/ae/mic
an/aes/thesia
an/aes/thetic
an/aes/thet/ist
an/aes/thet/ize
ana/gram
an/al/gesic
an/al/o/gous
an/al/ogy
ana/lyse
anal/y/sis
ana/lyst
ana/lyt/ical
an/ar/chist
an/ar/chy
an/ath/ema
an/at/omy
an/cestor
an/ces/tral
an/ces/try

an/chor
an/chor/age
an/chovy
an/cient
an/cil/lary
an/droid
an/ec/dote
an/er/oid
an/eur/ism
an/gel
an/ger
ang/ler
an/gli/cism
an/gora
an/grily
an/guish
an/gu/lar
ani/mal
ani/mate
ani/ma/tion
ani/mos/ity
ani/seed
ank/let
an/nal
an/neal
an/nex
an/nexe
an/ni/hil/ate
an/ni/hil/ation
an/ni/ver/sary
an/no/tate
an/nounce
an/nounce/ment
an/noun/cer
an/noy
an/noyed

an/nual
an/nually
an/nuity
an/nul
an/nul/ment
an/ode
an/od/ize
an/om/aly
anom/al/ous
an/ony/mous
an/ony/mously
an/orak
an/or/exia ner/vosa
an/other
an/swer
an/swer/able
an/swer/ing
an/tag/on/ism
an/tag/on/ist
an/tag/on/ize
Ant/arc/tic
ant/eater
ante/ce/dent
ante/date
ante/dil/u/vian
ante/lope
ante/natal
an/ten/na
an/terior
ante/room
an/them
ant/hill
an/thol/ogy
an/thra/cite
an/thro/po/logi/cal
an/thro/pol/ogist

an/thro/pol/ogy	apa/thetic	ap/pease/ment
an/ti/biotic	apa/thy	ap/pend
an/ti/body	aperi/ent	ap/pen/di/citis
an/tici/pate	aperi/tif	ap/pen/dix
an/tici/pa/tion	ap/er/ture	ap/per/tain
an/ti/climax	aph/or/ism	ap/pet/ite
an/ti/clock/wise	aph/ro/dis/iac	ap/pet/izer
an/tics	api/ary	ap/pet/iz/ing
an/ti/cy/clone	api/cul/ture	ap/plaud
an/ti/dote	ap/ing	ap/plause
an/ti/freeze	apla/sia	ap/pliance
an/ti/his/ta/mine	apoc/a/lyptic	ap/plic/able
an/tip/athy	apoc/ryphal	ap/pli/cant
an/tip/odes	apo/gee	ap/pli/ca/tion
an/ti/quar/ian	apol/it/ical	ap/ply
an/ti/quary	apo/lo/getic	ap/point
an/ti/quated	apo/lo/get/ically	ap/pointed
an/tique	apo/lo/gize	ap/point/ment
an/tiquity	apo/logy	ap/por/tion
an/tir/rhin/um	apo/plectic	ap/posite
an/ti/sep/tic	apo/plexy	ap/praise
an/ti/social	apos/tate	ap/praisal
an/ti/thesis	apos/trophe	ap/preci/able
ant/ler	ap/pal	ap/preci/ably
an/vil	ap/pal/ling	ap/preci/ate
an/xi/ety	ap/pal/lingly	ap/preci/ation
any/body	ap/par/atus	ap/preci/at/ive
any/how	ap/parel	ap/pre/hend
any/one	ap/par/ent	ap/pre/hen/sion
any/place	ap/par/ently	ap/pre/hen/sive
any/thing	ap/par/it/ion	ap/pren/tice
any/way	ap/peal	ap/pren/tice/ship
any/where	ap/peal/ing	ap/proach
aor/tic	ap/pear	ap/proach/able
apart/heid	ap/pear/ance	ap/proach/ing
apart/ment	ap/pease	ap/prob/ation

ap/pro/pri/ate
ap/pro/pri/ation
ap/prove
ap/prov/ing
ap/proxi/mate
ap/proxi/mation
ap/ri/cot
Ap/ril
ap/ron
ap/ti/tude
apt/ness
aqua/lung
aqua/marine
aquar/ium
Aquar/ius
aqua/tint
aque/duct
aqui/line
ar/ab/esque
Ara/bia
ar/able
arach/nid
arach/noid
Ara/maic
ar/bit/rar/ily
ar/bit/rary
ar/bit/rate
ar/bor
ar/cade
archae/olo/gical
archae/olo/gist
archae/ology
ar/chaic
arch/angel
arch/bishop
arch/ery

arche/typal
arche/type
archi/pel/ago
archi/tect
archi/tec/ture
archi/trave
arch/ives
arch/iv/ist
arch/way
arc/tic
ar/dent
ar/dently
ar/dour ar/dor (US)
ar/du/ous
ar/du/ously
Ar/gen/tina
ar/gon
ar/gu/able
ar/gue
ar/gu/ment
ar/gu/men/ta/tive
arid/ity
Ar/ies
ar/is/toc/ra/cies
ar/is/to/crat
ar/is/to/cratic
ar/ith/metic
ar/ith/meti/cal
ar/mada
ar/ma/ment
ar/ma/ture
arm/band
arm/chair
arm/ful
arm/is/tice
ar/mour

ar/mor (US)
ar/mour-plated
arm/oury
arm/pit
aro/matic
ar/range
ar/range/ment
ar/ray
ar/rears
ar/rest
ar/rive
ar/ro/gance
ar/rog/ant
ar/row
ar/senal
ar/sen/ic
ar/son
ar/terio/scler/osis
ar/tery
ar/tesian
art/ful
arth/ritis
ar/ti/choke
art/icle
ar/ticu/late
arti/ficial
artil/lery
ar/tisan
ar/tist
ar/tiste
ar/tis/tic
ar/tis/ti/cally
art/less
as/bes/tos
as/bes/tosis
as/cend

as/cend/ancy
as/cend/ant
as/cer/tain
as/cetic
as/cor/bic
as/cot
as/crip/tion
as/dic
asex/ual
ash/can (US)
ash/en
ash/lar
ash/pan
ash/tray
Asi/atic
as/in/ine
as/par/agus
as/pect
as/pen
as/per/ity
as/per/sions
as/phalt
as/phyxia
as/phyxi/ate
as/phyxi/ation
as/pir/ate
as/pire
as/pir/ation
as/pirin
as/sail/ant
as/sas/sin
as/sas/sin/ate
as/sas/sina/tion
as/sault
as/semble
as/sem/bly

as/sent
as/sert
as/ser/tion
as/ser/tive
as/sess
as/ses/sor
as/set
as/sidu/ous
as/si/du/ity
as/sign
as/sig/nation
as/sign/ment
as/simi/late
as/sist
as/sist/ance
as/sist/ant
as/sizes
as/so/ci/ate
as/sorted
as/sort/ment
as/suage
as/sume
as/sump/tion
as/sur/ance
as/sure
as/sur/edly
as/ter
as/ter/isk
as/ter/oid
asth/matic
as/tig/matic
as/tig/mat/ism
as/ton/ish
as/ton/ish/ing
as/ton/ish/ment
as/tound

astrin/gent
as/tro/loger
as/tro/logy
as/tro/naut
as/tro/nomer
as/tro/nomi/cal
as/tro/nomy
as/tute
asy/lum
asym/met/rical
asyn/chron/ous
at/av/is/tic
athe/ism
ath/lete
ath/let/ics
At/lan/tic
at/las
at/mo/sphere
at/mo/spheric
atom/izer
aton/al/ity
atone/ment
at/ro/cious
at/ro/city
at/tach
at/taché
at/tach/ment
at/tack
at/tain
at/tain/able
at/tain/ment
at/tempt
at/tend
at/tend/ance
at/tend/ant
at/ten/tion

at/ten/tive
at/tent/ively
at/tenu/ate
at/tic
at/tire
at/ti/tude
at/tor/ney
at/tract
at/tract/ive
at/tract/ively
at/tribu/table
at/tri/bute
at/tri/tion
au/ber/gine
au/burn
auc/tion
auc/tion/eer
au/da/cious
au/da/city
aud/ible
au/di/ence
au/dio-vis/ual
au/dit/ing
au/dit/ion
aud/itor
aud/it/or/ium
aug/ment
aug/ment/ation
au/gur
Au/gust
aur/icle
au/rora
aus/pi/ces
aus/pi/cious
aus/tere
aus/ter/ity

Aus/tral/asia
Aus/tra/lia
Aus/tra/lian
Aus/tria
au/then/tic
au/then/ti/cate
au/then/tic/ity
au/thor
auth/ori/tarian
auth/ori/ta/tive
au/thor/ity
au/thor/iza/tion
au/thor/ize
au/tis/tic
auto/bio/graph/ical
auto/bio/graphy
autoc/racy
auto/crat
auto/crat/ic/ally
auto/cue
auto/graph
auto/matic
auto/mati/cally
auto/ma/tion
auto/maton
auto/mo/bile
auton/omous
auton/omy
aut/opsy
au/tumn
au/tum/nal
aux/ili/ary
avail/abil/ity
avail/able
ava/lanche
av/ari/ce

av/ari/cious
av/enue
av/er/age
aver/sion
avi/ary
avi/ation
avo/cado
avoid/able
avoid/ance
avoir/du/pois
avow/able
avun/cu/lar
awaken/ing
aware/ness
aw/ful
awk/ward
awk/wardly
awk/ward/ness
awn/ing
ax/iom
ax/io/matic
aya/tol/lah
aza/lea
bab/bler
ba/bel
ba/boon
ba/by/ish
baby-sit/ter
bac/ca/rat
bac/cha/nal
bach/elor
ba/cil/lus
back/ache
back/bit/ing
back/bone
back/break/ing

bab/bler
ba/bel
ba/boon
ba/by/ish
baby-sit/ter
bac/ca/rat
bac/cha/nal
bach/elor
ba/cil/lus
back/ache
back/bit/ing
back/bone
back/break/ing
back/cloth
back/date
back/fire
back/gam/mon
back/ground
back/hand
back/ing
back/lash
back/less
back/log
back/pedal
back/side
back/stage
back/stairs
back/stroke
back/ward
back/ward/ness
back/water
back/woods (US)
back/yard
ba/con
bac/terio/logi/cal
bac/teri/olo/gist

bac/teri/ology
bac/terium
bad/min/ton
baf/fling
ba/ga/telle
bag/gage
bag/pipes
Ba/ha/mas
bail/iff
baili/wick
bake/house
ba/la/clava
ba/la/laika
bal/ance
bal/boa
bal/cony
bal/der/dash
bal/een
bale/ful
bal/lad
bal/last
ball/cock
bal/ler/ina
bal/let
bal/lis/tics
bal/loon
bal/loon/ing
bal/lot
ball/point
ball/room
bal/ly/hoo
ba/lo/ney
bal/sam
bal/us/ter
bal/us/trade
bam/boo

bam/boozle
ba/nana
band/age
ban/died
ban/dit
band/master
ban/do/lier
bands/man
band/stand
band/wagon
ban/ish
ban/ish/ment
ban/is/ters
ban/jo
bank/note
bank/rupt
bank/ruptcy
ban/ner
ban/quet
ban/shee
ban/tam
ban/ter
bap/tis/try
bap/tis/tery
bap/tize
bara/thea
bar/bar/ian
bar/baric
bar/bar/ous
bar/be/cue
bar/bell
bar/ber
bar/bit/ur/ate
bar/bule
bare/back
bare/faced

bare/foot
bare/headed
bare/ness
bar/gain
bar/gain/ing
ba/ri/tone
bar/ium
bark/ing
bar/ley
bar/maid
bar/man
bar/nacle
barn/yard
ba/ro/meter
ba/ro/met/ric
bar/on/ess
bar/onet
ba/roque
bar/rack
bar/rage
bar/rel
bar/ren
bar/ren/ness
bar/ri/cade
bar/rier
bar/ring
bar/ris/ter
bar/room (US)
bar/row
bar/ter
bas/alt
bas/cule
base/ball
base/board
base/less
base/ment

bash/ful
bash/fully
ba/sic
ba/sic/ally
ba/si/lica
ba/sin
ba/sis
bas/ket
bas/ket/ball
bas/ket/work
bas/set
bas/si/net
bas/soon
bas/tard
bas/tion
bath/mat
bath/robe
bath/room
bath/salts
bath/towel
bath/tub
bathy/sphere
bats/man
bat/tal/ion
bat/ted
bat/ten
bat/ter
bat/tery
bat/tle/field
bat/tle/front
bat/tle/ments
bat/tle/ship
bat/tling
baux/ite
bay/onet
bay/wood

ba/zaar
ba/zooka
beach/comber
beach/head
beach/wear
bead/ing
beag/ling
bean/bag
bear/able
beard/less
bear/garden
bear/ing
bear/skin
beast/li/ness
be/atif/ic
beau/ti/cian
beau/ti/ful
bea/ver
be/calmed
be/came
be/cause
be/come
be/dazzle
bed/clothes
bed/cover
bed/ding
be/deck
be/devil
bed/jacket
bed/lam
bed/pan
be/drag/gled
bed/ridden
bed/rock
bed/room
bed/side

bed/spread
bed/time
beef/burger
beef/eater
bee/hive
bee/keeper
bee/keep/ing
bees/wax
beef/bur/ger
beet/root
be/fore
be/fore/hand
be/friend
beg/gar
beg/garly
beg/ging
be/gin
be/gin/ner
be/gin/ning
be/go/nia
be/grudge
be/half
be/have
be/ha/vi/our
  be/ha/vi/or (US)
be/head
be/hest
be/hind
be/hold
be/holden
be/lated
be/lay
be/lea/guered
bel/fry
Bel/gian
Bel/gium

be/lie
be/lieve
be/little
bel/la/donna
bell-bot/toms
bell/boy bell/hop
  (US)
bel/li/cose
bel/li/ger/ent
bel/li/ger/ency
bel/low
bel/lows
bell/push
belly/ache
belly/flop
belly/ful
be/long
be/long/ings
be/loved
be/low
belt/ing
be/moan
be/muse
be/neath
be/ne/dic/tion
be/ne/fac/tor
be/ne/fac/tress
be/ne/fi/cent
be/ne/fi/cial
be/ne/fi/ci/ary
be/ne/fit
be/ne/vol/ence
be/ne/vol/ent
be/nign
bent/wood
be/queath

be/quest
be/rate
be/reaved
be/reave/ment
be/reft
beri/beri
ber/ry
ber/serk
be/ryl/lium
be/seech
be/set
be/set/ting
be/side
be/sides
be/siege
be/som
be/sot/ted
be/sought
be/spoke
bes/tial
be/stow
best/sel/ler
be/tray
be/trayal
bet/ter
bet/ting
be/tween
be/velled
bev/el/ling
bev/er/age
be/ware
be/wilder
be/wil/der/ment
be/witch
be/witch/ing
be/yond

223

bi/an/nual
bi/an/nually
bi/ased
bi/ath/lon
bib/li/cal
bib/lio/graph/ical
bib/lio/ma/nia
bib/lio/graphy
bib/lio/phile
bibu/lous
bi/car/bon/ate
bi/cen/ten/ary
bi/cen/ten/nial
bi/ceph/al/ous
bi/ceps
bi/colour
bi/corn
bi/cycle
bid/dable
bid/der
bi/det
bi/en/nial
bi/en/ni/ally
bi/fari/ous
bi/focal
bi/fo/li/ate
bi/fur/cate
bi/fur/ca/tion
big/am/ist
big/am/ous
big/amy
big/head
big/oted
big/otry
bi/kini
bi/lat/eral

bil/berry
bil/harzia
bi/ling/ual
bil/ious
bil/la/bong
bill/board (US)
bil/let
bill/fold (US)
bil/liards
bil/ling
bil/lion
bil/low
bill/poster
bi/met/al/lic
bi/mil/len/ary
bi/mil/len/nium
bi/nary
bind/ery
bind/ing
bind/weed
bin/nacle
bin/ocu/lar
bio/chem/ist
bio/chem/istry
bio/de/grad/able
bio/graph/ical
bio/graphy
bio/lo/gical
bio/lo/gist
bio/logy
bi/onic
bio/physics
bio/plasm
bi/par/ous
bi/par/ti/san
bi/ped

bi/plane
bird/seed
birth/day
birth/mark
birth/place
birth/right
bis/cuit
bi/sect
bi/sex/ual
bish/op/ric
bis/muth
bi/son
bis/tro
bitch/ily
bit/ing
bit/ten
bit/ter
bit/terly
bit/ter/ness
bit/tern
bitu/men
bi/valve
bi/vouac
bi/zarre
blab/ber/mouth
black/beetle
black/berry
black/bird
black/board
black/currant
black/fly
black/guard
black/head
black/ish
black/leg
black/list

black/mail
black/ness
black/out
black/smith
blad/der
blad/der/wrack
blame/less
blanc/mange
blan/dish/ments
blan/ket
blas/pheme
blas/phe/mer
blas/phem/ous
blas/phemy
bla/tant
blaz/ing
blaz/onry
blem/ish
bless/ing
blind/fold
blind/ness
bliss/ful
blis/ter
blith/er/ing
blitz/krieg
bliz/zard
block/ade
block/age
blood/bath
blood/curd/ling
blood/hound
blood/less
blood/shed
blood/shot
blood/stain
blood/stream

blood/thirsty
blos/som
blotch/ier
blot/ter
blow/fly
blow/lamp
blow/out
blub/ber
blud/geon
blue/bell
blue/berry (US)
blue/bottle
blue/print
blu/ish
blun/der
blun/der/buss
blun/der/ing
blus/ter
board/ing
board/room
boast/ful
boat/hook
boat/house
boat/swain
bob/bies
bob/bin
bobo/link
bob/sleigh
boc/age
bod/ice
bod/ies
bod/kin
body/guard
body/work
bo/gey
bog/gle

bo/gie
bo/gus
bois/ter/ous
bois/ter/ous/ness
bold/ness
bol/lard
boll/worm
bol/shie
bol/ster
bom/bard
bom/bard/ment
bom/bas/tic
bomb/shell
bon/anza
bon/bon
bond/age
bone/less
bone/shaker
bon/fire
bon/net
bo/nus
booby/trap
book/able
book/binder
book/bind/ing
book/case
book/ing
book/ish
book-keep/ing
book/let
book/maker
book/mar/ker
book/sel/ler
book/shelf
book/shop
book/stall

book/worm
boom/er/ang
boom/ing
boor/ish
boon/doggle
bor/acic
bora/cite
bor/dello
bor/der
bor/der/ing
bor/der/line
bor/eal
bore/dom
bore/hole
bor/ing
bor/row
bor/stal
bo/sun
bo/tan/ical
bot/an/ist
bot/any
bother/ation
bot/tle
bot/tle/neck
bot/tling
bot/tom
bot/tom/less
botu/lism
bou/doir
boul/der
boul/evard
boun/cing
boun/dary
boun/ti/ful
bou/quet
bour/bon (US)

bour/geois
bour/geoisie
bou/tique
bo/vine
bow/ler
bow/line
bowl/ing
bow/sprit
box/ing
box/room
boy/cott
boy/friend
boy/hood
brace/let
bra/chio/pod
brack/ish
brad/awl
brag/ging
brah/min
brain/child
braini/ness
brain/less
brain/power
brain/wash
brain/wave
bra/less
bran/dish
bras/si/ere
bra/vado
brav/ery
braz/enly
bra/zier
Bra/zil
bread/crumbs
bread/line
bread/win/ner

break/able
break/ables
break/ages
break/away
break/down
break/fast
break/ing
break/neck
break/through
break/up
break/water
breath/alyser
breath/ing
breath/less
breath/tak/ing
breed/ing
brevi/ary
brev/ity
brick/layer
brick/work
bride/groom
brides/maid
bridge/head
bridle/path
bridle/way
brief/case
brief/ing
brig/ade
briga/dier
brig/and
bright/ish
bright/ness
bril/liance
bril/liant
brim/ful
brim/ming

Brit/ain
brit/tle
brit/tle/ness
broad/cast
broad/cast/ing
broad/loom
broad/min/ded
bro/cade
broc/coli
bro/chure
bron/chial
bron/chitis
broom/stick
brother/hood
brow/beat
brown/ish
brow/ser
bru/nette
brush/wood
bru/tal
bru/tal/ity
brut/ally
bub/ble
bub/bling
bub/bly
buc/can/eer
bucket/ful
buck/teeth
buck/wheat
Bud/dhism
Bud/dhist
bud/ding
bud/dleia
bud/geri/gar
buf/falo
buf/fer

buf/fet
buf/foon
buf/foon/ery
bug/bear
bu/gler
build/ing
bul/bous
bulk/head
bull/dog
bull/doze
bul/let
bul/letin
bull/fighter
bull/finch
bull/frog
bul/lion
bul/lock
bull/ring
bul/rush
bumble/bee
bum/per
bump/tious
bun/ga/low
bun/gling
bun/ion
bunt/ing
buoy/ancy
buoy/ant
bur/den
bur/dock
bur/eau/cracy
bur/geon
burg/lar
bur/lesque
bur/row
bur/sar

bur/sary
bury/ing
bush/man
busi/ness
busi/ness/like
busi/ness/man
bus/man
bus/sing
bu/tane
but/cher
but/ler
but/ted
but/ter
but/tock(s)
but/ton
but/tress
buz/zard
by/gone
by/pass
by/stander
by/word
cab/a/ret
cab/bage
cab/in
cab/inet
cab/man
ca/boose
cack/ling
ca/co/graphy
ca/co/phony
cac/tus
ca/da/ver/ous
cad/die
cad/dis fly
cad/dy
ca/dence

ca/det
cad/mium
ca/du/ceus
ca/du/city
cae/sar/ean
caf/et/eria
caf/fein
ca/gey/ness
ca/hoots
cais/son
ca/jole
cake/walk
cal/a/boose (US)
cal/amine
ca/lam/it/ous
ca/lam/ity
cal/car/eous
cal/ci/fer/ous
cal/cium
cal/cu/lable
cal/cu/late
cal/cu/lation
cal/cu/lator
cal/cu/lus
ca/le/fac/tory
cal/en/dar
ca/len/dula
cali/brate
cal/ibre cali/ber (US)
cal/ico
ca/liph
call/boy
cal/li/grapher
cal/lig/raphy
call/ing
cal/li/pers

cal/lis/then/ics
cal/lous
cal/lus
calm/ness
cal/orie
cal/or/ific
calo/type
cal/um/ni/ate
cal/umny
ca/lypso
ca/lyx
ca/ma/ra/derie
cam/ber
cam/bium
ca/mel/lia
ca/meo
cam/era
cami/sole
camo/mile
cam/ou/flage
cam/paign
cam/pan/ile
cam/pa/nol/ogy
cam/pan/ula
cam/phor
camp/ing
camp/site
cam/pus
cam/shaft
Can/ada
ca/nal
ca/nary
can/asta
can/can
can/cel
can/cel/la/tion

can/cer
can/cer/ous
can/de/la/bra
can/des/cent
can/did
can/di/date
can/di/dature
can/died
can/dour can/dor
(US)
candy/floss
candy/tuft
can/ine
can/is/ter
can/ker
can/na/bis
can/ni/bal
can/ni/bal/ism
can/ni/bal/ize
can/nier
can/ning
can/non
can/non/ball
can/not
ca/noe
canoe/ing
canoe/ist
ca/noni/cate
can/on/ize
can/opy
can/tan/ker/ous
can/tata
can/teen
can/ter
cant/icle
can/ti/lever

can/ton
can/vas
can/vass
can/vas/sing
can/yon
cap/ab/il/ity
cap/able
cap/ably
ca/pa/ci/tance
ca/pa/citor
ca/pa/cious
ca/pa/city
ca/per
ca/per/cail/lie
ca/pil/lary
capi/tal
capi/tal/ism
capi/tal/ist
capi/tal/iz/ation
capi/ta/tion
ca/pitu/late
ca/pitu/lation
ca/pon
cap/puc/cino
ca/price
ca/pric/ious
Cap/ri/corn
cap/size
cap/stan
cap/sule
cap/tain
cap/taincy
cap/tion
cap/tiv/ate
cap/tive
cap/tiv/ity

cap/ture
capy/bara
ca/rafe
cara/mel
cara/pace
cara/van
cara/van/ning
cara/way
car/bine
car/bo/hy/drate
car/bolic
car/bon
car/bon/ate
car/bonic
car/bon/ifer/ous
car/boy
car/buncle
car/bur/ation
car/bur/et/tor
car/case car/cass
car/ci/no/gen
car/da/mom
card/board
car/diac
car/di/gan
car/dinal
car/dio/gram
car/dio/graph
car/di/ologist
car/di/ology
car/dio/vas/cu/lar
ca/reer
care/free
care/less
care/less/ness
ca/ress

care/taker
Ca/rib/bean
ca/ri/bou
ca/ri/ca/ture
ca/ril/lon
car/mine
carn/age
car/nal
car/na/tion
car/ni/val
car/ni/vore
car/ni/vor/ous
ca/ro/tid
ca/rou/sel
car/pal
car/pel
car/pen/ter
car/pet
car/pet/ing
car/port
car/pus
car/sick
car/riage
car/riage/way
car/rier
car/rion
car/rot
cart/horse
car/ti/lage
cart/load
car/to/grapher
car/to/graphy
car/ton
car/toon
cart/ridge
cart/wheel

229

car/very
car/ving
cary/atid
cas/cade
case/ment
cash/ier
cash/mere
cas/ing
cas/ino
cas/ket
cas/sava
cas/ser/ole
cas/sette
cas/sock
cas/ta/nets
cast/away
cast/ing
cas/tel/lated
cas/tig/ate
cas/trate
cas/ual
casu/alty
cata/clysm
cata/combs
cata/falque
cata/lepsy
cata/logue cata/log
(US)
cata/lyst
cata/ma/ran
cata/pult
cat/ar/act
ca/tarrh
ca/tas/trophe
cata/strophic
cat/call
catch/ment

catch/word
cat/echism
cat/ech/ize
cat/eg/ori/cal
cat/egory
cat/er/pil/lar
ca/ter/waul
cat/fish
cat/gut
ca/thed/ral
cath/er/ine wheel
cath/eter
cath/ode
cath/olic
cath/oli/cism
cat/kin
cat/sup (US)
cat/tery
cat/tle
cau/cus
caul/dron cal/dron
(US)
cau/li/flower
cause/way
caus/tic
caus/ti/cally
cau/ter/iz/ation
caut/er/ize
cau/tion
cau/tious
cav/al/cade
ca/va/lier
cav/alry
cave/fish
cave/man
cav/ern

cavi/ar(e)
cav/ity
ca/vort
cay/enne
cay/man
cease/fire
cease/less
ce/dar
ce/dilla
ceil/ing
cel/eb/rate
cel/eb/ration
cel/eb/rity
cel/ery
ce/les/tial
cel/ib/acy
cel/ib/ate
cel/lar
cel/list
cel/lo/phane
cel/lu/lar
cel/lu/lose
Cel/sius
ce/ment
cem/et/ery
ceno/taph
cen/ser
cen/sor
cen/sor/ious
cen/sor/ship
cen/sure
cen/sus
cen/ten/arian
cen/ten/ary
cen/ten/nial
cen/ti/grade

cen/ti/litre
  cen/ti/liter (US)
cen/ti/metre
  cen/ti/meter (US)
cen/ti/pede
cent/ral/ize
centre/piece
cen/tri/fugal
cen/tri/petal
cen/tur/ion
cen/tury
cepha/lo/pod
ce/ramic
ce/re/bel/lum
ce/reb/ral
ce/re/mon/ial
ce/re/mon/ious
ce/re/mony
cer/tain
cer/ti/fic/ate
cer/tify
cer/ti/tude
ce/ru/men
cer/vi/cal
cer/vix
ces/sa/tion
ces/sion
cess/pit
chaf/finch
cha/grin
chair/lift
chair/man
cha/let
chal/ice
chal/lenge
chal/leng/ing

cham/ber
cham/ber/maid
cham/ber/pot
cha/me/leon
cham/fer
cham/ois
cham/pagne
cham/pion
cham/pion/ship
chan/cel
chan/cel/lery
chan/cel/lor
chan/de/lier
chand/ler
change/able
change/over
chan/nel
chan/nelled
chan/ter/elle
chap/eron
chap/lain
chap/ter
char/ac/ter
char/ac/ter/istic
char/ac/ter/ize
cha/rade
char/coal
charge/able
char/ger
cha/risma
cha/ris/matic
char/it/able
char/ity
char/lady
char/la/tan
charm/ing

char/ter
char/woman
chas/sis
chas/tise
chas/tise/ment
chast/ity
chat/eau
chat/tel
chat/ter/box
chauf/feur
chau/vin/ism
chau/vin/is/tic
cheap/ness
cheat/ing
check/list
check/mate
check/out
check/up
cheek/bone
chee/ki/ness
cheer/ful
cheer/leader
cheer/less
cheese/cake
cheese/cloth
cheese/paring
chee/tah
chem/ical
che/mise
chem/is/try
cher/ish
che/root
cher/ubic
cher/ubs
cher/vil
chess/board

chessmen

chess/men
chest/nut
chev/ron
chi/cane
chick/weed
chic/ory
chief/tain
chif/fon
chil/blain
child/ren
child/ish/ness
child/like
chil/li/ness
chim/ney
chim/pan/zee
chin/chilla
Chi/nese
chi/nois/erie
chip/board
chip/munk
chi/po/lata
chip/pings
chi/ro/pod/ist
chir/rup
chis/elled
chis/el/ler
chi/sel/ling
chit/chat
chiv/al/rous
chlor/in/ate
chlor/ine
chloro/form
chloro/phyll
choc/olate
choir/boy
choir/master

cho/king
chol/era
cho/les/terol
chop/per
chop/sticks
cho/reo/graphy
cho/reo/grapher
chor/ister
chow/der
chris/ten
Chris/tian
Chris/ti/an/ity
Christ/mas
chro/matic
chro/mium
chro/mo/some
chron/icle
chron/icler
chro/no/logical
chro/no/logi/cally
chro/no/meter
chrys/alis
chrys/an/the/mum
church/goer
church/war/den
church/yard
chur/lish
chur/lish/ness
chut/ney
ci/cada
ci/gar
ci/gar/ette
cili/ate
cin/ders
cin/ema
cine/mato/gra/phic

cin/namon
cinque/foil
ci/pher
cir/clip
cir/cuit
cir/cuit/ous
cir/cu/late
cir/cum/cise
cir/cum/fer/ence
cir/cum/navi/gate
cir/cum/scribe
cir/cum/scrip/tion
cir/cum/spect
cir/cum/stance
cir/cum/stan/tial
cir/cum/vent
cir/cus
cir/rho/sis
cir/rus
cis/tern
cit/adel
ci/ta/tion
citi/zen
citi/zen/ship
cit/reous
cit/ric
cit/rus
civ/ico
civ/il/ian
civ/ility
civi/liz/ation
civ/il/ize
clad/ding
claim/ant
clair/voyant
clam/ber

clam/mier
clam/our
clam/our/ous
clam/or/ous (US)
clamp/down
clan/des/tine
clan/nish
clap/per
clap/per/board
clap/trap
cla/rify
cla/ri/net
cla/rin/et/tist
clar/ity
clasp/knife
clas/sic
clas/si/cal
clas/si/cism
classi/fi/ca/tion
clat/ter
claus/tro/phobia
clavi/chord
clav/icle
clean/ing
clean/li/ness
clean/sha/ven
clear/ance
clear/way
clea/vage
cle/ma/tis
clem/ency
clem/ent
clem/en/tine
clere/story
clergy/man
cler/ical

clever/ness
cli/ent
cli/en/tele
cliff/han/ger
cli/mate
cli/ma/to/logy
cli/max
cli/nic
clit/oris
clob/ber
clock/wise
clock/work
clois/ter
close/ness
clo/thing
cloud/burst
cloudi/ness
cloud/less
club/foot
club/house
clue/less
clum/sily
clum/si/ness
clus/ter
clut/ter
co/agu/late
co/alesce
co/al/es/cence
coal/field
coal/hole
co/ali/tion
coal/mine
coarse/ness
coast/guard
coast/line
co/balt

cob/bler
cob/ble(stone)
co/bra
cob/web
co/caine
coc/cyx
coch/in/eal
cock/ade
cock/atoo
cock/chafer
cock/erel
cock/ney
cock/pit
cock/roach
cock/sure
cock/tail
co/co/nut
co/coon
cod/dle
co/deine
co/di/cil
co/di/fy
co-di/rec/tor
co-edu/ca/tional
co/efficient
coel/ac/anth
co/erce
co/er/cion
co/exist
co/exist/ence
cof/fee
cof/fers
cof/fin
co/gent
cog/it/ate
cog/nate

cog/niz/ance
co/habit
co/here
co/her/ence
co/her/ent
co/hes/ive
co/hort
coif/fure
coin/age
co/in/cide
co/in/cid/ence
co/in/cid/ental
co/lan/der
cold/ness
cole/slaw
col/itis
col/lab/or/ate
col/lab/or/ation
col/lage
col/la/gen
col/lapse
col/lap/sible
col/lar
col/late
col/la/tor
col/lat/eral
col/league
col/lect
col/lect/ive
col/lect/or
col/lege
col/legi/ate
col/lide
col/lie
col/lier
col/liery

col/lis/ion
col/lo/quial
col/lo/quial/ism
col/lu/sion
co/logne
col/onel
co/lo/nial
co/lo/nial/ist
col/on/ist
col/on/ize
col/on/nade
col/ony
Col/or/ado beetle
col/or/ific
col/os/sal
col/os/sus
col/os/trum
col/our col/or (US)
col/our/ful
col/or/ful (US)
col/um/bine
col/umn
coma/tose
com/bat
com/bat/ant
com/bat/ive
com/bin/ation
com/bine
com/bust/ible
com/bus/tion
come/back
come/down
co/me/dian
com/edy
come/up/pance
com/fort

com/fort/able
com/forter
com/fort/less
com/mand
com/man/dant
com/man/deer
com/man/der
com/mand/ment
com/mando
com/mem/or/ate
com/mem/or/ation
com/mence
com/mence/ment
com/mend
com/mend/able
com/menda/tion
com/mend/at/ory
com/men/sur/ate
com/ment
com/men/tary
com/men/tator
com/merce
com/mer/cial
com/mer/cial/ize
com/mis/erate
com/mis/sar
com/mis/sion
com/mis/sion/aire
com/mis/sioner
com/mit
com/mit/ment
com/mit/tal
com/mit/tee
com/modi/ous
com/mod/ity
com/mo/dore

com/mon
com/moner
com/mon/place
com/mon/wealth
com/mo/tion
com/mu/nal
com/mune
com/mun/ic/able
com/muni/cate
com/muni/cation
com/muni/ca/tive
com/muniqué
com/mun/ism
com/mun/ity
com/mut/able
com/mu/ta/tion
com/mute
com/mu/ter
com/pact
com/pan/ion
com/pany
com/par/able
com/para/tive
com/pare
com/pari/son
com/part/ment
com/pass
com/pas/sion
com/pas/sion/ate
com/pati/bility
com/pat/ible
com/pat/riot
com/pel
com/pel/ling
com/pen/sate
com/pen/sa/tion

com/pére
com/pete
com/pet/ence
com/pe/tent
com/peti/tion
com/peti/tive
com/peti/tor
com/pile
com/pla/cent
com/plain
com/plaint
com/plais/ance
com/ple/ment
com/plete
com/pletely
com/plete/ness
com/pletion
com/plex
com/plex/ion
com/plex/ity
com/pli/ant
com/pli/cate
com/pli/ca/tion
com/pli/city
com/pli/ment
com/pli/men/tary
com/ply
com/pli/ance
com/pli/ant
com/pon/ent
com/pose
com/posi/tor
com/post
com/pos/ure
com/pound
com/pre/hend

com/pre/hen/sible
com/pre/hen/sion
com/pre/hen/sive
com/press
com/pres/sor
com/prise
com/prom/ise
com/pul/sion
com/pul/sory
com/punc/tion
com/pu/ta/tion
com/pute
com/puter
com/rade
com/rade/ship
con/cave
con/ceal
com/ceal/ment
con/cede
con/ceit
con/ceive
con/ceiv/able
con/cen/trate
con/cen/tra/tion
con/cen/tric
con/cept
con/cep/tion
con/cern
con/cern/ing
con/cert
con/cer/ted
con/cer/tina
con/certo
con/ces/sion
con/chol/ogy
con/cili/ate

235

con/cili/atory
con/cise
con/cise/ness
con/clave
con/clude
con/clu/sion
con/clu/sive
con/coct
con/coc/tion
con/comi/tant
con/cord
con/cord/ance
con/cor/dat
con/course
con/crete
con/cre/tion
con/cu/bine
con/cur
con/cur/rent
con/cus/sion
con/demn
con/dense
con/des/cend
con/de/scen/sion
con/di/ment
con/dition
con/dole
con/do/min/ium
con/done
con/dor
con/du/cive
con/duct
con/duc/tion
con/duc/tor
con/duc/tress
con/duit

con/fab
con/fect
con/fec/tion
con/fec/tion/ery
con/fed/er/acy
con/fed/er/ate
con/fed/er/ation
con/fer
con/fer/ence
con/fess
con/fes/sion
con/fes/sional
con/fes/sor
con/fetti
con/fide
con/fid/ant
con/fid/ante
con/fide
con/fi/dence
con/fi/den/tial
con/fine
con/firm
con/fir/ma/tion
con/fis/cate
con/fis/ca/tion
con/flag/ra/tion
con/flict
con/form
con/form/ist
con/form/ity
con/found
con/front
con/fron/ta/tion
con/fuse
con/fus/edly
con/fus/ing

con/fu/sion
con/geal
con/gen/ial
con/geni/tal
con/ges/ted
con/ges/tion
con/glom/er/ate
con/glom/era/tion
con/gratu/late
con/gratu/la/tions
con/gratu/la/tory
con/gre/gate
con/gre/ga/tion
con/gress
con/gres/sional
con/ical
con/ifer
con/if/er/ous
con/jec/ture
con/jec/tural
con/jugal
con/ju/gate
con/ju/gation
con/junc/tion
con/junc/ti/vitis
con/jun/cture
con/jure
con/jurer
con/jur/ing
con/ker
con/nect
con/nec/tion
con/ning tower
con/nive
con/niv/ance
con/nois/seur

con/note
con/quer
con/quer/ing
con/queror
con/quest
con/science
con/scien/tious
con/scious
con/scious/ness
con/script
con/scrip/tion
con/sec/rate
con/se/cra/tion
con/secu/tive
con/sen/sus
con/sent
con/se/quence
con/se/quen/tial
con/se/quently
con/serve
con/ser/va/tion
con/ser/va/tive
con/ser/va/tory
con/sider
con/sid/er/able
con/sid/er/ate
con/sid/er/ation
con/sid/er/ing
con/sign
con/sign/ment
con/sist
con/sist/ency
con/sist/ent
con/sist/ently
con/so/la/tion
con/sole

con/soli/date
con/soli/da/tion
con/sommé
con/son/ant
con/sort
con/sor/tium
con/spicu/ous
con/spir/ator
con/spir/at/or/ial
con/spire
con/stable
con/stab/ul/ary
con/stancy
con/stant
con/stel/la/tion
con/ster/na/tion
con/sti/pated
con/sti/pa/tion
con/stitu/ent
con/sti/tute
con/sti/tu/tional
con/strain
con/straint
con/strict
con/stric/tion
con/struct
con/struc/tive
con/struc/tor
con/strue
con/sul
con/su/lar
con/su/late
con/sult
con/sul/tant
con/sul/ta/tion
con/sul/ta/tive

con/sul/ting
con/sume
con/sumer
con/sum/mate
con/sum/ma/tion
con/sump/tion
con/sump/tive
con/tact
con/ta/gious
con/tain
con/tainer
con/tam/in/ate
con/tam/ina/tion
con/tem/plate
con/tem/pla/tion
con/tem/pla/tive
con/tem/por/ary
cont/emp/or/an/
eous
con/tempt
con/tempt/ible
con/temp/tu/ous
con/tend
con/ten/der
con/tent
con/tent/edly
con/ten/tion
con/ten/tious
con/test
con/tes/tant
con/text
con/ti/nent
con/ti/nen/tal
con/tin/gency
con/tin/gent
con/tinu/ally

237

con/tinu/ation
con/tinue
con/ti/nu/ity
con/tinu/ous
con/tort
con/tor/tion
con/tour
con/tra/band
con/tra/cep/tion
con/tra/cep/tive
con/tract
con/trac/tion
con/trac/tor
con/trac/tual
con/tra/dict
con/tra/dic/tion
con/tra/dic/tory
con/tralto
con/trap/tion
con/trari/ness
con/trary
con/trast
con/tra/vene
con/tra/ven/tion
con/tre/temps
con/trib/ute
con/tri/bu/tion
con/trite
con/tri/tion
con/trive
con/tri/vance
con/trol
con/trol/ler
con/tro/ver/sial
con/tro/versy
con/tu/sion

con/un/drum
con/ur/ba/tion
con/val/esce
con/val/es/cence
con/val/es/cent
con/vec/tion
con/vene
con/venor
con/veni/ence
con/veni/ent
con/vent
con/ven/tion
con/ven/tional
con/verge
con/ver/gence
con/ver/gent
con/ver/sant
con/verse
con/ver/sa/tion
con/ver/sion
con/vert
con/ver/ter
con/vert/ible
con/vex
con/vey
con/vey/ance
con/veyor
con/vict
con/vic/tion
con/vince
con/vin/cing
con/viv/ial
con/vo/ca/tion
con/voke
con/vol/vu/lus
con/voy

con/vulse
con/vul/sion
con/vul/sive
cool/ant
co/oper/ate
co/op/er/at/ive
co-ord/in/ate
co/pilot
cop/ing
cop/ious
cop/per
cop/pice
copy/right
copy/wri/ter
cor/dial
cordi/al/ity
cordi/ally
cor/dite
cor/don
cor/du/roy
cork/age
cork/screw
cor/mor/ant
cor/nea
cor/ner
cor/net
corn/flakes
corn/flour
cor/nice
corn/starch
co/rol/lary
co/rona
cor/on/ary
cor/on/ation
cor/oner
cor/onet

cor/poral
cor/por/ate
cor/por/ation
cor/por/eal
cor/pu/lence
cor/pu/lent
cor/puscle
cor/rect
cor/rec/tion
cor/rec/tive
cor/rel/ate
cor/re/la/tion
cor/res/pond
cor/res/pon/dence
cor/res/pon/dent
cor/res/pon/ding
cor/ri/dor
cor/rob/or/ate
cor/rob/or/ation
cor/rode
cor/ro/sive
cor/ru/gated
cor/rupt
cor/rupt/ible
cor/rup/tion
cor/set
cor/ti/sone
cos/me/tic
cos/mic
cos/mo/naut
cos/mo/pol/itan
cos/set
cost/li/ness
cos/tume
cot/tage
cot/ton

coty/ledon
couch/ette
coun/cil
coun/cil/lor
coun/sel
coun/sel/lor
count/down
coun/ten/ance
coun/ter
coun/ter/bal/ance
coun/ter/blast
coun/ter/charge
coun/ter/feit
coun/ter/foil
coun/ter/mand
coun/ter/meas/ure
coun/ter/pane
coun/ter/part
coun/ter/point
coun/ter/poise
coun/ter/sign
coun/ter/sink
coun/try
coun/try/side
coup/ling
cou/pon
cour/age
cour/ageous
cour/gette
cour/ier
cour/teous
cour/tesy
court/room
court/ship
court/yard
cov/en/ant

Cov/en/try
cov/er/age
cover/let
cov/ert
cov/et/ous
cow/ard
cow/ar/dice
cow/boy
cow/hand
cow/herd
cow/pat
cow/shed
cow/slip
cox/swain
coy/ness
coy/ote
crack/ling
craft/ily
crafti/ness
crafts/man
cram/pon
cran/berry
cra/nium
cra/ter
cra/vat
cray/fish
craz/ily
crazi/ness
cream/ery
cre/ate
cre/ation
cre/ative
cre/ativ/ity
cre/ator
crea/ture
cre/den/tials

239

cred/ible
credi/bil/ity
cred/ibly
credi/table
credi/tably
credi/tor
credu/lity
credu/lous
cre/ma/tion
cre/ma/tor/ium
cre/mate
creo/sote.
cres/cent
crest/fal/len
cre/vasse
crev/ice
crew/cut
crim/inal
crim/in/ology
crim/son
crip/ple
cri/sis
crisp/ness
cri/ter/ion
criti/cal
criti/cism
criti/cize
cro/chet
crock/ery
cro/co/dile
cro/cus
crook/edly
crop/per
cro/quet
cro/quette
cross/bar

cross/check
cross/eyed
cross/fire
cross/legged
cross/roads
cross/wind
crossword
crot/chet
crou/pier
crow/bar
cru/cial
cru/cible
cru/ci/fix
cru/ci/fix/ion
cru/cify
crude/ness
crum/pet
cru/sade
cru/sader
crus/ta/cean
cryp/tic
crys/tal
crys/tal/lize
crys/tal/lo/graphy
cu/bicle
cu/bism
cu/bist
cu/cum/ber
cud/dle
cud/gel
cul/in/ary
cul/min/ate
cul/mi/na/tion
cul/pable
cul/pa/bil/ity
cul/prit

cul/ti/vate
cul/ti/va/tion
cul/ti/va/tor
cul/ture
cul/tural
cum/ber/some
cumu/la/tive
cum/ulus
cu/nei/form
cun/ning
cup/board
cup/ful
cu/pid/ity
cur/able
cur/ate
cur/ator
cur/few
curi/os/ity
cur/iously
cur/lew
cur/rant
cur/rency
cur/rent
cur/ricu/lum
cur/ry/comb
cur/sory
cur/tail
cur/tain
cur/va/ture
cush/ion
cus/tard
cus/to/dian
cus/tody
cus/tom
cus/tom/arily
cus/tom/ary

cus/tomer
cus/toms
cut/icle
cut/lery
cut/let
cy/an/ide
cy/ber/net/ics
cyc/la/men
cyc/lic
cyc/li/cal
cyc/ling
cyc/list
cyc/lone
cyg/net
cyl/in/der
cym/bals
cyni/cal
cyni/cism
cy/press
Cy/prus
cys/ti/tis
Czecho/slo/vakia
dab/chick
dachs/hund
daf/fo/dil
dag/ger
da/guer/reo/type
dah/lia
dain/tily
dairy/maid
dairy/man
dal/ma/tian
dam/age
dam/ask
dam/na/tion
damn/ing

damp/ness
dam/sel
dam/son
dan/de/lion
dan/druff
dan/ger
dan/ger/ous
dan/gle
Dan/ish
dap/per
dark/ness
dark/room
dar/ling
dart/board
dash/board
dash/ing
date/less
daugh/ter
daunt/less
dav/en/port
day/break
day/dream
day/light
day/time
daz/zle
dea/con
de/ac/ti/vate
dead/line
dead/lock
dead/pan
deaf/ness
deal/ings
death/bed
death/trap
dé/bâcle
de/bar

de/base
de/bate
de/bauch/ery
de/ben/ture
de/bili/tate
de/bil/ity
de/bon/air
de/brief
deb/ris
de/bunk
dé/but
de/cade
dec/ad/ence
de/caf/fein/ated
de/can/ter
de/cap/it/ate
de/cath/lon
de/cay
de/cease
de/ceased
de/ceit
de/ceive
De/cem/ber
de/cent
de/cen/tral/ize
de/cep/tion
de/cep/tive
dec/ibel
de/cide
de/cid/edly
de/cidu/ous
deci/mal
deci/mate
de/cipher
de/cis/ion
de/cis/ive

241

deck/chair
de/claim
de/clare
dec/lar/ation
de/cline
de/clutch
de/coc/tion
de/code
de/com/mis/sion
de/com/pose
de/con/tam/in/ate
de/cor
dec/or/ate
dec/or/ations
dec/or/ator
de/cor/um
dec/or/ous
de/coy
de/crease
de/cree
de/crepit
ded/i/cate
ded/i/ca/tion
de/duce
de/duct
de/duc/tion
de/face
defa/ma/tion
de/fama/tory
de/fault
de/fault/er
de/feat
de/feat/ism
de/feat/ist
de/fe/cate
de/fect

de/fec/tion
de/fec/tive
de/fec/tor
de/fence de/fense
(US)
de/fend
de/fen/dant
de/fen/sive
de/fer
de/fer/ence
de/fer/en/tial
de/fi/ance
de/fiant
de/fi/ciency
de/fi/cient
de/fi/cit
de/file
de/fine
defi/nitely
defi/ni/tion
de/flate
de/flect
de/fo/li/ate
de/formed
de/form/ity
de/fraud
de/fray
de/freeze
de/frost
de/funct
de/fuse
de/gen/er/ate
de/grad/ation
de/grad/ing
de/gree
de/hy/drate

de/ity
de/jec/ted
de/ject/edly
de/jec/tion
de/lay
de/lec/table
del/eg/ate
dele/ga/tion
de/lete
de/le/tion
de/let/eri/ous
de/lib/er/ate
de/lib/er/ation
deli/cacy
deli/cate
de/li/ca/tes/sen
de/li/cious
de/light
de/light/ful
de/lin/eate
de/lin/quency
de/lin/quent
de/li/ri/ous
de/li/rium
de/liver
del/phin/ium
de/lude
de/luge
dema/gogue
de/mand
de/mand/ing
de/mar/ca/tion
de/mean/our
de/men/ted
dem/er/ara
demi/john

242

de/mil/it/ar/ize
de/mise
de/mister
de/mo/bil/ize
de/moc/racy
demo/crat
demo/cratic
demog/raphy
de/mol/ish
demo/lition
de/mon
dem/on/strable
dem/on/strate
dem/on/stra/tion
dem/on/stra/tor
de/moral/iz/ation
de/mor/al/ize
de/mur
de/mure
den/drite
de/nial
deni/grate
den/izen
Den/mark
de/nom/in/ation
de/nom/in/ator
de/note
de/nounce
den/sity
den/tist
den/tures
de/nun/ci/ation
de/odor/ant
de/odor/ize
de/part
de/part/ment

de/part/ure
de/pend
de/pend/able
de/pend/ant
de/pend/ency
de/pend/ent
de/pict
de/pila/tory
de/plete
de/plor/able
de/plore
de/ploy
de/popu/late
de/port
de/por/ta/tion
de/port/ment
de/pose
de/pos/it
de/pos/ition
de/posi/tor
de/posi/tory
de/pot
de/praved
de/pre/cate
de/pre/ci/ate
de/pre/ci/ation
dep/re/dation
de/press
de/pres/sant
de/pres/sing
de/pres/sion
dep/ri/va/tion
de/prive
de/pu/ta/tion
de/pute
de/puty

de/rail
de/rail/ment
de/ranged
der/el/ict
de/res/tric/ted
de/ride
de/ris/ible
de/ris/ion
de/ris/ive
de/ris/ory
de/riva/tive
de/rive
der/ma/ti/tis
de/roga/tory
der/rick
der/rin/ger
des/cant
des/cend
des/cen/dant
des/cent
de/scribe
de/scrip/tion
de/scrip/tive
de/sec/rate
de/sert (abandon)
des/ert (dry region)
de/ser/ted
de/ser/ter
de/serve
de/ser/vedly
de/ser/ving
de/sic/cate
de/sign
des/ig/nate
de/sir/able
de/sire

243

de/sist
desk/top
des/ol/ate
des/ola/tion
des/pair
des/per/ate
des/per/ation
des/pic/able
des/pise
des/pite
de/spoil
des/pond/ency
des/pond/ent
des/pot
des/potic
des/sert
des/tin/ation
des/tine
des/tiny
des/ti/tute
des/troy
des/troyer
de/struc/tion
des/truc/tive
des/ul/tory
de/tach
de/tach/able
de/tach/ment
de/tail
de/tain
de/tainee
de/tect
de/tec/tion
de/tec/tive
de/tec/tor
dé/tente

de/ten/tion
de/ter
de/ter/gent
de/teri/or/ate
de/teri/or/ation
de/ter/min/ation
de/ter/mine
de/ter/rent
de/test
de/test/able
det/on/ate
det/on/ation
de/ton/ator
de/tour
de/tract
det/ri/ment
det/ri/men/tal
deu/ter/ium
de/valu/ation
de/value
de/vas/tate
de/vas/ta/tion
de/velop
de/vel/oper
de/vel/op/ment
de/viate
de/vice
de/vil
de/vil/ish
de/vi/ous
de/vise
de/void
de/vol/ution
de/volve
de/vote
de/vo/tion

de/vour
de/vout
dex/ter/ity
dia/betes
dia/betic
dia/bol/ical
dia/dem
di/ag/nose
di/ag/nosis
di/ag/nos/tic
di/ag/onal
dia/gram
dia/gram/matic
dia/lect
dia/lec/tic
dial/ling
dia/logue
dia/meter
dia/met/ri/cally
dia/mond
di/an/thus
dia/per (US)
dia/phan/ous
dia/phragm
diar/rhoea diar/rhea
    (US)
di/ary
di/as/tole
dia/tribe
di/chot/omy
di/coty/le/don
dic/tate
dic/ta/tor/ial
dic/ta/tor/ship
dic/tion
dic/tion/ary

di/dac/tic
did/dle
did/geri/doo
die/sel
dif/fer
dif/fer/ence
dif/fer/ent
dif/fer/en/tial
dif/fer/en/ti/ate
dif/fi/cult
dif/fi/dence
dif/fi/dent
dif/frac/tion
dif/fuse
di/gest
dig/ger
dig/ging
di/git
di/gi/talis
dig/ni/fied
dig/nit/ary
dig/nity
di/gress
di/gres/sion
di/hed/ral
di/lap/id/ated
di/late
dil/at/ory
dil/emma
di/let/tante
di/li/gence
di/li/gent
di/lute
di/men/sion
di/men/sional
di/min/ish

di/minu/endo
dim/in/ution
dim/inu/tive
dim/ness
dim/ple
dingi/ness
din/ner
di/no/saur
dio/cese
di/ode
di/ox/ide
diph/theria
diph/thong
dip/loma
dip/lo/macy
dip/lo/matic
dip/lo/ma/tist
dip/so/mania
dip/so/ma/niac
di/rect
di/rection
di/rectly
di/rect/ness
di/rec/tor
di/rec/tory
di/ri/gible
dis/ab/il/ity
dis/ad/van/tage
dis/ad/van/ta/geous
dis/af/fec/ted
dis/agree
dis/agree/able
dis/agree/ment
dis/al/low
dis/ap/pear
dis/ap/pear/ance

dis/ap/point
dis/ap/point/ing
dis/ap/point/ment
dis/ap/proval
dis/ap/prove
dis/ap/prov/ingly
dis/arm
dis/arma/ment
dis/arm/ing
dis/ar/range
dis/ar/ray
dis/as/ter
dis/as/trous
dis/band
dis/belief
dis/be/liever
dis/bud
dis/burse
dis/card
dis/cern
dis/cern/ible
dis/charge
dis/ciple
dis/cip/lin/arian
dis/cip/lin/ary
dis/cip/line
dis/claim
dis/claimer
dis/close
dis/clos/ure
dis/col/our
dis/col/or (US)
dis/com/fit
dis/com/fort
dis/con/cert
dis/con/cer/ting

245

dis/con/nect
dis/con/so/late
dis/con/tent
dis/con/tinue
dis/con/tinu/ous
dis/cord
dis/cor/dant
dis/co/thèque
dis/count
dis/cour/age
dis/cour/age/ment
dis/cour/ag/ing
dis/course
dis/cour/teous
dis/cour/tesy
dis/cover
dis/credit
dis/credit/able
dis/creet
dis/crep/ancy
dis/cre/tion
dis/crim/in/ate
dis/crim/in/ation
dis/cus
dis/cuss
dis/cus/sion
dis/dain
dis/dain/ful
dis/ease
dis/em/bark
dis/en/chan/ted
dis/en/chant/ment
dis/en/gage
dis/en/tangle
dis/fav/our
  dis/fav/or (US)

dis/fig/ure
dis/fran/chise
dis/gorge
dis/grace
dis/grace/ful
dis/gruntled
dis/guise
dis/gust
dis/gust/ing
dis/har/mony
dish/cloth
dis/hear/ten
dish/ev/elled
dis/hon/est
dis/hon/our
dis/honor (US)
dis/hon/our/able
dish/washer
dis/il/lu/sion
dis/il/lu/sion/ment
dis/in/cen/tive
dis/in/clin/ation
dis/in/clined
dis/in/fect
dis/in/fec/tant
dis/in/gen/uous
dis/in/herit
dis/in/te/grate
dis/in/te/gration
dis/in/ter
dis/in/ter/ested
dis/jointed
dis/like
dis/lo/cate
dis/lo/cation
dis/lodge

dis/loyal
dis/mal
dis/mantle
dis/may
dis/miss
dis/mount
dis/obe/dience
dis/obe/dient
dis/obey
dis/order
dis/or/gan/ize
dis/ori/en/tate
dis/own
dis/par/age
dis/par/ate
dis/pas/sion/ate
dis/patch
dis/pel
dis/pen/sary
dis/pen/sation
dis/pense
dis/perse
dis/per/ser
dis/pir/ited
dis/place
dis/place/ment
dis/play
dis/please
dis/pleas/ure
dis/pos/able
dis/pose
dis/pos/sess
dis/pro/por/tion
dis/pro/por/tion/
  ate
dis/prove

dis/pute
dis/qualify
dis/quiet
dis/re/gard
dis/re/pair
dis/repu/table
dis/re/pute
dis/re/spect
dis/re/spect/ful
dis/rupt
dis/rup/tion
dis/sat/is/fac/tion
dis/sat/is/fied
dis/sect
dis/sem/in/ate
dis/sen/sion
dis/sent
dis/ser/ta/tion
dis/ser/vice
dis/si/dent
dis/simi/lar
dis/si/pate
dis/si/pa/tion
dis/so/ci/ate
dis/so/lute
dis/solve
dis/suade
dis/tance
dis/taste
dis/taste/ful
dis/tem/per
dis/tend
dis/til
dis/til/lery
dis/tinct
dis/tinc/tive

dis/tinctly
dis/tin/guish
dis/tin/guish/able
dis/tort
dis/tor/tion
dis/tract
dis/trac/tion
dis/traught
dis/tress
dis/tres/sing
dis/tri/bute
dis/tri/bu/tion
dis/tribu/tive
dis/tribu/tor
dis/trict
dis/trust
dis/turb
dis/use
dit/to
dit/ty
di/ur/etic
di/van
di/verge
di/ver/gence
di/verse
di/ver/sity
di/version
di/vide
di/vi/dend
di/vine
divin/ity
di/vis/ible
di/vi/sion
di/vis/ive
di/vorce
di/vor/cee

di/vulge
diz/zi/ness
do/cile
dock/yard
doc/tor
doc/tor/ate
doc/trin/aire
doc/tri/nal
doc/trine
docu/ment
docu/men/tary
dod/der
do/deca/he/dron
dog/gerel
dog/ma
dog/watch
dol/drums
dole/ful
dol/lar
dol/lop
dol/or/ous
dol/phin
dol/phin/ar/ium
do/main
dom/estic
do/mes/ti/cated
dom/es/ti/city
domi/ciled
dom/in/ant
dom/in/ate
dom/in/eer
dom/in/ion
dom/ino
do/nate
don/key
do/nor

247

door/keeper
door/knob
door/man
door/mat
door/step
door/way
dor/mant
dor/mer
dor/mit/ory
dor/mouse
dor/sal
do/sage
doss/house
dos/sier
do/tage
doubt/ful
doubt/less
dough/nut
dove/cote
dove/tail
dow/ager
dowel/ling
down/cast
down/fall
down/grade
down/hearted
down/hill
down/pour
down/right
down/stairs
down/stream
down/town
down/trodden
down/wards
dra/co/nian
drag/net

dra/gon
dra/gon/fly
dra/goon
dra/matic
drama/tist
drama/tize
dras/tic
drain/age
drain/pipe
dres/sage
dres/ser
dress/maker
drift/wood
drink/able
drip/ping
drom/ed/ary
drop/ping
drowsi/ness
drudg/ery
drug/gist
drum/lin
drum/mer
drum/stick
dry/ness
du/al/ism
dub/bin
du/bi/ous
du/bious/ness
duch/ess
duck/ling
duc/tile
duf/fel duf/fle
dumb/bell
dumb/found
dump/ling
dun/ga/rees

dun/geon
duo/denal
duo/denum
du/plex (US)
du/pli/cate
du/pli/ca/tion
du/pli/ca/tor
du/pli/city
dur/able
dur/ability
dura/tion
dur/ess
dur/ing
dust/bin
dust/man
dust/pan
duti/able
duti/ful
dy/ing
dy/nam/ic
dy/nam/ics
dy/na/mite
dy/namo
dyn/asty
dys/en/tery
dys/func/tion
dys/lexia
dys/lexic
dys/pep/sia
dys/pep/tic
dys/trophy
ear/ache
ear/drum
ear/mark
ear/phone
ear/ring

ear/shot
earn/est
earn/ings
earth/en/ware
earth/quake
ear/wig
east/bound
east/ern
east/wards
eat/ables
eaves/drop
ebul/li/ent
ec/cen/tric
ec/cen/tri/city
ec/cle/si/ast/ical
ech/elon
echo/lo/ca/tion
ec/lamp/sia
ec/lec/tic
ec/lipse
eco/logi/cal
eco/logy
econ/omic
econ/om/ics
econ/omize
econ/omy
ec/stasy
ec/to/plasm
ecu/men/ical
ec/zema
ed/ible
edi/fice
edi/tor
edi/tor/ial
edu/cate
edu/ca/tion

edu/ca/tional
ef/face
ef/fect
ef/fec/tive
ef/fem/in/ate
ef/fer/vesce
ef/fer/ves/cence
ef/fi/ca/cious
ef/fi/ci/ency
ef/ficient
ef/figy
ef/flor/esce
ef/flu/ent
ef/fort
ef/front/ery
ef/fus/ive
egal/it/ar/ian
egg/cup
egg/plant
egg/shell
egg/timer
ego/cen/tric
ego/ism
ego/ist
ego/tism
ego/tist
egre/gi/ous
eider/down
eight/een
eight/eenth
eigh/ti/eth
ei/stedd/fod
ejacu/late
ejec/tor
elab/or/ate
elas/tic/ity

el/bow
el/der
el/der/berry
el/ect
elec/tion
elec/toral
elec/tor/ate
elec/tric
elec/tri/cal
elec/tri/cian
elec/tri/city
elec/tri/fi/cation
elec/tro/cute
elec/troly/sis
elec/tron
elec/tronic
ele/gant
ele/giac
ele/ment
ele/men/tary
ele/phant
ele/vate
ele/va/tion
ele/va/tor
el/even
eli/cit
eli/gible
elim/in/ate
elim/in/ation
el/lipse
elo/cu/tion
elong/ate
elo/quence
elo/quent
elu/ci/date
elu/sive

249

ema/ci/ated
em/an/ate
em/an/ci/pate
em/an/ci/pa/tion
em/balm
em/bank/ment
em/bar/go
em/bark
em/bar/ka/tion
em/bar/rass
em/bar/rass/ment
em/bassy
em/bat/tled
em/bed
em/bel/lish
em/bers
em/bez/zle
em/bez/zle/ment
em/bit/tered
em/blem
em/bodi/ment
em/body
em/boss
em/brace
em/bro/ca/tion
em/broi/der
em/bryo
em/bry/onic
emen/da/tion
em/er/ald
emer/gency
emer/gent
emer/itus
emer/sion
em/ery
emi/grant

emi/grate
emi/nence
emi/nently
emol/li/ent
emolu/ment
emo/tion
emo/tive
em/peror
em/pha/sis
em/pha/size
em/phatic
em/pire
em/piri/cal
em/ploy
em/ploy/ment
em/por/ium
em/power
em/press
emu/late
emul/sion
en/able
en/act
en/amel
en/am/oured
en/camped
en/camp/ment
en/cap/su/late
en/case
en/ceph/al/itis
en/chan/ting
en/cir/cle
en/clave
en/close
en/com/pass
en/core
en/coun/ter

en/cour/age
en/cour/age/ment
en/croach
en/crust
en/cyc/lical
en/cyc/lo/pae/dia
en/cyc/lo/pe/dia
en/dan/ger
en/deav/our
en/dev/or (US)
en/demic
en/dive
end/less
en/dorse
en/dow
en/dow/ment
en/dure
end/ways
en/emy
en/er/getic
en/er/geti/cally
en/ergy
en/er/vate
en/fil/ade
en/fold
en/force
en/fran/chise
en/gage
en/gage/ment
en/gen/der
en/gine
en/gin/eer
Eng/land
Eng/lish/man
Eng/lish/woman
en/grave

en/gra/ving
en/grossed
en/gulf
en/hance
en/igma
en/ig/matic
en/joy
en/joy/able
en/joy/ment
en/large
en/large/ment
en/lighten
en/light/en/ment
en/list
en/mity
enor/mous
en/quire
en/rich
en/rol en/roll (US)
en/rol/ment
en/roll/ment (US)
en/semble
en/sign
en/slave
en/sue
en/sure
en/tab/la/ture
en/tail
en/tangle
en/tangle/ment
en/ter
en/ter/itis
en/ter/prise
en/ter/tain
en/ter/tainer
en/ter/tain/ment

en/thrall
en/thral/ling
en/throne
en/thuse
en/thu/si/asm
en/thusi/ast
en/thusi/astic
en/tice
en/tire
en/tirety
en/title
en/tity
en/to/mol/ogy
en/tour/age
en/trails
en/trance
en/tranc/ing
en/trant
en/treat
en/treat/ing
en/trench
en/tre/pre/neur
en/tre/pren/eur/ial
en/trust
en/twine
enu/mer/ate
enun/ci/ate
en/velop
en/vel/ope
en/vi/able
en/vi/ous
en/viron/ment
en/vi/rons
en/vis/age
en/voy
en/zyme

epaul/ette
eph/em/eral
epi/carp
epi/centre
epi/cure
epi/demic
epi/der/mis
epi/glot/tis
epi/gram
epi/lepsy
epi/lep/tic
epi/logue
epis/copal
epis/co/pa/lian
epi/sode
epi/taph
epi/thet
epit/ome
epit/om/ize
equ/able
equal/ity
equal/ize
equan/im/ity
equa/tor/ial
eques/trian
equi/dis/tant
equi/lat/eral
equi/lib/rium
equi/noc/tial
equi/nox
equip/ment
equi/table
equi/val/ent
equivo/cal
equi/vo/cate
erad/ic/ate

erect/ile
erec/tion
er/go/nomics
er/mine
erog/en/ous
er/rand
er/ratic
er/rati/cally
er/ratum
er/ron/eous
eru/dite
eru/di/tion
erup/tion
es/cal/ate
es/cal/ator
es/cap/ade
es/cape
es/capee
es/cape/ment
es/carp/ment
es/cort
Es/kimo
eso/phagus (US)
eso/teric
es/pal/ier
es/pec/ial
es/pion/age
es/plan/ade
es/presso
es/say
es/sence
es/sen/tial
es/tab/lish
es/tab/lish/ment
es/tate
es/teem

es/tim/able
es/tim/ate
es/tim/ation
es/trange
es/tu/ary
et/cet/eras
eter/nal
eter/nity
eth/er/eal
eth/ics
eth/nic
eth/nol/ogy
eti/quette
ety/mol/ogy
eu/cal/yptus
euch/ar/ist
eu/logy
eu/logize
eu/nuch
eu/phem/ism
eu/phoria
eu/reka
Eur/ope
Euro/pean
eu/than/asia
evacu/ate
evacu/ation
evalu/ate
evalu/ation
evan/es/cent
evan/gel/ical
evan/gel/ist
evap/or/ate
evap/or/ation
eva/sion
evas/ive

even/ing
even/song
event/ful
even/tual
eventu/al/ity
ever/green
ever/lasting
every/body
every/day
every/one
every/thing
every/where
evic/tion
evi/dence
evi/dently
evis/cer/ate
evoc/a/tive
evo/lu/tion
ex/acer/bate
ex/acer/ba/tion
ex/acti/tude
ex/ag/ger/ate
ex/ag/ger/ation
ex/al/ta/tion
ex/alted
ex/amine
ex/am/inee
ex/ample
ex/as/per/ate
ex/as/per/ation
ex/cav/ate
ex/ca/vation
ex/ca/va/tor
ex/ceed
ex/cel
ex/cel/lence

ex/cept
ex/cep/tion/able
ex/cep/tional
ex/cerpt
ex/cess
ex/ces/sive
ex/change
ex/chequer
ex/cise
ex/cis/ion
ex/cite
ex/cit/ability
ex/cit/able
ex/cite/ment
ex/claim
ex/clam/ation
ex/clude
ex/clu/sion
ex/clu/sive
ex/com/muni/cate
ex/com/muni/
  cation
ex/cre/ment
ex/cres/cence
ex/creta
ex/crete
ex/cru/ci/at/ing
ex/cur/sion
ex/cus/able
ex/cuse
ex-di/rec/tory
ex/ecrable
ex/ecrate
ex/ecute
ex/ecu/tion
ex/ecu/tioner

exec/u/tive
exec/u/tor
ex/ec/u/trix
ex/em/plary
ex/emp/lify
ex/empt
ex/emp/tion
ex/er/cise
ex/ert
ex/er/tion
ex/hale
ex/haust
ex/hibit
ex/hibi/tion
ex/hibi/tion/ist
ex/hil/ar/ate
ex/hil/ar/ation
ex/hort
ex/hume
ex/hu/ma/tion
ex/ile
ex/ist
ex/ist/ence
ex/odus
ex of/fi/cio
ex/on/er/ate
ex/on/er/ation
ex/or/bit/ant
ex/or/cism
ex/or/cize
ex/otic
ex/pand
ex/panse
ex/pan/sion
ex/pan/sive
ex/pa/ti/ate

ex/pat/ri/ate
ex/pect
ex/pec/tancy
ex/pec/tant
ex/pec/ta/tion
ex/pect/or/ant
ex/pe/di/ency
ex/pe/di/ent
ex/pe/dite
ex/pedi/tion
ex/pedi/tious
ex/pel
ex/pend/able
ex/pend/it/ure
ex/pense
ex/pen/sive
ex/peri/ence
ex/peri/ment
ex/peri/men/tal
ex/pert
ex/per/tise
ex/pire
ex/piry
ex/plain
ex/plan/ation
ex/plana/tory
ex/pletive
ex/plic/able
ex/pli/cit
ex/plode
ex/ploit
ex/ploi/ta/tion
ex/plore
ex/plora/tion
ex/plora/tory
ex/plo/sion

ex/po/nent
ex/port
ex/pose
ex/posé
ex/pos/tu/late
ex/po/sure
ex/pound
ex/press
ex/pres/sion
ex/pres/sive
ex/pressly
ex/press/way
ex/pro/pri/ate
ex/pro/pri/ation
ex/pul/sion
ex/pur/gate
ex/quis/ite
ex/tant
ex/tem/pore
ex/tem/por/ize
ex/tend
ex/ten/sive
ex/tent
ex/tenu/at/ing
ex/ter/ior
ex/term/in/ate
ex/ter/min/ation
ex/ter/nal
ex/tinct
ex/tinc/tion
ex/tin/guish
ex/tol
ex/tort
ex/tor/tion
ex/tor/tion/ate
ex/tra

ex/tract
ex/trac/tion
ex/tra/dite
ex/tra/di/tion
ex/tran/eous
ex/tra/ord/in/arily
ex/tra/ord/in/ary
ex/trap/o/late
ex/trap/ol/ation
ex/tra/va/gance
ex/trava/gant
ex/trava/ganza
ex/treme
ex/trem/ist
ex/trem/ity
ex/tri/cate
ex/tro/vert
ex/trude
ex/uber/ance
ex/uber/ant
ex/ude
ex/ult
ex/ult/ant
eye/ball
eye/bath
eye/brow
eye/ful
eye/lash
eye/lid
eye/liner
eye/piece
eye/shade
eye/sight
eye/sore
eye/strain
eye/wash

eye/wit/ness
fab/ric
fab/ri/cate
fab/ri/ca/tion
fa/bu/lous
face/cloth
face/lift
fa/ce/tious
fa/cial
fa/cile
fa/cili/tate
fa/cil/ity
fac/sim/ile
fac/tion
fac/tor
fac/tory
fac/tual
fac/ulty
fad/dist
fag/got
Fah/ren/heit
fail/ure
fair/ground
fair/ness
fairy/land
faith/ful
faith/less
fal/con
fal/la/cious
fal/lacy
fal/len
fal/lible
fall/out
fal/low
false/hood
fal/setto

fal/ter
fal/si/fy
fa/mil/iar
fam/ili/ar/ity
fam/ili/ar/ize
fam/ily
fam/ine
fam/ished
fam/ous
fan/atic
fan/at/ical
fan/cier
fan/dan/go
fan/fare
fan/light
fan/tas/tic
fan/tasy
far/away
far/ci/cal
fare/well
farm/house
farm/ing
farm/yard
far/rea/ching
far/thest
fas/cia
fas/cin/ate
fas/cina/tion
fas/cism
fas/cist
fash/ion
fash/ion/able
fas/tidi/ous
fa/tal/ism
fat/al/ity
fate/ful

fa/tigue
fat/ten
fat/ten/ing
fat/uous
fau/cet (US)
fault/less
fa/vour fa/vor (US)
fa/vour/able
fav/or/able (US)
fa/vour/ite
fav/or/ite (US)
fear/ful
fear/less
fear/some
feas/ible
feasi/bility
feath/er/weight
fea/ture
feb/rile
Feb/ru/ary
feck/less
fec/und
fed/eral
fed/era/tion
feeble/ness
feed/back
feel/ing
fe/licity
fe/line
fel/low
fel/low/ship
fe/male
fem/in/ine
fem/in/in/ity
fem/in/ist
fe/mur

fenc/ing
fen/der
fen/nel
fer/ment
fer/men/ta/tion
fe/ro/cious
fer/ret
fer/rous
fer/rule
fer/ry
fer/ry/man
fer/tile
fer/til/ity
fer/til/ize
fer/til/izer
fer/vent
fer/vour fer/vor
(US)
fes/ter
fest/ival
fes/tive
fes/toon
fet/ish
fet/lock
fet/ter
feud/al/ism
fe/ver/ish
fi/asco
fibre/glass
fib/ula
fic/tion
fic/tit/ious
fid/dle
fid/el/ity
fid/get
field/mouse

255

fields/man
field/work
fiend/ish
fierce/ness
fif/teen
fif/ti/eth
fig/ment
fig/ure
fig/ure/head
fila/ment
fil/bert
fili/buster
fili/gree
fil/ler
fil/let
fil/ter
fi/nal
fi/nal/ist
fi/nal/ity
fi/nal/ize
fi/nale
fi/nance
fin/an/cial
fin/an/cier
find/ings
fin/esse
fin/ger
fin/ger/nail
fin/ger/print
fin/ger/tip
fin/icky
fin/ish
fin/ite
Fin/land
fire/arm
fire/fly

fire/guard
fire/light
fire/man
fire/place
fire/proof
fire/side
fire/war/den
fire/wood
fire/work
fir/ma/ment
first/hand
fis/cal
fish/bone
fish/cake
fisher/man
fish/ery
fish/monger
fis/sion
fis/si/ped
fis/sure
fis/tula
fit/ful
fit/ment
fit/ness
fit/ting
fix/ation
fixa/tive
fiz/zle out
flab/ber/gast
flac/cid
fla/geo/let
flag/gel/ate
flag/pole
flag/rant
flag/ship
flag/stone

flam/boy/ant
flame/proof
flam/ingo
flam/mable
flan/nel
flap/ping
flash/back
flash/bulb
flash/cube
flasg/gun
flash/gun
flash/light
flash/point
flat/fish
flat/let
flat/ten
flat/ter
flatu/lence
flat/worm
flaut/ist
fla/vour fla/vor
(US)
flaw/less
fledg/ling
fleet/ing
flex/ible
flexi/bility
flint/lock
flip/pant
flip/per
flir/ta/tion
floc/cose
flood/gate
flood/light
floor/board
floor/cloth

floor/show
flor/es/cence
flo/ri/bunda
flo/rist
flo/ta/tion
flo/tilla
flot/sam
flour/ish
flour/mill
flower/bed
flower/pot
fluc/tu/ate
fluc/tu/ation
flu/ency
flu/ent
fluor/es/cence
fluor/escent
fluor/ide
fluor/ine
flus/ter
flu/tist
flut/ter
flyi/ng
fly/leaf
fly/over
fly/past
fly/sheet
fly/weight
fly/wheel
fod/der
foe/tus
fog/horn
fog/lamp
fo/li/age
fol/low
fol/ly

fo/ment
fon/dant
fond/ness
fon/due
food/stuff
fool/hardy
fool/ish/ness
fool/proof
fools/cap
foot/ball
foot/brake
foot/hills
foot/hold
foot/ing
foot/lights
foot/man
foot/note
foot/path
foot/plate
foot/print
for/age
for/bade
for/bear/ance
for/bid
for/bid/ding
force/ful
force/meat
for/ceps
for/cible
fore/arm
fore/bear
fore/bo/ding
fore/cast
fore/castle
fore/close
fore/father

fore/fin/ger
fore/front
fore/go
fore/gone
fore/ground
fore/hand
fore/head
fore/leg
fore/man
fore/most
fore/noon
for/en/sic
fore/runner
fore/see
fore/shadow
fore/sight
fore/skin
for/est
fore/stall
fore/taste
fore/tell
fore/thought
for/ever
fore/word
for/feit
for/gave
forg/ery
for/get
for/get/ful
for/give
for/go
for/got
for/lorn
form/al
for/mal/de/hyde
for/mat

257

for/mer
for/mid/able
for/mula
for/mu/late
for/sake
for/sythia
forth/coming
forth/right
forth/with
for/ti/fi/cation
for/tify
for/ti/tude
fort/night
fort/ress
for/tu/it/ous
for/tu/nate
for/ti/eth
for/tune
for/ward
fos/sick
fos/sil
fos/sil/ized
fos/ter
foun/da/tion
found/ries
foun/tain
four/poster
four/some
four/teen
fox/glove
fox/hound
fox/trot
frac/tion
frac/tious
frac/ture
fra/gile

fra/gil/ity
frag/ment
fra/grance
fra/grant
frame/work
fran/chise
frank/furter
fran/tic
fran/ti/cally
fra/ter/nal
fra/ter/nity
frat/er/nize
frat/ri/cide
fraudu/lent
freak/ish
free/hand
free/hold
free/lance
free/loader
free/mason
free/way
free/wheel
fre/quent
fre/quency
fresh/man
fresh/ness
fresh/water
fret/ful
fret/saw
fret/work
fric/tion
Fri/day
friend/li/ness
friend/ship
frig/ate
fright/en/ing

fri/gid
fri/gid/ity
friski/ness
frit/ter
fri/vol/ity
friv/ol/ous
friz/zle
frog/man
frog/march
front/age
fron/tier
front/is/piece
frost/bite
frost/ily
fru/gal
fruit/cake
fruit/ful
frump/ish
frus/trate
fuch/sia
fuel/ling
fu/git/ive
ful/crum
ful/fil
ful/fil/ment
full/ness
ful/some
fu/mi/gate
func/tion
fun/da/men/tal
fu/ner/al
fun/fair
fun/gi/cide
fun/gus
fu/nicu/lar
fun/nel

fun/nily
fur/nace
furn/ish
fur/ni/ture
fur/ore
fur/rier
fur/row
fur/ther
fur/ther/more
fur/ther/most
fur/tive
fusel/age
fu/sil/ier´
fu/sil/lade
fu/sion
fu/tile
fu/ture
gab/ar/dine
gad/about
gaf/fer
gain/ful
gain/say
ga/lac/tic
gal/axy
gal/lant
gal/lan/try
gal/leon
gal/lery
gal/ley
Gal/lic
gal/li/cism
gal/ling
gal/li/vant
gal/lon
gal/lop
gal/lows

gall/stone
Gal/lup poll
ga/lore
ga/loshes
ga/lumph
gal/van/ize
gal/va/nometer
gam/bit
gam/ble
gam/bol
game/keeper
games/man/ship
gam/ma rays
gam/mon
gam/my
ga/mut
gan/der
gang/ling
gang/lion
gang/plank
gan/grene
gan/gren/ous
gang/ster
gang/way
gan/net
gan/try
gaol/bird
gar/age
gar/bage
gar/ble
gar/den
gar/denia
gar/den/ing
garde/robe
gar/gan/tuan
gar/goyle

gar/ish
gar/land
gar/lic
gar/ment
gar/ner
gar/net
gar/nish
gar/ret
gar/ri/son
gar/rul/ous
gar/ter
gas/eous
gas/ket
gas/mask
gaso/line
gaso/meter
gas/works
gas/tric
gas/tro/en/ter/it/is
gas/tro/nome
gas/tro/pod
gat/eau
gate/crash
gate/post
gate/way
gather/ing
gaunt/let
gaz/ebo
ga/zelle
gaz/et/teer
ga/zump
gear/box
gear/lever
gear/stick
gear/shift (US)
gear/wheel

259

gel/at/in(e)
gel/at/in/ous
gel/ding
gel/ig/nite
Gem/ini
gem/stone
gen/darme
gen/der
genea/lo/gical
gen/eal/ogist
gen/eal/ogy
gen/eral
gen/er/alis/simo
gen/er/al/iz/ation
gen/er/ate
gen/er/ation
gen/er/ator
gen/eric
gen/er/ous
gen/er/os/ity
gen/esis
gen/et/ics
ge/nial
gen/ital
gen/it/ive
ge/nius
geno/cide
gen/teel
gen/til/ity
gen/tile
gentle/man
gentle/ness
gen/tri/fi/cation
genu/flect
genu/ine
geo/detic

geo/graphi/cal
geo/graphy
geo/logi/cal
geo/logy
geo/met/ri/cal
geo/metry
ge/ran/ium
ger/bil
geria/tri/cian
ge/ri/at/rics
ger/mane
Ger/many
ger/mi/cide
ger/min/ate
ge/ron/to/logy
ger/und
ges/ta/tion
ges/ticu/late
ges/ture
get/away
get-to/gether
gey/ser
gher/kin
gib/ber/ish
gib/bet
gib/bon
gib/lets
gid/di/ness
gi/gan/tic
gig/gle
gim/bals
gim/let
gim/mick
gin/ger
gin/ger/bread
ging/ham

gin/giv/itis
gin/seng
gir/affe
gir/der
girl/friend
giz/zard
gla/cial
gla/cier
gla/di/ator
gla/di/olus
glad/ness
glam/our glam/or (US)
glam/or/ize
glam/or/ous
glan/du/lar
glass/house
glass/ware
glau/coma
gla/zier
glee/ful
glen/garry
glim/mer
glis/ten
glit/ter
glob/ate
globe/trot/ter
globu/lar
glob/ule
glori/ous
glos/sary
glu/cose
glu/ten
glu/tin/ous
glut/ton
glot/ton/ous

gly/cer/in(e)
goal/keeper
goal/mouth
goal/post
gob/ble/de/gook
go-/be/tween
gob/let
gob/lin
god/child/ren
god-daugh/ter
god/dess
god/father
god/for/saken
god/mother
god/par/ents
god/send
god/son
gog/gle
gold/finch
gold/fish
gold/smith
gol/li/wog
gon/dola
good/bye
good/ness
good/night
good/will
goose/berry
gor/geous
gor/illa
gorm/less
gos/hawk
gos/ling
gos/pel
gos/sa/mer
gos/sip

got/ten (US)
gou/ache
gou/lash
gour/mand
gour/met
gov/ern
gov/ernor
grace/ful
grace/ful/ness
gra/cious
gra/di/ent
grad/ual
grad/uate
gradu/ation
graf/fiti
gram/mar
gram/mati/cal
gramo/phone
gran/ary
gran/dad
grand/child
grand/daugh/ter
gran/deur
grand/father
grand/par/ents
grand/son
grand/stand
gran/ite
granu/lar
granu/late
gran/ule
grape/fruit
grape/vine
graphi/cal
graph/ite
graph/ol/ogy

grass/hopper
grass/land
grass/roots
grass/widow
grate/ful
grati/fi/cation
grat/ify
grat/it/ude
gra/tu/itous
gra/tu/ity
grave/digger
grave/stone
grave/yard
grav/it/ate
grav/ity
grease/paint
grease/proof
green/ery
green/finch
green/fly
green/gage
green/grocer
green/house
green/ish
greet/ings
greg/arious
gren/ade
grey/hound
grey/lag
grid/iron
griev/ance
griev/ous
grim/ace
grind/ing
grind/stone
gro/cery

261

gro/tesque
ground/less
ground/nut
ground/sel
ground/sheet
grounds/man
ground/work
growl/ing
grub/bi/ness
grudg/ing
gru/el/ling
grue/some
grump/ily
guar/an/tee
guar/an/tor
guar/dian
guard/room
guards/man
guer(r)/illa
guess/work
guest/house
guf/faw
guid/ance
guide/book
guide/lines
guile/less
guil/lot/ine
gui/tar
gul/let
gull/ible
gul/li/bility
gum/boot
gump/tion
gurg/ling
gus/set
gut/ter

gut/tural
guy/rope
gym/khana
gym/nas/ium
gym/nast
gym/nas/tics
gyn/ae/co/logi/cal
gyn/ae/col/ogy
gy/rate
gy/ro/scope
hab/eas cor/pus
hab/er/dash/ery
hab/it/able
hab/itat
habi/ta/tion
hab/it/ual
hab/itu/ate
hack/neyed
hack/saw
had/dock
hae/mo/globin
hae/mo/philia
haem/or/rhage
haem/or/rhoids
hag/gard
hag/gis
hag/gle
hail/stone
hail/storm
hair/brush
hair/cut
hair/dres/ser
hair/less
hair/net
hair/raising
hair/spring

hair/style
hal/cyon
half/wit
hali/but
hali/tosis
hall/mark
hal/low
hal/lu/cin/ate
hal/lu/cin/ation
hal/lu/cin/atory
hal/lu/cino/gen
halo/gen
hal/ter
ham/burger
ham/let
ham/mer
ham/mock
ham/per
hamp/ster
ham/string
ham/strung
hand/bag
hand/ball
hand/clap
hand/cuff
hand/ful
han/di/cap
handi/craft
handi/work
hand/ker/chief
handle/bar
hand/ler
hand/made
hand/out
hand/rail
hand/shake

hand/some
hand/spring
hand/stand
hand/wri/ting
handy/man
hang/man
hang/nail
hang/over
han/ker
hanky/panky
han/som
hap/haz/ard
hap/less
hap/pen
hap/pily
hap/pi/ness
har/angue
har/ass
har/bin/ger
har/bour har/bor
(US)
hard/back
hard/board
hard/core
hard/ener
hard/liner
hard/ness
hard/ship
hard/work
hard/wor/king
hare/bell
hari/cot
har/le/quin
harm/less
har/mon/ica
har/mo/nium

har/mony
har/ness
har/poon
harp/si/chord
har/rier
har/row
harsh/ness
har/vest
hash/ish
has/sle
has/sock
has/tily
has/ti/ness
hatch/back
hatch/ery
hat/chet
hate/ful
haugh/tily
haul/age
haul/ier
hav/er/sack
haw/ker
haw/ser
haw/thorn
hay/fever
hay/maker
hay/making
hay/stack
hay/wire
haz/ard
haz/ard/ous
hazel/nut
head/ache
head/board
head/dress
head/land

head/light
head/line
head/long
head/mas/ter
head/mis/tress
head/phones
head/quar/ters
head/rest
head/room
head/scarf
head/set
head/ship
head/stone
head/strong
head/way
head/wind
health/ily
hear/say
heart/beat
heart/burn
heart/felt
heart/less
heart/search/ing
hearth/rug
heat/wave
hea/venly
hea/vi/ness
heavy/weight
Heb/rew
hec/tare
hec/tic
hec/tor
hedge/hog
hedge/row
hed/on/ist
heed/less

263

he/gem/ony
hein/ous
heir/ess
heir/loom
he/li/an/thus
heli/cop/ter
he/lio/trope
heli/pad
heli/port
he/lium
hel/le/bore
hel/met
helms/man
help/ful
help/less
hemi/sphere
hemi/spheri/cal
hem/line
hem/lock
hen/bane
hence/forth
hench/man
hen/house
hen/pecked
hepa/ti/tis
hep/ta/gon
her/ald
her/aldic
herb/aceous
her/bi/vore
her/biv/or/ous
here/abouts
here/after
here/with
her/edi/tary
her/ed/ity

her/esy
here/tic
heri/tage
her/maph/ro/dite
her/meti/cally
her/mit/age
her/nia
hero/ine
hero/ism
her/pes
her/ring
her/self
hesi/tant
hes/it/ate
hes/sian
het/ero/gen/eous
het/ero/sex/ual
hex/agon
hey/day
hi/atus
hi/ber/nate
hic/cup hic/cough
hid/den
hide/bound
hid/eous
hier/archi/cal
hier/archy
hiero/glyphics
high/ball
high/brow
high/lands
high/light
high/ness
high/road
high/way
high/way/man

hi/jack
hil/ari/ous
hil/arity
hill/billy
hil/lock
hill/side
hin/der
hin/drance
hind/most
hind/sight
hin/ter/land
hip/pie
hip/po/drome
hip/po/pota/mus
hip/sters
hire/ling
hir/sute
his/tol/ogy
his/torian
his/tori/cal
his/tory
his/tri/onic
hoard/ing
hoar/frost
hoarse/ness
hob/nailed
hob/nob
hog/manay
hogs/head
hold/all
holi/day
holi/ness
Hol/land
hol/low
hol/ly
hol/ly/hock

holo/caust
hol/ster
hom/age
hom/burg
home/less
home/sick/ness
home/work
hom/icide
hom/ily
hom/oe/opathy
hom/eopathy (US)
homo/geneous
hom/og/en/ize
homo/ol/o/gate
homo/sexual
hom/un/cu/lus
hon/est
honey/comb
honey/moon
honey/suckle
hon/or/ary
hon/our
hon/our/able
hon/or/able (US)
hood/lum
hood/wink
hoo/li/gan
hope/ful
hope/less
hop/field
hop/per
hop/scotch
ho/ri/zon
ho/ri/zontal
hor/mone
horn/beam

hor/net
horo/scope
hor/rible
hor/rific
hor/ror
horse/back
horse/box
horse/hair
horse/man
horse/play
horse/power
horse/radish
horae/rider
horse/shoe
horse/woman
hor/ti/cul/ture
hos/pit/able
hos/pital
hos/pit/al/ity
hos/tage
hos/tel
host/ess
hos/tile
hos/til/ity
hot/bed
hotch/potch
ho/tel
hot/house
hot/plate
hour/glass
house/boat
house/breaker
house/coat
house/ful
house/hold
house/keeper

house/maid
house/man
house/master
house/mistress
house/room
house/warming
house/wife
house/work
hov/er/craft
how/ever
hub/bub
hulk/ing
hul/la/ba/loo
hu/man
hu/mane
hu/man/ism
hu/man/it/ar/ian
hu/man/ity
hum/ble/ness
hum/bug
hum/drum
hu/merus
hu/mid
hu/midi/fier
hu/mili/ate
hum/ming/bird
hu/mour hu/mor
(US)
hump/backed
hu/mus
hunch/back
hun/dred
hun/dred/weight
Hun/gar/ian
hun/ger
hun/grily

265

hunts/man
hur/rah hur/ray
hur/ri/cane
hur/riedly
hurt/ful
hus/band
hus/bandry
husk/ily
huski/ness
hust/ings
hust/ler
hy/acinth
hy/brid
hy/dran/gea
hy/drant
hy/draulic
hy/dro/elec/tric
hy/dro/foil
hy/dro/gen
hy/drog/ra/pher
hy/droly/sis
hy/dro/phobia
hy/dro/plane
hy/dro/pon/ics
hy/dro/ther/apy
hy/giene
hy/grom/eter
hym/nal
hy/per/bole
hy/per/crit/ical
hy/per/mar/ket
hy/per/sen/sit/ive
hy/per/ten/sion
hy/phen/ate
hyp/no/sis
hyp/notic

hyp/no/tism
hyp/no/tize
hy/po/chon/dria
hy/po/crisy
hypo/crite
hy/po/der/mic
hy/po/ten/sion
hy/pot/en/use
hy/po/ther/mia
hy/pothe/sis
hy/po/theti/cal
hys/ter/ec/tomy
hys/teria
hys/teri/cal
hys/terics
ice/berg
ice/box
ice/cap
ice/field
ice/house
ici/ness
icono/clast
ideal/ism
ideal/ist
ideal/istic
ideal/ize
ident/ical
identi/fica/tion
iden/tify
identi/kit
iden/tity
ideo/logi/cal
ideol/ogy
ideo/matic
idio/syn/crasy
idi/otic

idle/ness
id/ol/atry
ig/loo
ig/neous
ig/nite
ig/noble
ig/no/mi/ni/ous
ig/nora/mus
ig/nor/ance
ig/nor/ant
ig/nore
il/legal
il/leg/ible
il/le/git/imate
il/li/cit
il/lit/er/acy
il/lit/er/ate
ill/ness
il/lo/gical
il/lu/min/ate
il/lusion
il/lus/trate
il/lus/tra/tive
il/lus/tri/ous
im/age
ima/gery
im/agin/ary
im/agin/a/tive
ima/gine
im/bal/ance
im/be/cile
im/bibe
im/bue
im/it/ate
imi/tat/ive
imi/ta/tor

im/macu/late
im/ma/nent
im/ma/ter/ial
im/ma/ture
im/meas/ur/able
im/me/di/ate
im/me/morial
im/mense
im/men/sity
im/merse
im/mi/grate
im/mi/grant
im/mi/nent
im/mob/ile
im/mobility
im/mobilize
im/mod/er/ate
im/moral
im/mor/tal
im/mor/tal/ity
im/mor/tal/ize
im/mov/able
im/mune
im/mun/ize
im/mut/able
im/pact
im/pair
im/pale
im/pal/pable
im/part
im/par/tial
im/pass/able
im/passe
im/pas/sioned
im/pass/ive
im/pa/tient

im/peach
im/peach/ment
im/pec/cable
im/pe/cu/ni/ous
im/ped/ance
im/pedi/ment
im/pede
im/pel
im/pend/ing
im/pen/et/rable
im/peni/tant
im/per/at/ive
im/per/cep/tible
im/per/fect
im/per/ial
im/per/ial/ist
im/peril
im/peri/ous
im/per/ma/nent
im/per/me/able
im/per/son/al
im/per/son/ate
im/per/son/ator
im/per/tin/ence
im/per/ti/nent
im/per/turb/able
im/per/vious
im/pe/tigo
im/petu/osity
im/petu/ous
im/petus
im/pinge
im/plac/able
im/plant
im/ple/ment
im/pli/cate

im/pli/cit
im/plore
im/ply
im/pol/ite
im/poli/tic
im/pon/der/ables
im/port
im/port/ance
im/port/ant
im/por/tu/nate
im/por/tune
im/pose
im/po/sition
im/poss/ible
im/pos/tor
im/pos/ture
im/po/tence
im/po/tent
im/pound
im/pov/er/ish
im/prac/tic/able
im/prac/tical
im/pre/cation
im/pre/cise
im/preg/nable
im/preg/nate
im/pre/sario
im/press
im/pres/sion
im/pres/sion/ism
im/pres/sive
im/prim/atur
im/print
im/prison
im/prob/able
im/promptu

267

improper

im/proper
im/pro/pri/ety
im/prove
im/prov/i/dent
im/pro/vis/ation
im/pro/vise
im/pu/dence
im/pru/dent
im/pu/dent
im/pugn
im/pulse
im/pu/nity
im/pure
im/pute
in/ab/il/ity
in/ac/cess/ible
in/ac/cur/acy
in/ac/cur/ate
in/ac/tive
in/ade/quate
in/ad/miss/ible
in/ad/ver/tent
in/ad/vis/able
in/alien/able
in/ane
in/an/im/ate
in/ap/plic/able
in/ap/pro/pri/ate
in/ap/ti/tude
in/ar/ticu/late
in/ar/tis/tic
in/at/ten/tion
in/at/ten/tive
in/aud/ible
in/aug/ur/ate
in/aus/pic/ious

in/born
in/bred
in/cal/cul/able
in/can/des/cent
in/cap/able
in/ca/paci/tate
in/ca/pa/city
in/car/cer/ate
in/car/nate
in/cau/tious
in/cen/di/ary
in/cense
in/cen/tive
in/cep/tion
in/cess/ant
in/cest
in/ces/tu/ous
in/ci/dent
in/ci/den/tal
in/cin/er/ate
in/cipi/ent
in/cision
in/cis/ive
in/cisor
in/cite
in/civ/il/ity
in/clem/ent
in/clin/ation
in/cline
in/clude
in/clu/sion
in/cog/nito
in/co/her/ent
in/come
in/coming
in/com/mu/ni/cado

in/com/par/able
in/com/pat/ible
in/com/pet/ent
in/com/plete
in/com/pre/hen/
sible
in/con/ceiv/able
in/con/clus/ive
in/con/gru/ous
in/con/se/quen/tial
in/con/sid/er/able
in/con/sid/er/ate
in/con/sis/tent
in/con/sol/able
in/con/spicu/ous
in/con/stancy
in/con/stant
in/con/ti/nent
in/con/tro/vert/ible
in/con/veni/ence
in/cor/por/ate
in/cor/rect
in/cor/rig/ible
in/cor/rupt/ible
in/crease
in/cred/ible
in/credu/lous
in/cre/ment
in/crim/in/ate
in/cu/bate
in/cu/bus
in/cul/cate
in/cum/bent
in/cur
in/cur/able
in/cur/ious

268

in/cur/sion
in/debted
in/de/cent
in/de/ci/pher/able
in/de/cision
in/de/ci/sive
in/dec/or/ous
in/deed
in/de/fati/gable
in/de/fen/sible
in/de/fin/able
in/def/in/ite
in/del/ible
in/del/ic/ate
in/dem/nify
in/dent
in/den/tures
in/de/pen/dent
in/des/crib/able
in/des/truc/tible
in/de/term/in/able
in/de/term/in/ate
in/dex
in/di/cate
in/dict
in/dif/fer/ent
in/di/gen/ous
in/di/gent
in/di/ges/tion
in/dig/nant
in/dig/nity
in/digo
in/dir/ect
in/dis/creet
in/dis/cretion
in/dis/crim/in/ate

in/dis/pen/sable
in/dis/posed
in/dis/put/able
in/dis/sol/uble
in/dis/tinct
in/dis/tin/guish/
    able
in/di/vid/ual
in/di/vis/ible
in/doc/trin/ate
in/do/lence
in/dom/it/able
in/door
in/dub/it/able
in/duce
in/duc/tion
in/dulge
in/dus/try
in/eb/ri/ate
in/ed/ible
in/ef/fable
in/ef/fec/tive
in/ef/fec/tual
in/ef/fi/cient
in/ele/gant
in/el/igible
in/ept
in/ep/ti/tude
in/equal/ity
in/equit/able
in/eradi/cable
in/ert
in/ertia
in/es/cap/able
in/es/sen/tial
in/es/tim/able

in/ev/it/able
in/ex/act
in/ex/cus/able
in/ex/haust/ible
in/ex/or/able
in/ex/pen/sive
in/ex/peri/enced
in/ex/pert
in/ex/plic/able
in/ex/press/ible
in/ex/tric/able
in/fal/lible
in/fal/li/bility
in/fam/ous
in/fant
in/fan/ti/cide
in/fan/tile
in/fan/try
in/fatu/ated
in/fect
in/fec/tious
in/fer
in/fer/ence
in/ferior
in/feri/or/ity
in/fer/nal
in/ferno
in/fer/tile
in/fest
in/fi/del/ity
in/fighting
in/fil/trate
in/fin/ite
in/fin/it/esi/mal
in/fini/tive
in/firm

269

in/firm/ary
in/flame
in/flate
in/fla/tion
in/flex/ible
in/flict
in/flow
in/flu/ence
in/flu/enza
in/flux
in/form
in/for/mal
in/form/ant
in/for/ma/tion
in/for/ma/tive
in/fra/struc/ture
in/fre/quent
in/fringe
in/furi/ate
in/fuse
in/geni/ous
in/genu/ity
in/genu/ous
in/got
in/grained
in/gra/ti/ate
in/grati/tude
in/gred/ient
in/grow/ing
in/habit
in/hale
in/her/ent
in/herit
in/habit
in/hi/bi/tion
in/hos/pit/able

in/human
in/hu/man/ity
in/im/ical
in/im/it/able
in/iqui/tous
in/iquity
ini/tial
ini/ti/ate
ini/ti/at/ive
in/ject
in/ju/di/cious
in/junc/tion
in/jure
in/just/ice
ink/ling
ink/well
in/laid
in/land
in/lay
in/let
in/mate
in/most
in/nards
in/nate
in/ner
in/nings
in/no/cence
in/no/cent
in/nocu/ous
in/nov/ate
in/no/va/tive
in/no/vator
in/nu/endo
in/nu/mer/able
in/ocu/late
in/of/fen/sive

in/op/er/able
in/op/er/ative
in/op/por/tune
in/or/din/ate
in/or/ganic
in/put
in/quest
in/quire
in/quisi/tive
in/roads
in/rush
in/sane
in/san/it/ary
in/san/ity
in/sa/ti/able
in/scribe
in/scrut/able
in/sect
in/sec/ti/cide
in/se/cure
in/sem/in/ation
in/sens/ible
in/sens/it/ive
in/sep/ar/able
in/sert
in/set
in/shore
in/side
in/si/di/ous
in/sight
in/sig/nia
in/sig/ni/fi/cant
in/sin/cere
in/sin/cerity
in/sinu/ate
in/sipid

in/sist
in/sol/ent
in/sol/uble
in/sol/vent
in/som/nia
in/spect
in/spec/tor/ate
in/spire
in/stab/il/ity
in/stall
in/stal/ment
in/stall/ment (US)
in/stance
in/stant
in/stan/ta/neous
in/stead
in/step
in/sti/gate
in/stil
in/stinct
in/sti/tute
in/sti/tu/tional
in/struct
in/struc/tive
in/struc/tor
in/stru/ment
in/stru/men/tal
in/sub/ord/in/ate
in/sub/stan/tial
in/suf/fer/able
in/suf/fi/cient
in/su/lar
in/su/lar/ity
in/su/late
in/su/lin
in/sult

in/su/per/able
in/sure
in/sur/gent
in/sur/mount/able
in/sur/rec/tion
in/tact
in/take
in/tan/gible
in/teger
in/teg/ral
in/te/grate
in/teg/rity
in/tel/lect
in/tel/lec/tual
in/tel/li/gence
in/tel/li/gent/sia
in/tel/li/gible
in/tem/per/ate
in/tend
in/tense
in/ten/sify
in/ten/sity
in/ten/sive
in/tent
in/ten/tion
in/ten/tional
in/ter
in/ter/act
in/ter/cede
in/ter/cept
in/ter/cep/tion
in/ter/ces/sion
in/ter/change
in/ter/com
in/ter/con/tin/ental
in/ter/course

in/ter/est
in/ter/face
in/ter/fere
in/ter/fer/ence
in/ter/im
in/ter/ior
in/ter/ject
in/ter/lock
in/ter/loper
in/ter/lude
in/ter/marry
in/ter/me/di/ary
in/ter/me/di/ate
in/term/in/able
in/ter/mingle
in/ter/mis/sion
in/ter/mit/tent
in/tern
in/ter/nal
in/ter/na/tional
in/ter/nee
in/tern/ment
in/ter/phone
in/ter/planetary
in/ter/play
in/ter/po/late
in/ter/pose
in/ter/pret
in/ter/pre/ter
in/ter/reg/num
in/ter/ro/gate
in/ter/ro/ga/tive
in/ter/rupt
in/ter/sect
in/ter/sperse
in/ter/stel/lar

271

in/ter/twine
in/ter/val
in/ter/vene
in/ter/view
in/ter/viewee
in/ter/weave
in/tes/tate
in/tes/ti/nal
in/tes/tine
in/ti/macy
in/ti/mate
in/tim/id/ate
in/tol/er/able
in/tol/er/ant
in/ton/ation
in/tone
in/toxi/cate
in/tran/si/gence
in/tran/si/gent
in/tran/si/tive
in/tra/venous
in/trepid
in/tri/cacy
in/tri/cate
in/trigue
in/trin/sic
in/tro/duce
in/tro/spec/tive
in/tro/vert
in/trude
in/tru/sion
in/tu/ition
in/tui/tive
in/un/date
in/ure
in/vade

in/valid
in/vali/date
in/valu/able
in/vari/able
in/vasion
in/vec/tive
in/veigle
in/vent
in/ven/tive
in/ven/tor
in/ven/tory
in/verse
in/ver/sion
in/vert
in/ver/te/brate
in/vest
in/ves/ti/gate
in/ves/ti/ga/tor
in/ves/ti/ture
in/vest/ment
in/ves/tor
in/vet/er/ate
in/vidi/ous
in/vi/gil/ate
in/vig/or/ate
in/vin/cible
in/vis/ible
in/vi/ta/tion
in/vite
in/vo/ca/tion
in/voice
in/voke
in/vol/un/tary
in/volve
in/vul/ner/able
in/ward

iod/ine
ion/ize
iono/sphere
iras/cible
ir/ate
Ire/land
iri/des/cent
irk/some
ironi/cal
ir/radi/ate
ir/ra/tional
ir/rec/on/cil/able
ir/re/deem/able
ir/re/fut/able
ir/regu/lar
ir/rele/vant
ir/re/li/gious
ir/rep/ar/able
ir/re/place/able
ir/re/press/ible
ir/re/proach/able
ir/re/sist/ible
ir/res/ol/ute
ir/re/spec/tive
ir/re/spon/sible
ir/re/triev/able
ir/rev/er/ent
ir/re/ver/sible
ir/re/vo/cable
ir/ri/gate
ir/ri/tant
ir/ri/tate
ir/rup/tion
iso/bar
iso/late
iso/la/tion

iso/sceles
iso/therm
iso/tope
Is/rael
is/sue
isth/mus
it/alic
item/ize
it/in/er/ant
it/in/er/ary
it/self
jab/ber
jack/ass
jack/boot
jack/daw
jack/eted
jack/pot
ja/cuzzi
jag/uar
jail/bird
ja/lopy
jam/boree
jam/ming
jan/itor
Janu/ary
ja/pon/ica
jar/gon
jas/mine
jaun/dice
jav/elin
jaw/bone
jay/walker
jeal/ousy
jeal/ously
jelly/bean
jelly/fish

jeop/ard/ize
jeo/pardy
jer/boa
je/re/miad
jer/kin
jer/sey
jes/ter
jet/sam
jet/ti/son
jew/el/ler
jig/saw
jin/go/ism
jit/ter/bug
jit/ters
job/ber
joc/ular
jocu/lar/ity
joc/und
jodh/purs
jog/ging
jog/trot
join/ery
jol/lity
jot/tings
jour/nal
jour/nal/ese
jour/nal/ism
jour/ney
jov/ial
jovi/ality
joy/ful
joy/less
joy/ride
joy/stick
ju/bil/ant
ju/bilee

judge/ment
ju/di/ca/ture
ju/di/cial
ju/di/ciary
ju/di/cious
jug/ger/naut
jug/gler
jug/ular
juici/ness
juke/box
junc/tion
junc/ture
ju/nior
ju/ni/per
jun/ket
juri/di/cal
jur/is/dic/tion
jur/is/pru/dence
jur/ist
jury/man
just/ice
justi/fi/able
just/ify
just/ness
ju/ven/ile
jux/ta/pose
jux/ta/posi/tion
kal/eido/scope
kami/kaze
kan/garoo
kao/lin
ka/pok
ka/put
kar/ate
katy/did
ke/bab

273

ked/geree
keep/ing
keep/sake
kel/vin
ken/nel
kerb/stone
  curb/stone (US)
ker/chief
ker/nel
kero/sene
kes/trel
ket/chup
ket/tle
ket/tle/drum
key/board
key/hole
key/note
kick/back
kid/nap
kid/nap/ping
kid/ney
kil/ling
kill/joy
kilo/cycle
kilo/gram
kilo/metre
kilo/meter (US)
kilo/watt
ki/mono
kin/der/gar/ten
kin/dle
kind/ness
kin/etic
king/dom
king/cup
king/fisher

king/pin
kin/ka/jou
kin/ship
kip/per
kit/bag
kit/chen
kitch/en/ette
kit/ten
kit/ti/wake
klep/to/mania
knap/sack
knee/cap
knick/er/bock/ers
knick/ers
knight/hood
knit/ting
knit/ware
knob/ker/rie
knock/out
know/ingly
know/ledge
ko/ala
koo/ka/burra
ku/dos
Ku/wait
la/bel
la/bor/at/ory
la/bori/ous
la/bour la/bor (US)
lab/ra/dor
la/bur/num
laby/rinth
la/cer/ate
la/cer/ation
lach/ry/mose
lacka/dais/ical

lack/lustre
lack/luster (US)
lac/onic
lac/quer
la/crosse
lac/tate
lac/tif/er/ous
lad/der
lady/bird lady/bug
  (US)
lady/killer
lady/like
lady/ship
la/goon
lam/bast
lamb/skin
la/ment
la/ment/able
lam/in/ated
lamp/light
lam/poon
lamp/shade
land/fall
land/lady
land/lord
land/lubber
land/mark
land/owner
land/scape
land/slide
lan/guage
lan/guid
lan/guish
lan/guor
lan/olin
lan/tern

lan/yard
lap/dog
lap/wing
lar/ceny
lar/der
lar/gesse
lar/yn/gi/tis
lar/ynx
las/ci/vi/ous
lash/ing
lassi/tude
latch/key
late/comer
late/ness
la/tent
lat/eral
la/tex
lati/tude
lat/rine
lat/ter
lat/tice
laud/able
lau/da/num
laugh/able
laugh/ter
laun/d(e)rette
laun/dro/mat
laun/dry
laur/eate
lav/at/ory
lav/en/der
lav/ish
law/ful
law/less
law/suit
law/yer

lawn/mower
lax/at/ive
lay/about
lay/man
lay/out
lazi/ness
lazy/bones
leader/ship
leafi/ness
leaf/let
leak/age
lean/ing
lean/ness
leap/frog
learn/ing
lease/hold
leath/ery
Leb/anon
lech/er/ous
lec/tern
lec/ture
led/ger
lee/ward
lee/way
left/overs
leg/acy
leg/al/ity
leg/ate
lega/tee
leg/ation
le/gend
leg/gings
leg/gy
le/gible
le/gib/il/ity
le/gion

le/gis/late
le/gis/la/ture
le/git/im/acy
le/git/im/ize
leg/ume
leis/ure
lem/on/ade
le/mur
length/ily
lengthi/ness
length/ways
le/ni/ency
len/ten
len/til
leo/pard
leo/tard
lepi/dop/ter/ist
lep/rosy
les/bian
les/see
les/sen
les/son
let/down
leth/argy
let/out
let/ter
let/ter/box
let/ter/head
let/ter/press
let/tuce
leu/kae/mia
leu/ke/mia (US)
lever/age
lev/eret
lev/it/ate
lev/ity

275

lexi/co/grapher
lexi/co/graphy
lex/icon
li/able
li/aison
li/ba/tion
li/bel
libel/lous
lib/eral
lib/er/al/ism
lib/er/ate
li/bido
lib/rary
lib/retto
li/cence
li/cense
li/cen/ti/ate
li/cen/ti/ous
li/chen
lic/orice (US)
lieu/te/nant
life/belt
life/boat
life/guard
life/jacket
life/less
life/like
life/long
life/time
liga/ment
liga/ture
light/house
light/ness
light/ning
light/weight
like/able

like/li/hood
like/ness
like/wise
li/lac
lim/ber
lime/light
lim/er/ick
lime/stone
lim/ous/ine
limi/ta/tion
lim/pet
lim/pid
limp/ness
linc/tus
lin/ear
lines/man
lin/ger
lin/gerie
lin/guist
lini/ment
lin/ing
link/age
link/man
lin/net
li/no/leum
lin/seed
lin/tel
lion/ess
lip/stick
lique/fac/tion
li/quefy
li/queur
li/quid
li/qui/date
li/quid/ity
li/qui/dizer

li/quor/ice
lis/ten
list/less
lit/any
lit/er/acy
lit/eral
li/ter/ary
lit/er/ate
lit/er/at/ure
li/tho/graph
li/ti/gant
li/ti/gate
li/tig/ious
lit/mus
lit/ter
lit/tle
lit/toral
lit/urgy
live/li/hood
live/li/ness
liv/ery
live/stock
liz/ard
loath/some
lob/ster
lo/cale
lo/cal/ity
lo/cate
lock/out
lock/smith
lock/up
lo/co/mo/tion
lo/co/mo/tive
lo/cust
lode/stone
lodg/ing

lo/ess
lofti/ness
lo/gan/berry
log/ar/ithm
log/book
log/ger/heads
logi/cal
lo/gis/tics
loin/cloth
loi/ter
lol/li/pop
lone/li/ness
lon/gev/ity
lon/gi/tude
long/shore/man
long/stand/ing
loo/fah
look/out
loop/hole
loose/leaf
lo/qua/cious
lo/quacity
lord/li/ness
lord/ship
lo/tion
lot/tery
loud/ness
loud/speaker
lour/ing
lov/able
love/li/ness
love/sick
low/brow
low/down
lower/ing
low/land

loy/ally
loy/alty
loz/enge
lub/ri/cant
lub/ri/cate
lu/cerne
lu/cid
luc/ra/tive
lu/di/crous
lug/gage
lug/hole
lu/gu/bri/ous
luke/warm
lul/laby
lum/bago
lum/ber
lum/ber/jack
lum/in/ous
lun/acy
lun/cheon
lunch/time
lu/pin
lus/cious
lus/trous
lux/uri/ance
lux/uri/ate
lux/uri/ously
lux/ury
lyri/cism
ma/cabre
ma/car/oni
ma/car/oon
ma/caw
ma/cerate
ma/chete
mach/in/ation

ma/chine
ma/chin/ery
ma/chin/ist
mack/erel
mack/in/tosh
mac/ro/bio/tic
mad/cap
mad/den
ma/deira
mad/house
mad/man
mad/ness
ma/donna
mad/ri/gal
mael/strom
maes/tro
mag/a/zine
ma/genta
mag/got
ma/gic
ma/gis/ter/ial
ma/gis/trate
mag/nan/im/ity
mag/nani/mous
mag/nate
mag/nes/ium
mag/net
mag/net/ism
mag/net/ize
mag/neto
mag/ni/fi/cation
mag/ni/fi/cent
mag/nify
mag/ni/tude
mag/nolia
mag/num

mag/pie
ma/hog/any
mai/den
mai/den/hair
mail/bag
mail/box
mail/man
main/land
main/spring
main/stay
main/stream
main/tain
main/ten/ance
mais/on/ette
ma/jes/tic
ma/jesty
ma/jor/ette
ma/jor/ity
make/shift
make/weight
mala/chite
mal/ad/jus/ted
mal/adroit
mal/ady
mal/aise
mal/a/prop/ism
mal/aria
Ma/lay/sia
mal/ed/ic/tion
mal/ev/ol/ence
mal/for/ma/tion
mal/func/tion
mal/ice
ma/lign
ma/lig/nancy
ma/lin/ger

mal/lard
mal/le/able
mal/let
mal/low
mal/nu/tri/tion
mal/odor/ous
mal/prac/tice
mal/treat
mam/mal
mam/mary gland
mam/moth
man/acle
man/age
man/age/ment
man/ager/ess
mana/gerial
man/da/rin
man/date
man/dible
man/do/lin
man/fully
man/gan/ese
man/ger
man/grove
man/handle
man/hole
man/hood
mani/cure
mani/curist
mani/fest
mani/fes/ta/tion
mani/festo
mani/fold
man/ipu/late
man/li/ness
man/ne/quin

man/ner
man/nish
man/oeuvre
man/euver (US)
man/power
man/sard
man/slaugh/ter
man/sion
man/tel/piece
man/tle
man/ual
man/u/fac/ture
man/ure
man/u/script
map/ping
mara/thon
mar/aud
mar/auder
mar/ble
mar/chion/ess
mar/gar/ine
mar/gin
mar/ginal
mar/guer/ite
mari/gold
mari/juana
mar/ina
mar/in/ade
mar/ine
mar/ion/ette
mar/ital
mari/time
mar/joram
mark/edly
mar/ket
mar/ket/able

marks/man
mar/ma/lade
mar/mo/set
mar/mot
mar/oon
mar/quee
mar/quetry
mar/riage
mar/riage/able
mar/row
mar/ry
mar/shal
marsh/mallow
mar/su/pial
mar/ten
mar/tial
mar/tin
mar/tinet
mar/tin/gale
mar/tini
mar/tyr
mar/vel
mar/vel/lous
mar/zi/pan
mas/cara
mas/cot
mas/cu/line
maso/chism
maso/chist
ma/son
mas/onic
mas/onry
mas/quer/ade
mas/sacre
mas/sage
mas/sif

mas/sive
mas/tec/tomy
mas/ter
mas/ter/ful
mas/terly
mas/ter/mind
mas/ter/piece
mas/ter/stroke
mast/head
mas/ti/cate
mas/tiff
mas/titis
mas/toid
mas/tur/bate
mata/dor
match/box
match/less
match/maker
match/stalk (US)
match/stick
match/wood
ma/ter/ial
ma/ter/ial/ist
ma/ter/ial/ize
ma/ter/nal
ma/ter/nity
math/ema/tician
math/e/matics
mat/inée
mat/ins
mat/ri/arch
mat/ri/cide
mat/ricu/late
mat/ri/mo/nial
mat/ri/mony
mat/rix

mat/ron
mat/ter
mat/ting
mat/tress
ma/ture
maud/lin
maun/der
mau/so/leum
mav/er/ick
mawk/ish
maxi/mize
max/imum
may/day
may/hem
may/on/naise
may/oress
may/pole
mea/dow
meagre/ness
meager/ness (US)
me/an/der
mean/ing/ful
mean/ing/less
mean/ness
mean/time
mean/while
meas/ur/able
meas/ure/ment
meas/ure
mech/anic
mech/an/ics
mech/an/ism
mech/an/ize
med/al/lion
med/dle
me/dia

279

me/di/ate
me/di/ator
med/ical
me/di/cated
me/di/cinal
me/di/cine
me/di/eval
me/di/ocre
me/di/oc/rity
me/di/tate
me/dium
med/lar
med/ley
meek/ness
meet/ing
me/ga/cycle
me/ga/lith
me/ga/lo/mania
me/ga/phone
mega/ton
mel/an/choly
mel/low
mel/low/ness
mel/odic
melo/drama
melo/dra/matic
mel/odious
mel/ody
melt/ing
mem/ber
mem/brane
me/men/to
mem/oir
mem/or/able
mem/or/an/dum
mem/or/ial

mem/ory
men/ace
men/ag/erie
men/da/cious
men/da/city
men/di/cant
men/folk
me/nial
men/in/gitis
meno/pause
men/strual
men/stru/ate
mens/wear
men/tal
men/tal/ity
men/tion
men/tor
mer/can/tile
mer/cen/ary
mer/cer
mer/chan/dise
mer/chant
mer/chant/man
merci/ful
mer/ci/less
mer/cury
mere/tri/cious
mer/gan/ser
mer/id/ian
me/ringue
me/rino
mer/it
mer/maid
mer/ri/ment
mer/ry
merry/maker

mes/mer/ize
mes/sage
mes/sen/ger
meta/bolic
met/ab/olism
meta/carpus
me/tal/lic
me/tal/lur/gist
me/tal/work
meta/mor/phose
meta/mor/pho/sis
meta/phor
meta/phori/cal
meta/phy/sics
meta/tarsus
met/eor
met/eoric
met/eor/ite
met/eor/ology
me/thane
met/eor/olo/gist
methy/lated spi/rits
meth/odi/cal
met/icu/lous
met/ri/cal
met/ri/cate
met/ro/nome
met/rop/olis
met/ro/poli/tan
met/tle
Mex/ico
mez/zan/ine floor
mi/asma
Mich/ael/mas daisy
mi/crobe
mi/cro/cosm

mi/cro/fiche
mi/cro/film
mi/cro/light
mi/cron
mi/cro/phone
mi/cro/scope
mi/cro/wave
mid/day
mid/dle
mid/dle/weight
mid/dling
mid/get
mid/land
mid/night
mid/riff
mid/ship/man
mid/stream
mid/sum/mer
mid/way
mid/wife
mid/winter
mi/graine
mi/grant
mi/grate
mi/gra/tion
mil/dew
mild/ness
mile/age
mile/stone
mi/li/tant
mi/li/tancy
mi/li/tar/ism
mi/li/tary
mi/li/tate
mil/itia
milk/man

mill/pond
mill/stone
mil/len/nium
mil/let
mil/li/gram
mil/li/metre
mil/li/meter (US)
mil/liner
mil/lion
mil/li/pede
mim/icry
mim/osa
min/aret
mince/meat
min/cing
mind/ful
mind/less
mine/field
mine/layer
min/eral
min/er/al/ogist
min/es/trone
mine/sweeper
min/ia/ture
mini/bus
min/im/ize
min/imum
min/ion
mini/skirt
min/ister
min/is/ter/ial
min/is/ter/ing
min/is/try
min/now
min/ster
min/strel

min/uet
min/us/cule
mi/nute (*adj*)
min/ute (*n*)
mi/nute/ness
mi/nu/tiae
mir/acle
mir/acu/lous
mir/age
mir/ror
mis/ad/ven/ture
mis/an/thrope
mis/an/thropic
mis/apply
mis/ap/pre/hend
mis/ap/pre/hen/
  sion
mis/ap/pro/pri/ate
mis/be/have
mis/be/hav/iour
mis/cal/cu/late
mis/car/riage
mis/carry
mis/cast
mis/cel/lan/eous
mis/chance
mis/chief
mis/chiev/ous
mis/con/cep/tion
mis/con/duct
mis/con/struc/tion
mis/con/strue
mis/count
mis/creant
mis/cue
mis/deed

mis/de/mean/our
mis/de/meanor (US)
mis/di/rect
mis/er/able
mi/ser/li/ness
mis/ery
mis/fire
mis/fit
mis/for/tune
mis/giv/ing
mis/guided
mis/hap
mis/in/form
mis/in/ter/pret
mis/judge
mis/lay
mis/lead
mis/man/age
mis/nomer
mis/ogy/nist
mis/place
mis/print
mis/pro/nounce
mis/pro/nun/ci/
  ation
mis/quo/ta/tion
mis/quote
mis/read
mis/rep/re/sent
mis/sal
mis/sel
mis/shapen
mis/sile
mis/sing
mis/sion
mis/sion/ary

mis/sive
mis/spell
mis/state/ment
mis/sus
mis/take
mis/taken
mis/ter
mis/time
mis/tle/toe
mis/took
mis/tress
mis/trust
mis/un/der/stand
mis/use
miti/gate
mit/ten
mix/ture
mne/monic
mo/bile
mo/bil/ity
mo/bil/iz/ation
mo/bil/ize
moc/casins
mock/ery
mock/ing
mock/ing/bird
mod/er/ate
mod/er/ation
mod/er/ator
mod/ern
mod/er/nity
mod/ern/ize
mod/est
mod/icum
mod/ify
mod/ish

mod/ulate
modu/lar
mod/ule
mo/hair
moist/ness
moist/ure
mo/lar
mo/las/ses
mole/cule
mole/skin
mo/lest
mol/lify
mol/lusc mol/lusk
  (US)
mol/ly/coddle
mo/ment
mo/men/tary
mo/men/tous
mo/men/tum
mon/arch
mon/ar/chic
mon/archy
mon/as/tery
mon/as/tic
Mon/day
mone/tar/ist
mone/tary
money/box
money/lender
mon/gol
mon/gol/ism
mon/goose
mon/grel
mon/itor
mon/key
mono/chrome

mon/ocle
mon/ocu/lar
mon/og/amous
mon/og/amy
mono/gram
mono/graph
mono/lith
mono/logue
mono/mania
mono/nu/cle/osis
mono/phonic
mon/op/ol/ize
mon/op/oly
mono/rail
mono/syl/lable
mono/tone
mon/ot/on/ous
mon/ot/ony
mon/ox/ide
mon/soon
mon/ster
mon/stro/sity
mon/strous
mon/tage
monu/ment
moodi/ness
moon/beam
moon/light
moon/lit
moon/stone
moor/ing
moor/land
mo/ped
mor/aine
mor/ale
mor/al/ist

mor/al/ity
mor/al/ize
mor/ass
mora/tor/ium
mor/bid
mor/bid/ity
mor/dant
mori/bund
morn/ing
mo/rocco
mor/ose
mor/phia
mor/phine
mor/phol/ogy
mor/ris dance
mor/sel
mor/tal
mor/tal/ity
mor/tar
mort/gage
mort/ga/gee
mort/ga/gor
mor/tice
mor/tic/ian
mor/tify
mor/tise
mor/tuary
mo/saic
Mos/lem
mos/quito
mo/tel
moth/balls
moth/eaten
moth/er
moth/er/hood
moth/er/less

mo/tif
mo/tion
mo/ti/vate
mo/tive
mot/ley
mo/tor
motor/bike
motor/boat
motor/cade
motor/car
motor/cycle
motor/ist
motor/ize
motor/way
mot/tled
mouldi/ness
mould/ing
moun/tain
mouse/trap
mous/tache
mus/tache (US)
mouth/ful
mouth/organ
mouth/piece
mouth/wash
mouth/water/ing
mov/able
move/ment
mu/cus
mud/dle
mud/flat
mud/guard
muf/fin
muf/fle
mug/ging
mu/latto

283

mul/berry
mule/teer
mul/let
mul/lion
mul/ti/col/oured
mul/ti/far/ious
mul/ti/na/tional
mul/tiple
mul/ti/pli/cation
mul/ti/pli/city
mul/ti/ply
mul/ti/racial
mul/ti/storey
mul/ti/tude
mul/ti/tu/din/ous
mun/dane
mu/nici/pal
mu/nici/pal/ity
mu/ni/fi/cence
mu/ni/tions
mur/der
mur/derer
mur/der/ess
mur/der/ous
mur/ki/ness
mur/mur
mus/cle
mu/seum
mush/room
mu/sician
Mus/lim
mus/lin
mus/quash
mus/sel
mus/tang
mus/tard

mus/ter
musti/ness
mu/tate
mu/ti/late
mu/tin/eer
mu/tin/ous
mu/tiny
mut/ter
mut/ton
mu/tual
muz/zle
my/opia
my/self
mys/teri/ous
mys/tery
mys/tic
mys/ti/cism
mys/tify
mys/tique
myth/ol/ogy
myxo/ma/to/sis
na/celle
nag/ging
nail/brush
nail-bit/ing
naked/ness
name/less
name/sake
na/palm
naph/tha
nap/kin
nap/ping
nar/cis/sus
nar/cotic
nar/rate
nar/ra/tion

nar/ra/tive
nar/ra/tor
nar/row
na/sal
nas/ti/ness
nas/tur/tium
na/tion
na/tion/al/ist
na/tion/al/ity
na/tion/wide
na/tive
na/tiv/ity
nat/ter
nat/ural
nat/ur/al/ism
nat/ur/al/ist
nat/ur/ally
nat/ure
nat/ur/ism
nat/ur/ist
naugh/ti/ness
nau/sea
nau/seate
nau/seous
nau/tical
nau/ti/lus
navi/gable
navi/gate
navi/gation
navi/gator
Nea/pol/itan
near/ness
neat/ness
neb/ula
nebu/lous
ne/ces/sary

ne/ces/sit/ate
ne/ces/sit/ous
ne/ces/sity
neck/band
neck/lace
neck/tie
nec/ro/mancy
nec/tar
nec/tar/ine
needle/point
need/less
needle/woman
needle/work
ne/far/ious
ne/gate
nega/tive
neg/lect
neg/lect/ful
neg/li/gence
neg/li/gible
ne/go/ti/ate
ne/gro
neigh/bour
neigh/bor (US)
nei/ther
neo/lithic
nep/ot/ism
nerve/less/ness
ner/vous
nest/ling
net/ball
Nether/lands
nether/most
net/ting
net/tle
net/work

neu/ral/gia
neur/ol/ogist
neur/ol/ogy
neu/ro/sis
neur/otic
neu/ter
neu/tral
neu/tral/ity
neu/tra/lize
neu/tron
never/more
never/the/less
new/born
new/comer
new/fangled
new/ness
news/agent
news/caster
news/letter
news/man
news/paper
news/print
news/reel
news/worthy
new/ton
nib/ble
nice/ness
ni/cety
nick/name
ni/co/tine
Ni/geria
nig/gardly
nig/gle
nig/gling
night/cap
night/clothes

night/dress
night/in/gale
night/mare
night/shade
nim/ble
nim/bus
nin/com/poop
nine/pins
nine/teen
nine/ti/eth
nip/per
nip/ple
ni/trate
ni/tro/gen
nit/wit
nob/ble
no/bil/ity
no/ble
noble/man
no/body
noc/tur/nal
noc/turne
nod/ule
noise/less
nois/ily
no/mad
no/men/cla/ture
nom/inal
nom/in/ate
nom/inee
non/a/gen/arian
non-ag/gres/sion
non-al/co/holic
non/align/ment
non/chal/ance
non/chal/ant

non/com/bat/ant
non-com/mis/sioned
non-com/mit/tal
non/con/form/ist
non/de/script
non/en/tity
non/ex/ist/ent
non-fic/tion
non-pay/ment
non/plussed
non-re/fund/able
non-resi/dent
non-re/turn/able
non/sense
non/sen/si/cal
non-smo/ker
non-star/ter
non-vio/lence
nor/mal
nor/mal/ity
north/bound
north/ern
north/ward
Nor/way
nose/bag
nose/bleed
nose/dive
nose/gay
nos/tal/gia
nos/tril
not/ab/il/ity
not/able
not/ary
no/ta/tion
note/book
note/case

note/paper
note/worthy
noth/ing
noth/ing/ness
no/tice
no/tice/able
no/ti/fi/able
no/tify
no/tor/iety
no/tor/ious
not/with/standing
nour/ish
nour/ish/ment
nov/elty
No/vem/ber
nov/ice
now/a/days
no/where
nox/ious
noz/zle
nu/bile
nu/clear
nu/cleus
nu/dism
nu/dist
nu/ga/tory
nug/get
nuis/ance
nul/lify
num/ber
num/ber/less
numb/ness
numb/skull
num/er/acy
nu/me/ral
nu/meri/cal

nu/mer/ous
nu/mis/mat/ics
nu/mis/ma/tist
nup/tial
nurse/maid
nur/sery
nur/sery/man
nur/ture
nut/case
nut/crack/ers
nut/meg
nut/shell
nu/tri/ent
nu/tri/ment
nu/tri/tious
nu/tri/tive
nuz/zle
ny/lon
nym/pho/mania
nym/pho/maniac
oaf/ish
oast/house
oat/cake
oat/meal
ob/dur/acy
ob/dur/ate
obedi/ence
obedi/ent
ob/el/isk
ob/fus/cate
obit/uary
ob/ject
ob/jec/tion
ob/jec/tive
ob/jec/tor
ob/late

286

ob/lig/at/ory
ob/lige
ob/lig/ing
ob/lique
ob/lit/er/ate
ob/liv/ion
ob/long
ob/nox/ious
obo/ist
ob/scene
ob/scure
ob/scur/ity
ob/sequi/ous
ob/serv/ance
ob/ser/va/tory
ob/serve
ob/ser/ver
ob/sess
ob/ses/ive
ob/so/les/cent
ob/so/lete
ob/stacle
ob/stet/ric
ob/stet/rician
ob/stin/ate
ob/strep/er/ous
ob/struct
ob/struc/tive
ob/tain
ob/trude
ob/tru/sive
ob/tuse
ob/verse
ob/vi/ate
ob/vi/ous
oc/ca/sion

oc/cas/ional
oc/ci/dent
oc/cult
oc/cu/pant
oc/cu/pation
oc/cupy
oc/cur
oc/cur/rence
ocean/ography
oc/ta/gon
oc/tane
oc/tave
oc/tavo
oc/tet
Oc/to/ber
oc/to/gen/ar/ian
oc/to/pus
oc/u/lar
odd/ment
odi/ous
odo/meter
odor/ous
odour/less
Oed/ipus com/plex
oeso/phagus
of/fal
off/cut
of/fence
of/fen/sive
of/fer
of/fice
of/fi/cial
of/ficial/ese
of/fi/cious
of/fing
off-li/cence

off/set
off/shore
off/side
off/spring
off/stage
of/ten
oil/field
oil/rig
oil/skin
oil/slick
oil/tan/ker
oint/ment
old-fash/ioned
ol/fac/tory
oli/garchy
ol/ive
Olym/pic
om/buds/man
om/elette
om/in/ous
om/ni/bus
om/ni/po/tence
om/nis/cient
om/niv/or/ous
on/coming
on/er/ous
one/self
one-up/man/ship
on/ion
on/looker
on/rush
on/set
on/slaught
on/ward
opa/city
opal/es/cent

open/cast
open/ing
open/ness
op/era
oper/able
oper/ate
oper/atic
oper/ative
oper/ator
oph/thal/mic
oph/thal/mol/ogist
op/in/ion
op/os/sum
op/po/nent
op/por/tune
op/por/tun/ist
op/pose
op/po/site
op/press
op/pres/sor
op/pro/brium
op/ti/cal
op/tic/ian
op/tim/ism
op/ti/mist
op/ti/mum
op/tion
op/to/metrist (US)
opu/lence
or/acle
or/ange
orange/ade
or/ang-ut/ang
ora/tion
ora/tori/cal
ora/torio

or/bit
or/chard
or/ches/tra
or/ches/trate
or/chid
or/chis
or/dain
or/deal
or/der
or/der/li/ness
or/di/nal
or/di/nance
or/din/ary
or/din/ation
ord/nance
or/gan
or/gan/ism
or/gan/ist
or/gan/ize
or/gasm
ori/ent
ori/ental
ori/en/tate
ori/en/teer/ing
ori/fice
ori/gin
ori/ginal
ori/gin/ate
ori/gin/ator
ori/ole
or/na/ment
or/nate
orn/ith/ol/ogist
orn/ith/ology
or/phan
or/phan/age

or/tho/dox
or/tho/graphy
or/tho/paedic
os/cil/late
os/ier
os/mo/sis
os/prey
os/sify
os/ten/sible
os/ten/ta/tious
os/teo/arth/ritis
os/teo/path
os/tra/cism
os/tra/cize
os/trich
other/wise
other/worldly
ot/ter
ot/to/man
our/selves
out/back
out/bid
out/board
out/break
out/build/ings
out/burst
out/cast
out/cry
out/dated
out/doors
out/er/most
out/fit
out/going
out/grow
out/ing
out/land/ish

out/last
out/law
out/lay
out/line
out/live
out/look
out/lying
out/man/oeuvre
out/man/euver (US)
out/moded
out/number
out/patient
out/post
out/pour/ings
out/put
out/rage
out/ra/geous
out/rider
out/right
out/set
out/shine
out/side
out/size
out/skirts
out/smart
out/spo/ken
out/stand/ing
out/stay
out/vote
out/ward
out/weigh
out/wit
ova/tion
over/all
over/awe
over/bal/ance

over/bear/ing
over/board
over/cast
over/charge
over/coat
over/come
over/crowded
over/dose
over/draft
over/draw
over/eat
over/es/ti/mate
over/ex/posed
over/fed
over/flow
over/grown
over/hang/ing
over/haul
over/head
over/heat
over/joyed
over/land
over/lap
over/leaf
over/load
over/look
over/night
over/pass
over/play
over/power
over/pro/duc/tion
over/rate
over/reach
over/re/act
over/ride
over/rule

over/run
over/seas
over/seer
over/shadow
over/shoes
over/shoot
over/sight
over/sleep
over/spend
over/state
over/step
over/stuffed
over/sub/scribed
over/take
over/tax
over/throw
over/time
over/tones
over/ture
over/turn
over/view
over/ween/ing
over/weight
over/whelm
over/work
over/wrought
ovu/late
own/er/ship
ox/ide
ox/id/ize
oxy/acet/yl/ene
oxy/gen
oy/ster
pace/ma/ker
pace/set/ter
pachy/derm

pa/ci/fier
pa/ci/fism
paci/fist
pa/cify
pack/age
pack/ing
pad/ding
pad/dle
pad/dock
pad/dy field
pad/lock
pae/dia/tri/cian
pa/gan
pag/eant
pag/in/ate
pa/goda
pain/ful
pain/kil/ler
pain/less
pains/taking
paint/work
pa/jamas (US)
Pak/istan
pal/ace
pal/at/able
pal/ate
pa/la/tial
pal/at/ine
pal/aver
pale/ness
pal/eo/lithic
Pal/es/tine
pal/ette
pal/in/drome
pal/ing(s)
pal/is/ade

pall/bearer
pal/let
pal/li/ate
pal/lia/tive
pal/lid
pal/lor
pal/mate
pal/mis/try
pal/pable
pal/pi/tate
pal/try
pam/pas
pam/per
pamph/let
pana/cea
pan/ache
pan/cake
pan/chro/matic
pan/creas
pan/demic
pan/de/mo/nium
pan/der
pan/egyric
pan/el/list
pan/nier
pan/oply
pan/or/ama
pan/ta/loons
pan/theism
pan/ther
pan/ties
pan/to/graph
pan/to/mime
pan/try
pa/pacy
pa/per

paper/back
paper/chase
paper/clip
paper/knife
paper/weight
pap/rika
pa/py/rus
par/able
para/bola
para/bolic
para/chute
par/ade
para/dise
para/dox
par/af/fin
para/gon
para/graph
para/keet
par/al/lax
par/al/lel
par/al/lel/ogram
para/lyse
par/alytic
para/meter
para/military
para/mount
para/noia
par/an/oiac
par/an/oid
para/pet
para/pher/na/lia
para/phrase
para/plegia
para/site
para/sol
para/trooper

par/boil
par/cel
parch/ment
par/don
par/ent
par/en/tage
par/en/the/sis
pa/ri/ah
pa/ri/etal
par/ish
par/ish/ioner
par/ity
par/lance
par/ley
par/lia/ment
par/lia/men/tar/ian
par/lour par/lor
  (US)
pa/ro/chial
par/ody
par/ole
par/oxysm
par/quet
par/ri/cide
par/rot
par/ry
par/sec
par/si/mony
pars/ley
pars/nip
par/son
par/take
par/ting
par/terre
par/tial
par/ti/ci/pant

par/ti/ci/pate
par/ti/ci/pa/tory
par/ti/ciple
par/ticle
par/ti/col/oured
par/tic/ular
par/ti/san
par/ti/tion
part/ner
par/tner/ship
part/ridge
par/tur/ition
pass/able
pas/sage
pass/book
pas/sen/ger
pas/sion
pas/sion/ate
pas/sive
pas/siv/ity
pass/over
pass/port
pass/word
pas/tel
pas/teur/ize
pas/tiche
pas/tille
pas/time
pas/tor
pas/try
pas/ture
patch/work
pa/tent
pa/ten/tee
pa/ter/nal
pa/ter/nity

pa/thetic
path/fin/der
path/ogen
path/ol/ogy
pa/thos
path/way
pa/tience
pa/tient
pat/ina
pa/tis/serie
pat/ois
pat/rial
pat/ri/arch
pat/ri/cian
pat/ri/cide
pat/ri/mony
pat/riot
par/riot/ism
pat/rol
pat/rol/man
pat/ron
pat/ron/age
pat/ron/ize
pat/ter
pat/tern
pau/city
pau/per
pave/ment
pav/il/ion
pay/able
pay/check
pay/load
pay/master
pay/ment
pay/roll
peace/able

291

peace/ful
peace/maker
pea/cock
pea/nut
pea/sant
peb/ble
pec/ca/dillo
peck/ish
pec/tin
pec/toral
pecu/late
pe/cu/liar
pe/cu/li/arity
pe/cu/ni/ary
peda/gogi/cal
ped/ant
ped/an/tic
ped/dle
ped/es/tal
ped/es/trian
pe/dia/trician
pedi/cure
pedi/gree
ped/lar
peel/ings
peep/hole
peer/age
pee/wit
pej/ora/tive
pel/ican
pel/let
pel/met
pe/nal
pe/nal/ize
pen/alty
pen/ance

pen/chant
pen/cil
pen/dant
pen/ding
pen/du/lum
pen/etrate
pen/etra/tion
pen/guin
pe/ni/cil/lin
pen/in/sula
pen/in/sular
peni/tent
peni/ten/tiary
pen/knife
pen/ni/less
penny/worth
pen/sion
pen/sive
pen/ta/gon
pen/tag/onal
pen/tath/lon
pent/house
pen/ul/tim/ate
pen/um/bra
pen/ury
pe/ony
pep/per
pep/per/corn
pep/per/mill
pep/per/mint
pep/tic
per/am/bu/lator
per/ceive
per/cen/tile
per/cep/tible
per/cep/tive

per/co/late
per/cus/sion
pere/grine
per/emp/tory
per/en/nial
per/fect
per/fec/tion
per/fidy
per/for/ate
per/form
per/form/ance
per/fume
per/func/tory
per/haps
peri/lous
peri/meter
peri/odic
peri/pat/etic
peri/pheral
peri/phery
peri/scope
per/ish
per/ish/ables
peri/ton/itis
peri/winkle
per/jure
per/ma/nency
per/ma/nent
per/man/gan/ate
per/me/able
per/me/ate
per/miss/ible
per/mis/sion
per/mit
per/mu/ta/tion
per/ni/cious

per/nick/ety
per/ox/ide
per/pen/dic/ular
per/pe/trate
per/pet/ual
per/petu/ate
per/petu/ity
per/plex
per/quis/ite
per/se/cute
per/se/vere
per/sist
per/sis/tent
per/son
per/son/able
per/sonal
per/son/al/ity
per/soni/fi/cation
per/son/nel
per/spec/tive
per/spex
per/spic/acious
per/spic/acity
per/spi/cu/ity
per/spire
per/suade
per/suas/ive
per/tain
per/ti/na/cious
per/tin/ent
per/turb
per/use
per/vade
per/vas/ive
per/verse
per/vert

pes/sary
pes/si/mism
pes/ti/cide
pes/til/ence
pe/tard
pe/tite
pe/ti/tion
pet/rel
pet/rify
pet/ro/chem/ical
pet/ro/dollar
pet/rol
pet/ro/leum
pet/ti/coat
pet/ti/ness
pet/u/lant
pe/tunia
pew/ter
phal/anx
phal/lus
phan/tom
phar/ma/ceu/ti/cal
phar/ma/cist
phar/ma/co/poeia
phar/macy
phar/yn/gitis
phar/ynx
phea/sant
phe/nom/enon
phil/an/thro/pist
phil/an/thropy
phil/at/ely
phil/har/monic
Phil/ip/pines
phil/is/tine
phil/lum/en/ist

philo/logical
philo/logy
philo/soph/ical
philo/sophy
phle/bi/tis
pho/bia
pho/netic
pho/ney
pho/no/graph
phos/phate
phos/phor
phos/phor/es/cence
phos/phorus
photo/copy
photo/elec/tric
photo/genic
photo/graph
photo/stat
phras/eology
phren/ol/ogy
phys/ical
phys/ician
phys/ics
physi/og/nomy
physi/ology
physio/ther/apy
phys/ique
pian/ist
pi/ano
piano/forte
pian/ola
pi/azza
pic/ar/esque
pic/ca/lilli
pic/colo
pick/axe

pick/pocket
pic/nic
pic/to/graph
pic/tor/ial
pic/ture
pictur/esque
pid/gin
pie/bald
piece/meal
piece/work
pi/geon
pi/geon/hole
piggy/back
piggy/bank
pig/let
pig/ment
pig/skin
pig/sty
pig/tail
pike/man
pil/as/ter
pil/chard
pile/driver
pil/fer
pil/grim
pil/grim/age
pil/lage
pil/lar
pill/box
pil/lion
pil/low
pil/low/case
pil/low/slip
pi/lot
pim/ento pim/iento
  (US)

pim/ple
pin/afore
pin/ball
pin/cers
pin/cush/ion
pine/apple
pin/ion
pink/eye
pin/nace
pin/nacle
pin/nate
pin/point
pin/prick
pin/stripe
pi/on/eer
pipe/line
pi/per
pip/ette
pi/ping
pi/quant
pi/ranha
pi/rate
pi/rati/cal
pir/ou/ette
Pis/ces
pis/tachio
pis/til
pis/tol
pis/ton
pit/cher
pitch/fork
pit/eous
pit/fall
pit/head
piti/able
pit/iful

piti/less
pit/tance
pit/ter/pat/ter
pi/tu/it/ary
plac/ard
pla/cid/ity
pla/cate
pla/cebo
pla/centa
pla/cid
pla/gi/ar/ism
pla/gi/ar/ize
plain/clothes
plain/ness
plain/tiff
plain/tive
plan/et/ar/ium
plank/ton
plan/ning
plan/tain
plan/ta/tion
plas/ter
plas/tic
plat/eau
plate/layer
plate/let
plat/form
plat/inum
plat/it/ude
pla/toon
plat/ter
platy/pus
plau/dits
plaus/ible
play/boy
play/ful

play/ground
play/group
play/thing
play/time
play/wright
pleas/ant
pleas/antry
pleas/ure
pleb/is/cite
plec/trum
plen/ary
ple/ni/po/ten/ti/ary
pleni/tude
plen/teous
plen/ti/ful
pleth/ora
pleur/isy
pli/able
pli/ant
pli/ers
plim/solls
plough/man
plug/hole
plu/mage
plumb/line
plum/met
plun/der
plu/ral
plu/to/crat
plu/to/nium
ply/wood
pneu/matic
pneu/monia
pocket/ful
pod/ium
poe/tic

pog/rom
poign/ancy
poign/ant
poin/set/tia
point/edly
point/less
poi/son
poi/son/ous
Pol/and
po/lar
pole/axe
pole/cat
po/lemic
po/lice
po/lice/man
po/lice/woman
pol/icy
po/lio/my/el/itis
pol/ish
Pol/ish
pol/ite
pol/ite/ness
pol/iti/cal
pol/it/ician
pol/it/ics
pol/len
pol/lin/ate
pol/ling
pol/lute
pol/ter/geist
poly/an/thus
poly/ester
poly/gam/ist
poly/gam/ous
poly/gamy
poly/glot

poly/gon
poly/mer
poly/sty/rene
poly/syl/lable
poly/tech/nic
poly/thene
poly/un/sat/ur/ated
poly/ure/thane
po/man/der
pome/gran/ate
pom/mel
pom/pom
pom/pous
pon/cho
pon/der
pon/tiff
pon/tifi/cate
pon/toon
pony/tail
poor/ness
pop/lar
pop/lin
popu/lace
popu/lar
popu/lar/ity
popu/late
por/cel/ain
por/cu/pine
por/no/graphic
por/nog/raphy
por/ous
por/poise
por/ridge
port/able
por/tal
port/cul/lis

295

portent

por/tent
por/ter
port/fo/lio
port/hole
por/tico
por/tion
por/trait
por/trait/ure
por/tray
Por/tu/gal
pos/eur
po/si/tion
pos/it/ive
pos/sess
pos/ses/sive
pos/sib/il/ity
pos/sible
post/age
post/box
post/code
post/date
pos/ter/ior
post/er/ity
post/gradu/ate
post/hum/ous
post/man
post/mark
post/mas/ter
post/mis/tress
post/pone
post/pone/ment
post/script
pos/tu/late
pos/ture
post/war
pot/ash

pot/as/sium
po/tato
po/tency
po/ten/tate
po/ten/tial
po/ten/ti/ometer
po/tion
pot/shot
pot/ter
poul/tice
poul/try
pound/age
pov/erty
pow/der
power/ful
power/less
pow/wow
prac/tic/able
prac/tical
prac/ti/cality
prac/tice
prac/tise
prac/ti/tioner
prag/matic
praise/worthy
pre/amble
pre/bend/ary
pre/car/ious
pre/cau/tion
pre/cede
pre/ce/dent
pre/cept
pre/cinct
pre/cious
pre/ci/pice
pre/cipi/tate

pre/cipi/tous
pré/cis
pre/cise
pre/clude
pre/co/cious
pre/co/city
pre/con/ceive
pre/con/cep/tion
pre/cur/sor
pre/date
pre/dator
pre/de/cease
pre/de/ces/sor
pre/des/tine
pre/de/ter/mine
pre/dica/ment
pre/dict
pre/dict/able
pre/di/lec/tion
pre/dis/pose
pre/dis/po/si/tion
pre/dom/in/ant
pre/dom/in/ate
pre-emi/nent
pre-emp/tive
pre/fab/ri/cated
pre/face
pre/fect
pre/fer
pre/fer/able
pre/fer/en/tial
pre/fer/ment
pre/fix
preg/nancy
preg/nant
pre/hen/sile

296

pre/his/tory
pre/judge
pre/judice
pre/ju/dicial
pre/late
pre/lim/in/ary
pre/lude
prem/ature
pre/med/it/ate
prem/ier
prem/ière
pre/mise
pre/mises
pre/miss
pre/mium
pre/molar
pre/mon/ition
pre/natal
pre/oc/cu/pa/tion
pre/para/tory
pre/pare
pre/pay
pre/pon/der/ance
prep/osition
pre/pos/ses/sing
pre/pos/ter/ous
pre/requis/ite
pre/rog/at/ive
pres/cient
pre/scribe
pre/scrip/tion
pre/sence
pre/sent
pre/sen/ti/ment
pre/ser/va/tive
pre/serve

pre/side
presi/dent
pres/id/ium
pres/sure
pres/tige
pre/sume
pre/sump/tuous
pre/sup/pose
pre/tence
pre/tend
pre/ten/sion
pre/ten/tious
pre/text
pret/tily
pret/tiness
pret/zel
pre/vail
preva/lent
pre/vari/cate
pre/vent
pre/ven/tive
pre/view
pre/vi/ous
priest/hood
prima bal/ler/ina
pri/mar/ily
pri/mary
pri/mate
prim/eval
prim/it/ive
prim/rose
prim/ula
prin/cipal
prin/ci/pal/ity
prin/ciple
print/ing

prior/ess
pri/or/ity
pris/matic
pri/son
pris/tine
pri/vacy
pri/vate
pri/vation
privi/lege
prob/able
pro/bate
pro/ba/tion
prob/lem
prob/le/mat/ical
pro/bos/cis
pro/ceed
pro/ceeds
pro/cess
pro/claim
proc/la/ma/tion
pro/cliv/ity
pro/cras/tin/ate
pro/cre/ate
pro/cur/ator
pro/cure
prod/igal
pro/dig/ious
prod/igy
prod/uce (*n*)
pro/duce (*v*)
pro/duc/tive
pro/fane
pro/fess
pro/fes/sion
pro/fes/sor
pro/fi/cient

297

pro/file
profit/able
pro/fit/eer
prof/li/gate
pro/forma
pro/found
pro/fund/ity
pro/fuse
pro/geny
pro/ges/ter/one
prog/nos/ti/cate
pro/gramme
pro/gram (US)
pro/gress
pro/gres/sive
pro/hibit
pro/hib/ition
pro/ject
pro/jec/tile
pro/jec/tor
pro/lapse
pro/le/tar/iat
pro/lific
pro/lix
pro/logue
pro/long
pro/lon/gation
prom/en/ade
prom/in/ence
pro/mis/cu/ous
pro/mise
prom/is/sory
prom/on/tory
pro/mote
pro/motion
prom/ul/gate

pro/noun
pro/nounce
pro/nun/ci/ation
pro/pa/ganda
pro/pa/gate
pro/pane
pro/pel
pro/pel/ler
pro/pen/sity
prop/erly
prop/erty
proph/ecy
pro/phetic
pro/phy/lac/tic
pro/phy/laxis
pro/pi/ti/ate
pro/por/tion
pro/por/tion/ate
pro/pose
pro/pound
pro/prie/tary
pro/pri/etor
pro/pri/ety
pro/pul/sion
pro/rogue
pro/saic
pro/scen/ium
pro/scribe
pro/sec/ute
pro/sec/utor
pro/sody
pros/pect
pros/pec/tus
pros/per
pros/per/ity
pros/tate

pros/ti/tute
pros/trate
pro/tag/on/ist
pro/tect
pro/tégé
pro/tein
pro/test
Prot/es/tant
pro/to/col
pro/ton
pro/to/plasm
pro/to/type
pro/trac/ted
pro/trude
pro/tub/er/ance
prov/en/ance
prov/erb
pro/vide
provi/dence
provi/den/tial
prov/ince
prov/in/cial
pro/vis/ion
pro/viso
pro/voca/tive
pro/voke
prow/ess
prox/im/ity
pru/dence
prud/ery
pru/dish/ness
pseph/ology
pseu/do/nym
psy/che/delic
psy/chia/trist
psy/chi/atry

psy/chic
psy/cho/ana/lysis
psy/chol/ogy
psy/cho/path
psy/cho/sis
psy/cho/som/atic
pu/berty
pu/bic
pub/lic
pub/li/can
pub/li/cation
pub/li/cist
pub/lish
pud/ding
pud/dle
puer/ile
puf/fin
pug/il/ist
pug/nac/ious
pul/let
pul/ley
pull/man
pull/over
pul/pit
pul/sar
pul/ver/ize
pum/ice (stone)
pum/mel
pump/kin
punc/tili/ous
punc/tual
punc/tu/ate
punc/ture
pun/dit
pun/gent
pun/ish

pun/net
pun/ter
pu/pate
pu/pil
pup/pet
pup/pet/eer
pur/chase
pur/ga/tory
pur/ify
pur/itan
pur/port
pur/pose
pur/ser
pur/sue
pur/suit
pur/veyor
push/bike
push/chair
push/ing
push/over
pu/sil/lan/im/ous
pussy/cat
pu/ta/tive
pu/trefy
pu/trid
put/ter
puz/zle
py/jamas
py/lon
pyr/amid
pyr/ites
pyro/ma/niac
pyro/tech/nics
py/thon
quad/rangle
quad/rant

quad/ra/phonic
quad/ri/lat/eral
quad/ru/ped
quad/ruple
quad/ru/pli/cate
quag/mire
quali/fi/ca/tion
qual/ify
quan/ti/ta/tive
qual/ity
quan/dary
quan/gos
quan/tify
quan/tity
quan/tum
quar/an/tine
quar/rel
quar/ry
quar/ter
quar/ter/light
quar/tet(te)
quar/to
quat/rain
qua/ver
quay/side
queer/ness
queru/lous
ques/tion
ques/tion/able
ques/tion/naire
quib/ble
quick/lime
quick/sand
quick/silver
qui/es/cent
quiet/ness

quin/ine
quin/tes/sence
quin/tet(te)
quin/tuple
quin/tu/plets
quix/otic
quiz/master
quiz/zical
quo/ta/tion
quo/tient
rab/bini/cal
rab/bit
rab/ble
rac/coon
race/course
race/horse
race/track
ra/cial/ism
ra/cism
rack/et/eer
rac/quet
ra/dar
ra/dial
ra/di/ance
ra/di/ate
ra/di/ator
rad/ical
ra/dio
radio/ac/tive
radi/ogra/pher
radi/ology
radio/ther/apy
rad/ish
rad/ium
rad/ius
raf/fia

raf/fish
raf/fle
raf/ter
ra/ga/muf/fin
rag/lan
rag/out
rail/ings
rail/road (US)
rail/way
rail/way/man
rai/ment
rain/bow
rain/coat
rain/drop
rain/fall
rain/water
rai/sin
ram/ble
rame/kin
ra/mi/fica/tion
ram/page
ram/pant
ram/part
ram/shackle
ran/cid
ran/cour
ran/cor/ous
ran/dom
ran/sack
ran/som
ra/pa/cious
ra/pa/city
ra/pier
rap/ist
rap/port
rap/ture

rap/tur/ous
rare/bit
rare/fied
rar/ing
ras/cal
rasp/berry
rat/chet (wheel)
rate/able
rate/payer
ra/ther
rat/ify
ra/tio
ra/tion
ra/tional
ra/tion/ale
ration/al/ize
rat/tan
rat/tle
rat/tle/snake
rau/cous
rav/age
rav/en/ous
ra/vine
ra/vi/oli
rav/ish
raw/hide
razz/ma/tazz
re/act
re/ac/ti/vate
read/able
re/ad/dress
readi/ness
re/ad/just
re/agent
re/align
real/is/tic

real/ize
real/tor (US)
re/an/im/ate
re/ap/pear
rear/guard
re/arm
re/ar/ma/ment
re/ar/range
rea/son
reas/on/able
re/as/semble
re/as/sure
re/bate
re/bel/lion
re/bound
re/buff
re/build
re/buke
re/but
re/cal/ci/trant
re/call
re/cant
re/cap/itu/late
re/cap/ture
re/cast
re/cede
re/ceipt
re/ceive
re/cent
re/cept/acle
re/cep/tion
re/cep/tion/ist
re/cep/tive
re/cess
re/ces/sion
re/cid/iv/ist

re/cipe
re/cipi/ent
re/cip/ro/cate
reci/pro/city
re/ci/tal
re/cita/tive
re/cite
reck/less
re/claim
re/cline
re/cluse
rec/og/ni/tion
rec/og/nize
rec/og/niz/ance
re/coil
re/col/lect
re/com/mend
re/com/pense
re/com/pose
re/con/cile
re/con/dite
re/con/di/tion
re/con/nais/sance
re/con/noitre
re/con/sider
re/con/sti/tute
re/con/struct
rec/ord (*n*)
re/cord (*v*)
re/count
re/coup
re/course
re/cover
rec/re/ation
re/crim/ina/tion
re/cru/des/cence

re/cruit
rec/tal
rect/angle
rec/tan/gu/lar
rec/tify
rec/ti/tude
rec/tor
rec/tory
rec/tum
re/cum/bent
re/cu/per/ate
re/cur
re/cur/rent
re/cycle
red/cur/rant
re/dec/or/ate
re/deem
re/demp/tion
re/deploy
red/head
red/ol/ent
re/double
re/doubt/able
re/dound
re/dress
re/duce
re/dun/dant
red/wood
re/elect
re/enter
re/fect/ory
re/fer
re/fer/ral
ref/er/en/dum
re/fill
re/fine

re/fin/ery
re/fit
re/flate
re/flect
re/flec/tor
re/flex
re/flex/ive
re/float
re/form
re/for/ma/tory
re/frac/tion
re/fract/ory
re/frain
re/fresh
re/fri/ger/ator
re/fuel
re/fuge
re/fu/gee
re/fund
re/furbish
re/fuse
re/fute
re/gain
re/gal
re/gale
re/galia
re/gard
re/gard/less
re/gatta
re/gen/er/ate
re/gent
ré/gime
re/gi/ment
re/gion
reg/is/ter
reg/is/trar

reg/is/try
re/gress
re/gres/sion
re/gret
re/gret/table
regu/lar
regu/lar/ity
regu/late
re/gur/gi/tate
re/hab/il/it/ate
re/hash
re/hearse
re/im/burse
re/in/car/na/tion
rein/deer
re/in/force
re/in/state
re/it/er/ate
re/ject
re/joice
re/join
re/join/der
re/ju/ven/ate
re/kindle
re/lapse
re/late
re/la/tion
rel/at/ive
re/lat/iv/ity
re/lax
re/lay
re/lease
re/leg/ate
re/lent
rel/ev/ant
re/li/ance

re/li/able
rel/ict
re/lief
re/li/gion
re/lin/quish
re/lish
re/lo/cate
re/luc/tant
re/main
re/mand
re/mark
re/mark/able
re/med/ial
rem/edy
re/mem/ber
re/mem/brance
re/mind
rem/in/is/cence
re/miss
re/mis/sion
re/mit
re/mit/tance
rem/nant
rem/on/strate
re/morse
re/mote
re/mount
re/mov/able
re/move
re/mun/er/ate
re/nais/sance
ren/der
ren/dez/vous
ren/di/tion
ren/eg/ade
renege

re/new
ren/net
re/nounce
ren/ov/ate
re/nown
re/nun/ci/ation
re/open
re/or/gan/ize
re/ori/en/tate
re/paid
re/pair
re/par/ation
re/par/tee
re/pat/ri/ate
re/pay
re/peal
re/peat
re/pe/chage
re/pel
re/pel/lent
re/pent
re/per/cus/sion
rep/er/toire
rep/er/tory
re/pe/ti/tion
re/phrase
re/place
re/play
re/plen/ish
re/plete
rep/lica
rep/li/cate
re/ply
re/port
re/pose
re/posi/tory

re/pos/sess
rep/re/hen/sible
rep/re/sent
rep/re/sen/ta/tive
re/press
re/prieve
rep/ri/mand
re/print
re/pri/sal
re/prise
re/proach
rep/ro/bate
re/pro/duce
re/pro/graphics
re/proof
re/prove
rep/tile
re/pub/lic
re/pu/di/ate
re/pug/nant
re/pulse
re/pul/sive
repu/table
re/pute
repu/tedly
re/quest
re/quiem
re/quire
re/quis/ite
re/quisi/tion
re/run
res/cind
res/cue
re/search
re/semble
re/sent

re/serve
re/ser/vist
res/er/voir
re/shuf/fle
re/side
res/id/en/tial
res/idue
re/sign
resig/na/tion
re/si/li/ent
re/sist
re/sis/tor
re/sit
res/ol/ute
re/solve
res/on/ant
re/sorb
re/sort
re/sound
re/source
re/spect
re/spect/able
re/spect/ful
re/spect/ive
res/pira/tion
re/spire
res/pite
re/splen/dent
re/spond
re/spon/dent
re/spon/sib/il/ity
re/spon/sible
rest/aurant
res/ti/tu/tion
res/tive
rest/less

res/tora/tive
re/store
re/strain
re/straint
re/strict
rest/room
re/sume
re/sume
ré/sumé
re/sur/face
re/sur/gent
re/sur/rect
re/sus/ci/tate
re/tail
re/tain
re/tali/ate
re/tard
re/ten/tion
re/think
re/ti/cent
re/ti/cu/late
ret/ina
ret/inue
re/tire
re/tort
re/touch
re/trace
re/tract
re/tread
re/treat
re/trench
re/trial
re/tri/bu/tion
re/trieve
re/tro/act/ive
re/tro/grade

re/tro/spect
re/turn
re/unify
re/union
re/value
re/vamp
re/veal
re/veille
rev/el/ler
re/venge
rev/enue
re/ver/be/rate
re/vere
re/ver/ence
rev/er/end
rev/erie
re/ver/sal
re/verse
re/vers/ible
re/vert
re/view
re/vile
re/vise
re/vis/ion/ism
re/visit
re/viv/al/ist
re/vive
re/voke
re/volt
re/volu/tion
re/volve
re/vue
re/vul/sion
re/ward
rhap/sody
rheo/stat

rhe/sus
rhet/oric
rheum/at/ism
rheu/ma/toid
rhine/stone
rhi/no/ceros
rho/do/den/dron
rhom/bus
rhu/barb
ri/bald
rib/bon
rich/ness
rick/ets
rick/shaw
ri/co/chet
rid/dance
rid/dle
rider/less
ri/di/cule
ri/di/cu/lous
riff/raff
rig/ging
right/eous
right/ful
right/ness
ri/gid/ity
rig/mar/ole
rig/our
rim/less
ring/leader
ring/let
ring/mas/ter
ring/side
ring/worm
ri/ot/ous
ri/par/ian

rip/cord
ri/poste
rip/ple
ris/ible
ri/sotto
ris/sole
ri/val
river/side
road/block
road/hog
road/side
road/way
road/works
road/worthy
rob/ber
ro/bot
ro/bust
rock/ery
rock/ing
ro/dent
roent/gen
roguish/ness
roll/call
roll/mop
Ro/man
ro/mance
Ro/man/esque
Ro/mania
ro/man/tic
ro/man/ti/cize
Ro/many
rook/ery
room/mate
ro/sary
ros/eate
rose/mary

ros/ette
ros/ter
ros/trum
ro/tate
ro/tor
rot/ten
rot/ter
ro/tund
ro/tunda
rough/age
rough/ness
rough/shod
roul/ette
round/about
roun/del
round/house
roust/about
rou/tine
rov/ing
row/lock
roy/al/ist
roy/alty
rub/ber
rub/bish
rub/ble
ru/bella
ru/bi/cund
rub/ric
ruck/sack
ruc/tions
rud/der
rudi/ments
ruf/fian
ruf/fle
rug/ged
rug/ger

ruin/ous
ru/min/ant
ru/min/ate
rum/mage
ru/mour
rum/pus
run/away
run/down
run/way
rup/ture
rus/set
Rus/sia
rus/tic
rust/ling
ru/ta/baga
ruth/less
Sab/bath
sab/bat/ical
sab/otage
sab/oteur
sac/charin
sack/ing
sack/cloth
sac/ra/ment
sac/red
sac/ri/fice
sac/ri/fi/cial
sac/ri/lege
sac/ri/le/gious
sac/ris/tan
sac/risty
sac/ro/sanct
sad/den
sad/dle
sad/dle/bag
sa/dism

305

sa/dis/tic
saf/ari
safe/guard
saf/fron
sa/ga/cious
sa/ga/city
Sa/git/tar/ius
sail/boat
sail/cloth
saint/li/ness
sa/la/cious
sa/lami
sal/ary
sale/able
sale/room
sales/man
sales/woman
sa/li/ent
sa/line
sa/liva
sa/li/vate
sal/low
sal/ly
sal/mon
sal/mon/ella
sa/loon
sal/sify
salt/petre salt/peter
  (US)
sa/lu/bri/ous
sa/luki
sal/u/tary
sa/lute
sal/vage
sal/va/tion
sal/ver

Sam/ari/tan
samo/var
sam/pan
sam/phire
samp/ler
sam/urai
san/at/or/ium
san/it/ar/ium (US)
sanc/tify
sanc/ti/mon/ious
sanc/tion
sanc/tity
sanc/tu/ary
sanc/tum
san/dal
san/dal/wood
sand/bag
sand/bank
sand/paper
sand/piper
sand/stone
sand/wich
san/guin/ary
san/guine
san/it/ary
san/ita/tion
sap/ling
sap/per
sap/phire
sap/wood
sara/band
sar/casm
sar/cas/tic
sar/coma
sar/co/phagus
sar/dine

sar/donic
sa/rong
sar/tor/ial
Sas/sen/ach
sat/chel
sat/el/lite
sa/ti/ate
sat/ire
sat/ir/ical
sat/is/fac/tion
sat/isfy
sat/suma
sat/ur/ate
Sat/ur/day
sat/ur/nine
sauce/pan
sau/cer
sauer/kraut
saun/ter
saus/age
sav/age
sav/ag/ery
sav/eloy
sav/ings
sav/iour sav/ior
  (US)
sav/our sav/or (US)
sa/voy
saw/dust
saw/mill
saxo/phone
saxo/phon/ist
scab/bard
sca/bi/ous
scaf/fold
scal/lion

scal/lop
scal/ly/wag
scal/pel
scam/per
scan/dal
scan/dal/mon/ger
scan/dal/ous
scan/ner
Scan/din/avia
scan/sion
scan/tily
scape/goat
scap/ula
scar/city
scare/crow
scare/mon/ger
scar/ify
scar/let
scath/ing
scat/ter
scat/ter/brain
sca/venge
scav/en/ger
scen/ario
sce/nery
scep/tic skep/tic
   (US)
sched/ule
sche/matic
schis/ma/tic
schizo/phre/nia
schnit/zel
schol/arly
scholar/ship
schol/astic
school/book

school/girl
school/chil/dren
school/mas/ter
school/mis/tress
school/tea/cher
sci/at/ica
sci/ence
sci/en/ti/fic
scin/til/late
scis/sors
scler/osis
scof/fing
scorch/ing
score/board
scorn/ful
Scor/pio
scor/pion
Scot/land
scoun/drel
scout/master
scrap/book
scream/ing
screen/play
screen/wri/ter
screw/driver
scrib/ble
scrim/mage
scrip/ture
scro/tum
scrub/bing
scrump/tious
scru/pu/lous
scru/tin/ize
scuf/fle
scul/lery
sculp/tor

sculp/ture
scup/per
scur/ril/ous
scut/tle
sea/board
sea/farer
sea/food
sea/gull
seal/ant
seal/skin
sea/man
seam/less
seam/stress
sé/ance
sea/port
search/ing
search/light
sea/shore
sea/sick
sea/side
sea/son
sea/weed
sea/worthy
se/ca/teurs
se/cede
se/ces/sion
se/clu/ded
sec/ond
sec/ond/ary
se/cond/hand
se/cond/ment
sec/recy
sec/ret
sec/re/tary
se/cre/tive
se/crete

307

sec/tar/ian
sec/tion
sec/tor
secu/lar
se/cure
se/cur/ity
se/dan
se/date
se/da/tion
sed/a/tive
sed/en/tary
sedi/ment
se/di/tion
se/duce
se/duc/tion
seed/bed
seed/ling
seeds/man
seem/ing
seep/age
see/saw
seg/ment
seg/re/gate
seis/mic
seis/mo/graph
seis/mol/ogy
seiz/ure
sel/dom
sel/ect
sel/en/ium
sel/fish
self/less
sel/lo/tape
sel/vedge
se/man/tic
sema/phore

sem/blance
se/men
se/mes/ter (US)
semi/breve
semi/circle
semi/conductor
semi/tone
sem/inal
sem/inar
sem/inary
Sem/itic
se/mo/lina
sen/ate
sena/tor
se/nile
se/nior
se/ni/or/ity
sen/sa/tion
sense/less
sens/ible
sen/sit/ive
sen/sit/iv/ity
sen/sor
sen/sual
sen/su/ous
sen/tence
sen/ten/tious
sen/ti/ment
sen/ti/nel
sen/try
se/pal
sep/ar/ate
sep/ar/at/ism
se/pia
sep/sis
Sep/tem/ber

sep/tet
sep/tic
sep/ti/caemia
sep/tua/gen/arian
sep/tup/let
se/pul/chre
se/pul/cher (US)
se/quel
se/quence
se/quin
se/quoia
ser/en/ade
se/rene
ser/geant
ser/ial
ser/ious
ser/mon
ser/pent
ser/rated
ser/vant
ser/vice
ser/vice/man
ser/vi/ette
ser/vile
ser/vi/tude
ses/sion
set/back
set/tee
set/ter
set/ting
set/tle
set/tle/ment
set/tler
sev/en/teen
sev/enty
sev/eral

sev/er/ance
se/vere
se/ver/ity
sew/age
sex/ist
sex/tant
sex/tet
sex/ton
sex/tup/let
sex/ual
shab/bi/ness
shadi/ness
sha/king
shal/lot
shal/low
shame/faced
shame/ful
shame/less
sham/poo
sham/rock
shape/less
share/holder
sharp/ener
sharp/ness
sharp/shooter
shat/ter
sha/ving
sheep/dog
sheep/ish
sheep/shank
sheep/skin
sheikh/dom
shel/lac
shell/fish
shel/ter
shep/herd

shep/herd/ess
sher/bet
sher/iff
shifti/ness
shift/less
shim/mer
shin/ing
ship/builder
ship/mate
ship/ment
ship/owner
ship/ping
ship/shape
ship/wreck
ship/yard
shirt/sleeves
shock/ing
shod/di/ness
shoe/horn
shoe/lace
shoe/maker
shoe/string
shoot/ing
shop/floor
shop/keeper
shop/lif/ter
shop/ping
shop/walker
short/age
short/bread
short/cake
short/coming
short/en/ing
short/fall
short/hand
short/horn

shot/gun
shoul/der
shoul/der/blade
shovel/ful
show/boat
show/case
showi/ness
show/man
show/man/ship
show/piece
show/room
shower/proof
show/ery
shrap/nel
shred/der
shrew/ish
shrewd/ness
shrink/age
shrub/bery
shrun/ken
shud/der
shuf/fle
shut/eye
shut/ter
shut/tle
shut/tle/cock
shy/ness
sib/il/ant
sick/bay
sick/ness
side/board
side/burns
side/car
side/light
side/line
side/long

side/show
side/step
side/track
side/walk (US)
side/ways
si/enna
si/esta
sif/ter
sight/less
sight/screen
sight/seeing
sight/seer
sig/nal
sig/nal/man
sig/na/ture
sign/board
sig/net
sig/ni/fi/cance
sig/nify
sign/post
sil/age
si/lence
sil/hou/ette
sil/ica
sil/icon
sil/ic/one
sil/ic/osis
silk/screen
silk/worm
sil/li/ness
sil/ver
sil/ver/side
sil/ver/smith
sil/ver/ware
sim/ilar
sim/ile

sim/mer
simp/li/fy
simu/late
sim/ul/tan//eous
sin/cere
sine/cure
sin/ful
sin/gle/breasted
sin/gle/decker
sin/gle/handed
sing/let
sing/song
sin/gu/lar
sin/is/ter
sin/ner
sinu/ous
si/nus
si/nu/si/tis
si/phon
si/ren
sir/loin
sis/ter
sit/ter
situ/ate
six/pence
six/teen
six/ti/eth
skate/board
ske/dad/dle
skel/eton
sketch/ing
sketch/pad
skew/bald
ski/boots
skil/ful skill/ful
    (US)

skil/let (US)
skin/diver
skin/flint
skip/per
skir/mish
skirt/ing
skit/tish
skull/cap
sky/div/ing
sky/lark
sky/line
sky/scraper
slack/ness
sla/lom
slan/der
slant/ing
slant/wise
slap/dash
slap/stick
slaugh/ter
slaugh/ter/house
sla/vish
sledge/ham/mer
sleepi/ness
sleep/ing
sleep/less
sleep/walk
slen/der
slight/ingly
sling/shot
slip/case
slip/pery
slip/stream
slip/way
slob/ber
slo/gan

slog/ger
slop/pily
slov/enly
slow/coach
slow/worm
slug/gish
slum/ber
slum/ber/wear
sly/ness
small/holder
small/pox
smat/ter/ing
smelt/ing
smith/er/eens
smoke/less
smoke/screen
smoul/der
smug/gler
snack/bar
snap/dragon
snap/shot
snea/kers (US)
snig/ger
snip/pet
snob/bery
snob/bish
snor/kel
snow/ball
snow/bound
snow/drift
snow/drop
snow/fall
snow/flake
snow/plough
snuf/fle
snug/gle

soak/ing
soap/suds
sober/ness
sob/ri/ety
soc/cer
so/ci/able
so/cial
so/ci/ety
so/ci/ol/ogy
sod/den
so/dium
so/journ
sol/ace
sol/der
sol/dier
sol/emn
sol/em/nity
sol/en/oid
so/li/cit
sol/ici/tor
sol/ici/tous
soli/dar/ity
sol/id/ity
sol/id/ify
soli/dus
so/li/lo/quy
so/lit/aire
sol/it/ary
solo/ist
sol/stice
sol/uble
sol/u/tion
sol/vency
sol/vent
som/brero
some/body

some/how
some/one
som/er/sault
some/thing
some/time
some/times
some/where
som/nam/bu/lism
som/no/lence
son/ata
song/ster
son/net
son/or/ous
soph/ist/icate
soph/omore (US)
sop/or/ific
sop/rano
sor/bet
sor/cery
sor/did
sor/ghum
sor/or/ity (US)
sor/rel
sor/row
sor/row/ful
sor/ter
sor/tie
sort/ing
soul/ful
soul/less
sound/ing
sound/less
sound/ness
sound/proof
sound/track
south/bound

south/erner
south/paw
south/wards
sou/venir
sov/er/eign
space/craft
space/man
space/sav/ing
space/ship
space/suit
spa/cious/ness
spa/ghetti
Span/iard
span/iel
Span/ish
span/ner
spar/ing
spark/ing
spark/ler
spar/row
spar/row/hawk
spar/tan
spas/modic
spas/tic
spa/tial
spat/ter
spat/ula
spear/head
spear/mint
spe/cial
spe/cies
spe/ci/fi/ca/tion
spe/cify
spe/ci/men
spe/cious
spec/tacle

spec/tacu/lar
spec/ta/tor
spec/trum
spec/ulate
speech/less
speed/boat
speed/ometer
speed/way
spe/le/ology
spell/bound
spel/ling
spend/thrift
sphag/num
spheri/cal
spi/der
spil/lage
spina bif/ida
spin/ach
spin/dle
spin/drift
spine/less
spin/na/ker
spin/ner
spin/neret
spin/ney
spin/ster
spi/ral
spiri/tual
spiri/tual/ism
spite/ful
splen/did
splen/dour
splin/ter
splut/ter
spo/ken
spoil/sport

spoke/shave
spokes/man
spo/li/ation
sponge/bag
spon/sor
spon/tan/eous
spoon/feed
spoon/ful
spor/adic
spor/ran
spor/ting
sports/man
sports/man/ship
sports/wear
spot/less
spot/light
spread/eagled
spring/board
spring/bok
spring/clean
springi/ness
spring/like
spring/time
sprink/ler
spuri/ous
sput/ter
spu/tum
squad/ron
squan/der
squat/ter
squeam/ish
squee/gee
squir/rel
sta/bil/ize
stac/cato
sta/dium

stage/coach
stage/craft
stage/hand
stag/ger
stag/fla/tion
stag/nant
stag/nate
stain/less
stair/car/pet
stair/case
stal/ac/tite
stal/ag/mite
stale/mate
stale/ness
stall/holder
stal/lion
stal/wart
sta/men
stam/ina
stam/mer
stam/pede
stamp/ing
stan/chion
stan/dard
stand/offish
stand/pipe
stand/point
stand/still
sta/phy/lo/coc/cus
star/board
star/dom
star/fish
star/gazer
star/light
star/ling
star/va/tion

state/less
state/ment
state/side (US)
states/man
sta/tion
sta/tioner
sta/tion/mas/ter
sta/tis/ti/cal
sta/tis/tics
statu/ary
statu/esque
stat/ure
sta/tus
stat/ute
stead/fast
stead/ily
steak/house
steal/thy
steam/boat
steam/roller
steam/ship
steel/works
steeple/chase
steeple/jack
steer/ing
stel/lar
sten/cil
sten/gun
steno/grapher
sten/torian
step/brother
step/child
step/daughter
step/father
step/ladder
step/mother

step/sister
step/son
ste/reo
ste/reo/phonic
ste/reo/scope
ste/reo/type
ster/ile
ster/il/ize
ster/ling
stern/ness
stern/wheeler
ster/num
ster/oid
stetho/scope
steve/dore
stew/ard
stew/ard/ess
sticki/ness
stickle/back
stick/ler
stif/fen
stiff/ness
stig/mata
stil/etto
still/born
still/ness
stimu/lant
stimu/late
stimu/lus
sting/ray
stingi/ness
sti/pend
sti/pen/di/ary
stip/ple
stipu/late
stir/ring

313

stir/rup
stock/ade
stock/broker
stock/car
stock/ing
stock/ist
stock/man
stock/pile
stock/pot
stock/tak/ing
stoi/cism
sto/len
stom/ach
stone/crop
stone/mason
stone/wall
stone/ware
stop/cock
stop/gap
stop/over
stop/page
stop/per
stor/age
store/house
store/keeper
story/line
story/teller
stout/ness
stove/pipe
stow/away
strad/dler
strag/gler
straight/for/ward
strait/jacket
strait/laced
strange/ness

stran/gu/la/tion
strap/less
strap/ping
stra/ta/gem
stra/tegic
stra/tegi/cal
strat/ify
stra/to/sphere
straw/berry
stream/line
stream/lining
street/cat
strenu/ous
strep/to/coc/cus
strep/to/my/cin
stric/ture
strike/breaker
strik/ing
stri/dent
strin/gent
strip/ing
strip/per
strip/tease
stro/bo/scope
strol/ler
strong/hold
stron/tium
struc/ture
strug/gling
strych/nine
stub/ble
stub/born
stu/dent
stu/dio
stu/di/ous
stuf/fing

stuf/fi/ness
stul/tify
stun/ning
stu/pe/fac/tion
stu/pefy
stu/pen/dous
stu/pid
stur/geon
stut/ter
sty/lish
sty/lis/tics
sty/lize
sty/lus
sty/mie
styp/tic
sub/al/tern
sub/aqua
sub/com/mit/tee
sub/con/scious
sub/con/ti/nent
sub/con/tract
sub/cu/ta/ne/ous
sub/div/ide
sub/due
sub/edit
sub/head/ing
sub/ject
sub ju/dice
sub/junc/tive
sub/lease
sub/let
sub/lieu/ten/ant
sub/lim/ate
sub/lime
sub/lim/in/al
sub/mach/ine gun

sub/mar/ine
sub/merge
sub/mer/sion
sub/mis/sion
sub/mit
sub/nor/mal
sub/ord/in/ate
sub/poena
sub/scribe
sub/scrip/tion
sub/se/quent
sub/ser/vient
sub/side
sub/sid/iary
sub/si/dize
sub/sidy
sub/sist
sub/soil
sub/stance
sub/stan/dard
sub/stan/tial
sub/stan/ti/ate
sub/stant/ive
sub/sta/tion
sub/sti/tute
sub/stra/tum
sub/ten/ant
sub/ter/fuge
sub/ter/ra/nean
sub/title
sub/tract
sub/urb
sub/urbia
sub/ven/tion
sub/ver/sion
sub/way

sub/zero
suc/ceed
suc/cess
suc/cinct
suc/cour
suc/cu/lent
suc/cumb
such/like
sud/den
suf/fer
suf/fice
suf/fi/cient
suf/fix
suf/fo/cate
suf/frage
sug/gest
sug/ges/tible
sui/cide
suit/ability
suit/case
sul/len
sul/phur sul/fur
  (US)
sul/tan
sul/try
sum/mar/ize
sum/mary
sum/mar/ily
sum/mer
sum/mer/house
sum/mer/time
sum/mery
sum/mit
sum/mon
sump/tu/ous
sun/bathe

sun/beam
sun/burn
sun/dae
Sun/day
sun/deck
sun/dial
sun/down
sun/drenched
sun/dry
sun/flower
sun/glasses
sun/lamp
sun/less
sun/light
sun/rise
sun/set
sun/shade
sun/shine
sun/spot
sun/stroke
sun/tan
sun/trap
su/per
su/per/abund/ance
su/per/an/nu/ated
su/perb
su/per/charged
su/per/cili/ous
su/per/fi/cial
su/per/fine
su/per/flu/ous
su/per/high/way
  (US)
su/per/hu/man
su/per/im/pose
su/per/in/tend

su/per/ior
su/per/lat/ive
su/per/man
su/per/mar/ket
su/per/nat/ur/al
su/per/nova
su/per/num/er/ary
su/per/power
su/per/sede
su/per/son/ic
su/per/sti/tion
su/per/struc/ture
su/per/tan/ker
su/per/vene
su/per/vise
su/per/woman
su/pine
sup/per
sup/per/time
sup/plant
sup/ple
sup/ple/ment
sup/pli/ca/tion
sup/ply
sup/port
sup/pose
sup/pos/edly
sup/pos/it/ory
sup/press
sup/pres/sor
su/pra/na/tional
su/prem/acy
su/preme
su/premo
sur/charge
sure/ness

sur/face
surf/board
surf/boat
sur/feit
sur/geon
sur/gi/cal
sur/li/ness
sur/mise
sur/mount
sur/name
sur/pass
sur/plice
sur/plus
sur/prise
sur/real/ism
sur/ren/der
sur/rep/ti/tious
sur/round
sur/tax
sur/veil/lance
sur/vey
sur/vive
sus/cept/ible
sus/pect
sus/pend
sus/pen/ders
sus/pen/sion
sus/pi/cion
sus/pi/sious
sus/tain
sus/ten/ance
su/ture
swag/ger
swal/low
swash/buck/ling
swas/tika

sweat/shirt
Swe/den
sweep/ing
sweep/stake
sweet/bread
sweet/heart
sweet/ness
sweet/shop
swel/ter
swift/ness
swim/ming
swim/suit
swinge/ing
swing/ing
switch/back
switch/board
Swit/zer/land
swol/len
sword/fish
swords/man
sword/stick
sy/ca/more
sy/co/phant
syl/labic
syl/lable
syl/la/bub
syl/la/bus
sym/bi/osis
sym/bol
sym/metry
sym/pa/thize
sym/pathy
sym/phony
sym/po/sium
symp/tom
symp/to/matic

syn/agogue
syn/chro/mesh
syn/chro/nize
syn/co/pate
syn/di/cate
syn/drome
sy/nod
syn/onym
syn/ony/mous
syn/op/sis
syn/tax
syn/thesis
syn/thetic
syph/ilis
syr/inge
sys/tem
sys/te/matic
sys/temic
tab/er/nacle
tab/leau
table/cloth
table/land
table/spoon
tab/let
tab/loid
ta/boo
tabu/lar
tabu/la/tor
tacho/graph
ta/cit
taci/turn
tact/ful
tact/less
tac/ti/cian
tac/tics
tac/tile

tad/pole
taf/feta
tail/back
tail/board
tail/gate
tail/less
take/away
take/over
tal/ent
tal/is/man
talk/ative
talk/ing
tall/boy
tam/bour/ine
tame/ness
tam-o'shan/ter
tam/per
tam/pon
tan/dem
tan/gent
tan/gen/tial
tan/ger/ine
tan/gible
tank/ard
tan/nery
tan/nin
tan/tal/ize
tan/trum
tap/es/try
ta/pi/oca
ta/pir
tap/pet
tap/ping
ta/ran/tula
tar/get

tar/iff
tar/mac
tar/nish
tar/pau/lin
tar/ra/gon
tar/sus
tar/tan
tar/tar
tar/tare sauce
tart/ness
task/mas/ter
tas/sel
taste/ful
taste/less
tat/ters
tat/ting
tat/tle
tat/too
tat/ty
Tau/rus
tau/tol/ogy
tav/ern
taw/dry
tax/able
taxi/dermy
tax/man
taxi/meter
tax/payer
tea/bag
tea/cake
tea/cloth
tea/cup
tea/leaf
tea/pot
tea/room
tea/spoon

tea/time
team/ster
team/work
tear/ful
tea/sel
tech/nical
tech/nique
tech/no/crat
tech/no/logi/cal
te/di/ous
teen/age
tee/ter
tee/ter-tot/ter (US)
tee/total
tele/cast
tele/com/mu/ni/
  ca/tions
tele/gram
tele/graph
tel/egra/phist
tele/pathy
tele/phone
tel/eph/on/ist
tele/photo lens
tele/printer
tele/scope
tele/vision
tel/ling
tell/tale
te/mer/ity
tem/per
tem/pera
tem/pera/ment
tem/per/ance
tem/per/ate
tem/pest

tem/pes/tuous
tem/plate
tem/poral
tem/por/ary
temp/ta/tion
ten/able
ten/acious
ten/acity
ten/ant
ten/den/tious
ten/der
ten/der/hearted
ten/der/loin
ten/don
ten/dril
tene/ment
ten/fold
ten/nis
ten/sion
ten/sile
tent/acle
tent/at/ive
ten/ter/hooks
tenu/ous
ten/ure
te/pee
ter/cen/ten/ary
ter/mi/nal
ter/min/ate
ter/min/ology
ter/minus
ter/mite
ter/race
ter/ra/cot/ta
ter/rain
ter/ra/pin

ter/rest/rial
ter/rible
ter/rier
ter/ri/fic
ter/rit/ory
ter/ror
ter/ror/ism
ter/tiary
Tery/lene
testa/ment
test/icle
test/ify
tes/ti/mony
tet/anus
tet/ra/hed/ron
text/book
text/ual
tex/tile
tex/ture
Thai/land
thank/ful
thank/less
thanks/giving
theat/ri/cal
them/selves
theo/do/lite
theo/lo/gian
theo/logy
the/orem
theor/eti/cal
the/ory
thera/peu/tic
thera/pist
ther/apy
there/after
there/upon

ther/mi/onic
ther/mo/dy/nam/ics
ther/mo/meter
ther/mo/nu/clear
Ther/mos (flask)
ther/mo/stat
the/sau/rus
thick/set
thim/ble/ful
thin/ness
thin/nings
thinga/ma/jig
think/ing
thir/teen
thir/ti/eth
this/tle/down
thor/acic
thor/ough
thor/ough/bred
thor/ough/fare
thor/ough/going
thor/ough/ness
thought/ful
thought/less
thou/sand
thrash/ing
thread/bare
thread/like
thread/worm
three/fold
three/some
thresh/old
throm/bo/sis
through/out
through/put

through/way
throw/away
throw/back
thumb/nail
thumb/tack
thun/der
thun/der/ous
thun/der/struck
Thurs/day
thy/roid (gland)
ti/ara
tick/er/tape
tick/ing
tick/lish
tid/dler
tid/dly
tide/mark
tide/way
tid/ings
tidi/ness
tie/pin
ti/ger
ti/gress
tight/fit/ting
tight/rope
til/ler
tim/ber
tim/ber/yard
time/keeper
time/lag
time/less
time/piece
time/server
time/table
tim/or/ous

tim/pani
tinc/ture
tin/der
tin/ker
tin/sel
tip/ple
tip/ster
tip/toe
tir/ade
tired/ness
tire/less
tire/some
tis/sue
ti/tanic
tit/bit tid/bit (US)
tit/il/late
tit/iv/ate
ti/tra/tion
tit/ter
tit/tle tat/tle
titu/lar
toad/stool
toast/mas/ter
toast/rack
to/bacco
to/bog/gan
to/day
toe/nail
tof/fee
to/gether
toi/let
tol/er/able
tol/er/ate
toma/hawk
to/mato
tom/bola

319

tom/boy
tom/fool
to/mor/row
tom/tom
tongue/twister
to/night
ton/nage
ton/sil
ton/sil/litis
ton/sure
tooth/ache
tooth/brush
tooth/comb
tooth/less
tooth/paste
tooth/pick
to/paz
to/pi/ary
top/less
to/po/graphy
to/po/logy
top/side
top/soil
torch/light
tor/ment
tor/men/tor
tor/nado
tor/pedo
tor/pid
tor/rent
tor/ren/tial
tor/rid
tor/sion
tor/toise
tor/toise/shell
tor/tu/ous

tor/ture
to/tal/it/arian
to/tal/ity
to/tal/iz/ator
to/tem pole
tot/ter
tou/can
touch/down
touchi/ness
touch/paper
touch/stone
tough/ness
tou/pee
tour/na/ment
tour/ni/quet
to/wards
tow/el/ling
tow/path
towns/folk
town/ship
towns/man
towns/woman
towns/people
tox/aemia tox/emia
  (US)
toxi/col/ogy
tra/chea
tra/cheot/omy
track/less
tract/able
trac/tion
trac/tor
trade/mark
trades/man
trades/people
trade/wind

tra/di/tion
traf/fic
traf/fi/cator
trag/edy
train/ing
trai/tor
tra/ject/ory
tram/car
tram/way
tram/po/line
tran/quil
tran/quil/lizer
trans/act
trans/at/lan/tic
tran/scend
trans/con/tin/ental
tran/scribe
tran/script
tran/sept
trans/fer
trans/figure
trans/fix
trans/form
trans/fuse
tran/ship
tran/si/ence
tran/sis/tor
tran/sit
trans/it/ive
trans/it/ory
trans/late
trans/lit/er/ate
trans/lu/cent
trans/mis/sion
trans/mit
trans/mute

tran/som
trans/parency
trans/par/ent
tran/spire
trans/plant
trans/port
trans/pose
trans/ship
trans/ur/anic
trans/verse
trans/vest/ite
tra/peze
tra/pez/ium
trap/per
trap/pings
trau/matic
tra/vel/lator
tra/vel/ler
tra/verse
trav/esty
treach/ery
tread/mill
trea/son
treas/ure
treat/ment
treat/ise
tree/creeper
tree/less
tree/top
tre/foil
trel/lis
tre/mend/ous
tremu/lous
tren/chant
tre/pan
tre/phine

trep/ida/tion
tres/pass
tres/ses
tri/angle
tri/an/gular
tribes/man
tri/bunal
tri/bu/tary
trib/ute
trick/ster
tri/col/our
tri/cycle
tri/dent
tri/en/nial
trig/ger
tri/go/no/metry
tril/lion
tri/logy
tri/maran
trim/ming
trin/ity
trin/ket
tri/par/tite
tri/pod
trip/per
trip/tych
tri/umph
tri/um/phant
tri/um/vir/ate
triv/ial
trog/lo/dyte
Tro/jan
trol/ley
trom/bone
tro/phies
trop/ical

trouble/maker
trouble/shooter
trouble/some
trouble/spot
trous/seau
tru/ant
truck/load
truc/ulence
tru/ism
trum/pet
trun/cated
trun/cheon
trus/tee
trust/ful
trust/worthy
truth/ful
tu/ber/cu/lar
tuber/cu/losis
tube/less
tu/bu/lar
Tues/day
tug/boat
tu/ition
tum/ble/down
tum/my/ache
tu/mour tu/mor
(US)
tu/mult
tu/mu/lus
tun/dra
tung/sten
tu/nic
Tu/nisia
tun/nel
tur/ban
tur/bid

321

tur/bine
tur/bot
tur/bu/lent
tur/een
tur/gid
Tur/key
tur/meric
tur/moil
turn/coat
turn/over
turn/pike
turn/stile
turn/table
tur/nip
tur/pen/tine
tur/quoise
tur/ret
tur/tle
tur/tle/dove
tus/sock
tu/tor
tux/edo
twen/ti/eth
twi/light
twit/ter
two/penny
twp/some
ty/coon
tym/panum
type/setter
type/writer
typ/ist
ty/po/graphy
ty/phoid
ty/phoon
ty/phus

typ/ical
tyr/anny
tyr/an/nical
tyr/an/nous
ty/rant
ubi/quit/ous
ud/der
ug/li/ness
ul/cer
ul/cer/ous
ul/ter/ior
ul/ti/mate
ul/ti/matum
ul/tra/marine
ultra/vio/let
um/ber
um/bil/ical
um/brage
um/brella
um/pire
ump/teen
un/abated
un/able
un/abridged
un/ac/cept/able
un/ac/coun/ted for
un/ac/com/pan/ied
un/ac/count/able
un/ac/cus/tomed
un/ac/quain/ted
un/adop/ted
un/adul/ter/ated
un/af/fec/ted
un/aided
un/al/loyed
un/al/ter/able

un/am/bigu/ous
un/an/im/ous
una/nim/ity
un/an/nounced
un/answer/able
un/ap/pet/izing
un/ap/proach/able
un/armed
un/ash/amed
un/asked
un/as/sum/ing
un/at/tached
un/at/tain/able
un/at/ten/ded
un/at/trac/tive
un/au/thor/ized
un/avoid/able
un/aware
un/awares
un/bal/anced
un/bear/able
un/beat/able
un/be/known
un/be/liev/able
un/bend
un/biased
un/bleached
un/bolt
un/bosom
un/boun/ded
un/break/able
un/bridled
un/broken
un/burden
un/busi/ness/like
un/but/ton

322

un/called for
un/canny
un/cared for
un/ceas/ing
un/cere/mo/ni/ous
un/cer/tain
un/chal/lenged
un/change/able
un/char/it/able
un/checked
un/civ/il/ized
un/claimed
un/clas/si/fied
un/clean
un/clut/tered
un/coil
un/com/fort/able
un/com/mit/ted
un/com/mon
un/com/mu/nic/at/ive
uncom/pli/ment/ary
un/com/prom/ising
un/con/cealed
un/con/cerned
un/con/ditional
un/con/nected
un/con/scious
un/con/scion/able
un/con/trol/lable
un/con/ven/tional
un/cooked
un/co/op/er/ative
un/cork
un/cor/rec/ted
un/cor/rob/or/ated

un/couth
un/cover
un/crossed
un/crush/able
unc/tion
un/cul/tiv/ated
un/cut
un/dam/aged
un/daun/ted
un/de/cided
un/de/fen/ded
un/demo/cratic
un/deni/able
un/der/achieve
un/der/arm
un/der/car/riage
un/der/charge
un/der/clothes
un/der/coat
un/der/cover
un/der/cur/rent
un/der/cut
un/der/de/vel/oped
un/der/dog
un/der/done
un/der/es/tim/ate
un/der/ex/posed
un/der/fed
un/der/felt
un/der/foot
un/der/gar/ment
un/der/go
un/der/gradu/ate
un/der/ground
un/der/growth
un/der/hand(ed)

un/der/lay
un/der/lie
un/der/line
un/der/ling
un/der/manned
under/men/tioned
un/der/mine
un/der/neath
un/der/nour/ished
un/der/paid
un/der/pants
un/der/pass
un/der/priv/ileged
un/der/rate
un/der/seal
un/der/sell
un/der/shirt
un/der/side
un/der/signed
un/der/sized
un/der/slung
un/der/staffed
un/der/stand
un/der/state
un/der/stood
un/der/study
un/der/take
un/der/taker
un/der/tone
un/der/tow
un/der/value
un/der/water
un/der/wear
un/der/weight
un/der/went
un/der/world

un/der/write
un/de/served
un/desir/able
un/detec/ted
un/de/vel/oped
un/did
un/dies
un/dig/ni/fied
un/di/lu/ted
un/dis/charged
un/dis/tin/guished
un/di/vided
un/doubted
un/dreamt of
un/dress
un/drink/able
un/due
un/du/late
un/dy/ing
un/earned
un/earth
un/easi/ness
un/easy
un/eat/able
un/eco/nom/ic(al)
un/edu/cated
un/em/ployed
un/end/ing
un/en/light/ened
un/en/vi/able
un/equal
un/equi/vocal
un/er/ring
un/eth/ical
un/even
un/event/ful

un/ex/cep/tion/able
un/excep/tional
un/ex/pected
un/ex/plored
un/ex/posed
un/ex/pur/gated
un/fail/ing
un/fair
un/faith/ful
un/fa/mil/iar
un/fasten
un/fa/vour/able
un/feel/ing
un/fit
un/flin/chingly
un/fold
un/fore/seen
un/for/get/table
un/for/tu/nate
un/foun/ded
un/freeze
un/fre/quented
un/friendly
un/furl
un/fur/nished
un/gainly
un/get/at/able
un/godly
un/gracious
un/grate/ful
un/guar/ded
un/gu/late
un/happy
un/harmed
un/healthy
un/heard of

un/help/ful
un/her/al/ded
un/hinged
un/holy
un/hook
un/hoped for
un/hurt
uni/corn
un/iden/ti/fied
uni/fica/tion
uni/form
uni/lat/eral
un/im/por/tant
un/in/formed
un/in/hab/it/able
un/in/hib/ited
un/ini/ti/ated
un/in/tel/lig/ible
un/in/ter/rup/ted
un/in/vited
union/ist
uni/sex
uni/son
uni/valve
uni/ver/sal
uni/verse
uni/ver/sity
un/just
un/jus/ti/fied
un/kempt
un/kind
un/known
un/laden
un/lady/like
un/law/ful
un/leash

un/leavened
un/less
un/like
un/lim/ited
un/load
un/lock
un/looked for
un/lucky
un/man/age/able
un/manned
un/mar/ried
un/mask
un/men/tion/able
un/mis/tak(e)/able
un/mit/ig/ated
un/moved
un/musi/cal
un/nat/ural
un/ne/ces/sary
un/nerve
un/no/ticed
un/num/bered
un/ob/ser/vant
un/ob/struc/ted
un/ob/tain/able
un/ob/tru/sive
un/oc/cu/pied
un/of/ficial
un/op/posed
un/or/tho/dox
un/pack
un/paid
un/pal/at/able
un/par/al/leled
un/par/don/able
un/pat/ri/otic

un/person
un/pick
un/placed
un/pleasant
un/popu/lar
un/pre/ce/den/ted
un/pre/ju/diced
un/pre/med/it/ated
un/pre/pared
un/pre/pos/ses/sing
un/pre/ten/tious
un/prin/cipled
un/print/able
un/pro/duc/tive
un/pro/fes/sional
un/pro/fit/able
un/pro/nounce/able
un/pro/tec/ted
un/pro/voked
un/quali/fied
un/quest/ion/able
un/quote
un/ravel
un/real
un/reas/on/able
un/rec/og/niz/able
un/re/corded
un/re/fined
un/re/lated
un/re/li/able
un/re/lieved
un/re/mit/ting
un/re/quited
un/re/served
un/res/er/vedly
un/rest

un/rivalled
un/roll
un/ruf/fled
un/ruly
un/safe
un/said
un/sal/ted
un/sat/is/fac/tory
un/sat/is/fied
un/sav/oury
un/sav/ory (US)
un/scathed
un/scien/ti/fic
un/scramble
un/screw
un/scru/pu/lous
un/sealed
un/seat
un/seen
un/sel/fish
un/set/tle
un/sightly
un/skilled
un/soci/able
un/soc/ial
un/so/licited
un/solved
un/soph/is/ti/cated
un/sound
un/spar/ing
un/speak/able
un/spoilt
un/stable
un/steady
un/stick
un/stop/pable

325

un/suc/ces/sful
un/suit/able
un/sure
un/sus/pec/ted
un/swerv/ing
un/sym/pa/thetic
un/tapped
un/ten/able
un/think/able
un/tidi/ness
un/tidy
un/tie
un/til
un/timely
un/told
un/to/ward
un/true
un/trust/worthy
un/truth/ful
un/us/able
un/used
un/us/ual
un/varn/ished
un/veil
un/wary
un/well
un/whole/some
un/wieldy
un/wil/ling
un/wind
un/wise
un/wit/tingly
un/won/ted
un/work/able
un/wor/thy
un/wound

un/wrap
un/writ/ten
un/zip
up/braid
up/bring/ing
up/date
up/end
up/grade
up/heaval
up/hill
up/hold
up/hol/ster
up/keep
up/land
up/lift
up/per
up/per/most
up/pity
up/right
up/rising
up/roar
up/root
up/set
up/shot
up/side down
up/stage
up/stairs
up/stan/ding
up/start
up/stream
up/take
up/tight
up/turn
up/ward
ur/anium
ur/ban

ur/bane
ur/chin
ur/eter
ur/ethra
ur/gent
ur/inal
urin/ate
ur/ine
us/able
us/age
use/ful
use/less
ush/er/ette
us/urer
uten/sil
util/ity
util/ize
ut/most
uto/pia
ut/ter
ut/ter/ance
ut/ter/most
uxori/ous
va/cancy
va/cate
vac/cin/ate
vac/cine
va/cil/late
vac/uous
vac/uum
vaga/bond
vag/ar/ies
va/gina
vag/rant
vague/ness
val/en/tine

vali/ant
vali/date
val/ley
val/our
valu/able
value/less
val/vu/lar
vam/pire
van/dal
van/guard
va/nilla
van/ish
van/ity
van/quish
van/tage point
va/por/ize
vari/ability
vari/ance
vari/cose vein
varie/gated
vari/ety
vari/ous
var/nish
vas/ec/tomy
vat/man
vec/tor
ve/gan
ve/get/able
ve/ge/tar/ian
ve/he/mence
ve/hicle
vel/lum
ve/lo/city
ve/lour
vel/vet
ve/nal

ven/detta
vend/ing
ven/eer
ven/er/able
ven/er/ate
ven/er/eal
ve/ne/tian blind
ven/geance
ven/ial
ven/ison
ven/om
ven/ous
ven/ti/late
ven/tral
ven/tricle
ven/tri/lo/quist
ven/ture
ver/acious
ver/anda(h)
ver/bally
ver/batim
ver/bena
ver/biage
ver/bose
ver/dict
ver/di/gris
ver/ger
veri/fi/able
ve/ri/si/mil/it/ude
ver/it/able
ver/mi/celli
ver/mil/ion
ver/min
ver/mouth
ver/na/cu/lar
ver/ruca

ver/sa/tile
ver/si/fi/ca/tion
ver/sion
ver/so
ver/sus
ver/te/bra
ver/te/brate
ver/tex
ver/ti/cal
ver/tices
ver/tigo
ves/icle
ves/pers
ves/sel
ves/ti/bule
ves/tige
ves/ti/gial
vest/ments
ves/try
vet/eran
vet/er/in/ary
vex/ation
vi/able
via/duct
vi/brate
vi/bur/num
vic/ar/age
vi/cari/ous
vice/re/gal
vice/roy
vi/cini/ty
vi/cious
vi/cis/si/tude
vic/tim
vic/tor
vic/tor/ious

vid/eo/cas/sette
vid/eo/tape
view/fin/der
view/point
vi/gil/ant
vig/our
vil/ify
vil/lage
vil/lain
vin/di/cate
vin/dic/tive
vin/egar
vine/yard
vin/tage
vi/nyl
vi/ola
vi/ol/ate
vi/ol/ence
vi/olet
vi/olin
vi/ol/on/cello
vi/per
vir/gin
vir/ginia creeper
vir/ile
viro/logy
vir/tual
vir/tue
vir/tu/oso
viru/lence
vis/cera
vis/cos/ity
vis/cous
vis/count
vise/like (Am)
vis/ible

vi/sion
visi/ta/tion
vi/sor
vis/ual
vi/tal
vit/amin
viti/ate
vit/reous
vit/rify
vit/riol
vi/tup/era/tion
vi/va/cious
viv/id/ness
vi/vi/par/ous
vi/vi/sec/tion
vo/cabu/lary
vo/cal
vo/ca/tion
vo/ci/fer/ate
vo/cif/er/ous
voice/less
vol/at/ile
vol/cano
vo/li/tion
vol/ley
vol/ley/ball
vol/tage
vol/uble
vol/ume
vol/un/tary
vol/un/teer
vol/up/tu/ous
voo/doo
vo/ra/cious
vor/tex
vo/tary

vo/tive
vouch/safe
voy/age
vul/can/ize
vul/can/ology
vul/gar
vul/ner/able
vul/ture
wad/ding
waf/fle
wag/gon
wag/tail
wains/cot
waist/line
wait/ing
wait/ress
wake/ful
walk/about
walk/out
walk/over
walk/way
wal/laby
wal/let
wall/flower
wal/lop
wal/low
wall/pa/per
wal/nut
wal/rus
wan/der
wan/der/lust
want/ing
wan/ton
ward/ress
ward/robe
ward/room

ware/house
war/fare
war/head
war/horse
war/like
war/mon/ger
warn/ing
war/paint
war/path
war/rant
war/ring
war/rior
war/ship
wart/hog
war/time
wash/able
wash/basin
wash/bowl
wash/cloth
wash/day
wash/down
washer/woman
wash/ing
wash/leather
wash/out
wash/room
wash/stand
wasp/ish
wast/age
waste/ful
was/trel
watch/dog
watch/ful
watch/ing
watch/ma/ker
watch/man

watch/word
water/colour
water/course
water/cress
water/fall
water/fowl
water/front
water/less
water/level
water/logged
water/mark
water/proof
water/shed
water/side
water/spout
water/tight
water/way
water/works
wave/band
wave/length
wa/ver/ing
wax/works
way/farer
way/lay
way/side
way/ward
weak/en/ing
weak/ling
weak/ness
wea/pon
wea/sel
wea/ther/cock
wea/ther/man
wea/ther/proof
web/footed
wed/ding

Wed/nes/day
weed/kil/ler
week/day
week/end
wee/vil
weigh/bridge
weight/ing
weight/less
weight/lifter
wel/come
weld/ing
wel/fare
well/being
wel/ling/ton boots
wel/ter
wel/ter/weight
west/bound
west/ern/ize
west/bound
wet/ness
wet/ting
whale/boat
whale/bone
what/so/ever
wheat/sheaf
wheelbar/row
wheel/base
wheel/chair
wheel/wright
where/abouts
where/fore
wher/ever
where/upon
where/withal
whet/stone
whim/per

329

whimsical

whim/si/cal
whip/hand
whip/lash
whip/pet
whip/ping
whirl/pool
whirl/wind
whis/ker
whis/key (US)
whis/per
whistle/stop tour
white/bait
white/wash
white/wood
whit/ing
whit/low
Whit/sun
whole/hearted
whole/meal
whole/sale
whole/some
whop/per
wick/ed/ness
wick/er/work
wicket/kee/per
wide/spread
wid/ow/hood
wig/wam
wil/der/ness
wild/fire
wild/fowl
wild/life
wil/ful
wil/lies
wil/ling
wil/low

wil/low herb
will/power
wind/bag
wind/break
wind/burn
wind/cheater
wind/fall
wind/lass
wind/mill
win/dow
wind/pipe
wind/screen
wind/shield
wind/sock
wind/swept
wind/ward
win/dow/ledge
win/dow/sill
wine/glass
wing/less
wing/span
win/now
win/some
wire/less
wis/dom
wise/crack
wish/bone
wish/ful
wis/atria wis/teria
wist/ful
witch/craft
with/draw
with/ers
with/hold
with/out
with/stand

wit/ness
wiz/ard
wiz/ened
woe/be/gone
woman/hood
women/folk
won/der
wood/car/ving
wood/craft
wood/land
wood/pecker
wood.shed
woods/man
wood/wind
wood/work
wood/worm
wool/len
work/able
work/force
work/ing
work/man
work/man/ship
work/out
work/room
work/shop
wor/ri/some
wor/ship
wor/sted
wrap/ping
wreck/age
wrest/ler
wrest/ling
writ/ing
wrong/doer
wrong/doing
wrong/ful

xeno/phobe
xylo/phone
yard/age
yard/arm
yard/stick
yawn/ing
year/book
year/ling
yel/low
yel/low/ham/mer
yel/low/ish
yes/ter/day

yes/ter/year
Yid/dish
yo/del
yog/hurt yog/urt
yon/der
York/shire pud/ding
your/self
Yugo/slavia
Yule/tide
yum/yum
Zam/bia
zeal/ous

zen/ith
zig/zag
Zim/babwe
zip/per
zir/con/ium
zod/iac
zom/bie
zoo/logy
zuc/chini
zwie/back (US)

Glossary

One cannot make an omelette without breaking eggs, and by the same token one cannot explain punctuation without introducing a few grammatical terms. We have tried to keep these to a minimum, and usually they are explained at their first appearance. However, to get around the necessity of the reader hunting for that first appearance, we have collected the most important terms in this brief glossary. Please note that this is far from being a complete list of terms used in grammar.

absolute construction a phrase that is independent of or isolated from the syntax of the main clause of a sentence. Such constructions often contain a present participle. In the sentence 'The time of the next meeting having been agreed, the committee adjourned its proceedings', the words 'the time of the next meeting having been agreed' form an absolute construction.

adjectival subordinate clause a subordinate clause that functions grammatically as an adjective. Relative clauses are typical adjectival clauses. In the sentence 'Jane is the girl who lives next door', the words *who lives next door* describe the kind of girl Jane is, in the same way as the word *favourite* does in the sentence 'Jane is my favourite girl.'

adjective one of a class of words in a language that denote a certain characteristic or attribute of a noun or pronoun. Adjectives are describing words and can be placed before the noun or pronoun they describe or can be linked to it by certain verbs. The word 'sick' is an adjective in these two sentences: 'Bonzo is a sick dog' and 'My dog Bonzo is sick.'

See also **attributive**. (Note that certain adjectives may be placed directly after the noun they belong to: e.g. 'everlasting' in the sentence 'Through Jesus we may attain life everlasting.'

adverb any of a class of words that restrict or specify the action denoted by a verb or the attribute specified by an adjective. Adverbs can also modify (that is, qualify the effects of) other adverbs or even whole sentences. Examples of adverbs are 'obviously', 'fast', 'very', 'easily', in the sentence 'Obviously, because she was fit, she could run fast very easily.'

adverbial clause a subordinate clause that functions as an adverb within a sentence: for example, in the sentence 'You cannot remain within this society, because you do not wholeheartedly share its views', the last eight words represent an adverbial phrase modifying the rest of the sentence.

adverbial phrase a group of words that lacks a finite verb and functions as an adverb within a sentence. Such phrases often contain a preposition, as in 'down the street' in the sentence 'She ran naked down the street', or as in 'in that case' in the sentence 'In that case, I'll have beans on toast.'

affix a combination of letters added to a word or root to make a derived word or an inflected form. For example, the letters *-ly* form an affix that can be added to certain adjectives to produce the corresponding adverbs: e.g. *beautiful* plus the affix *-ly* gives the adverb *beautifully*. The affix *de-* placed in front of a verb or noun produces a word of opposite meaning: e.g. demobilize, de-icer. An affix added to the end of a word is a suffix; one added to the beginning of a word is a prefix.

affix boundary the point in a word between an affix and the word or root that precedes or follows it. In end-of-line hyphenation, one of the principles is that the hyphen should be placed at an affix boundary, as it is for example in the

333

hyphenated words *quick-ly* or *de-mobilize*.

agent person or thing that is the doer of the action specified by the verb in a clause or sentence. In both of the following sentences, the words *my wife Helen* function as an agent: 'My wife Helen bought a new car yesterday'; 'This new Audi was bought yesterday by my wife Helen.'

agent-noun any of a class of nouns formed from words, often verbs, by the addition of a suffix such as *-er*, *-or*, *-ist*, etc. Typical agent-nouns are *worker, actor, therapist*, etc.

apposition a grammatical construction in which a noun or a phrase functioning as a noun is placed directly after another noun in order to explain or modify its meaning. In the following sentence, the words 'Britain's prime minister' are said to be in apposition to 'Mrs Thatcher': 'On 14 July, Mrs Thatcher, Britain's prime minister, visited Paris.'

appositional comma a comma, usually one of a pair, that marks off the words that are in apposition to a preceding noun. Note the appositional commas around 'Britain's prime minister' in the example in the previous entry.

attributive (of an adjective or its position in a sentence or clause) directly preceding the noun that the adjective is modifying. In the sentence 'She wore a revealing dress', the adjective 'revealing' is in attributive position.

clause a group of words that consists of a subject, a finite verb, and (usually) a predicate but is not necessarily a complete sentence. The two chief types of clause are the main clause (or *co-ordinate clause*) and the **subordinate clause**.

close punctuation a type of punctuation marked by liberal use of punctuation marks, especially commas. Close punctuation can lead to excessive use of such stops as the comma and is now generally regarded as unhelpful and old-fashioned. *See also* **open punctuation**.

comma fault a punctuation error noted by some writers in the United States in which a comma is used to link two independent clauses in a sentence instead of a semicolon. *See* the chapter on Comma.

comma of address a comma (often one of a pair) used to mark off the name of a person being addressed from the rest of the sentence; for example, in the sentence 'Come in, John, and meet the other guests', the commas around 'John' are commas of address. Also called a vocative comma.

common collocation a phrase or group of words that follows a set pattern or word order and is in common use but is not normally classed as an idiom. Typical common collocations are 'fish and chips' and 'in abeyance'. *See* **idiom**.

compound word a word made up from two or more existing words, e.g. *bloodstream* (from *blood* and *stream*). Compound words may or may not be written with a hyphen. *See* the chapter on Hyphen.

conjunction any of a class of words that serve to connect two or more words, phrases or clauses. *See* **co-ordinating conjunction; subordinating conjunction**.

conjunctive adverb an adverb or adverbial phrase that functions like a conjunction in that it connects what has gone before with the following clause or sentence. Typical conjunctive adverbs are however, moreover, in addition, in that case, etc. *See* the chapter on Semicolon.

co-ordinate clause one of two or more clauses in a sentence that share the same level of importance within the sentence and are connected by co-ordinating conjunctions. *See* **co-ordinating conjunction**.

co-ordinating conjunction a type of conjunction that serves to introduce a co-ordinate clause. Typical co-ordinating conjunctions are *and, but, either, for, neither, nor*. *See also* **subordinating conjunction**.

defective question a question that is an elliptical or grammatically incomplete sentence; this is a term employed in this book but is not in general linguistic use. A typical defective question might be 'The gate? What gate?'

direct question a straightforward question ending in a question mark. The sentence 'Do you like oranges?' is a typical direct question.

direct speech the verbatim quotation of what someone said. Such a quotation is enclosed within quotation marks. For a full explanation of direct speech, *see* the chapter on Quotation Marks.

direct statement a straightforward sentence that is neither a question nor an exclamation and is therefore followed by a full point. *See* the chapter on Full Point.

elliptical connected with or resulting from ellipsis (of sentences, questions, etc.) and so condensed that the sentence is grammatically incomplete and the full meaning has to be supplied from the context.

finite verb a verb that appears in a form that has an ending showing the grammatical features by which it is linked to its subject in a sentence. These features include number (that is, whether the subject is singular or plural), person (that is, whether the subject is in the first, second or third person) and tense (that is, whether the action described by the verb is in the past, present or future tense).

gender any of up to three categories to which the nouns of a language may belong. In modern English, gender is generally correlated with sex, so that all male animate things (*man, boy, ram*, etc.) are classed as masculine, all female animate things (*woman, girl, ewe*, etc.) are said to be feminine, and all inanimate things (*chair, book, cup*, etc.) are considered to be neuter. Some English nouns, such as *car* and *ship*, are sometimes regarded as feminine and take the feminine pronoun *she*. In languages other than English, and in older stages of the English language itself, gender is a purely grammatical classification based on such criteria as the endings that different nouns have. German has three genders:

masculine, feminine and neuter. But French and the Celtic languages (e.g. Welsh and Irish) have only two: masculine and feminine.

genitive case a form of pronouns and certain nouns that denotes possession, ownership or some other form of association usually indicated by the word *of*. In Old and Middle English, masculine and neuter nouns added the suffix *-es* to form their genitive cases, and this form survives as the *'s* still used today but now extended to feminine nouns too. *See* the chapter on Apostrophe.

gerund a verbal noun that indicates an action or state and ends in *-ing*. Although a noun, the gerund retains its verb's ability to take an object, as in the sentence 'Killing him will be easy; getting away from the scene will be virtually impossible.' It is easy to confuse the gerund with the present participle, which also ends in -ing but functions as an adjective. In the sentence 'Jane's walking down the street with Tony made me very angry', the word 'walking' is a gerund because it denotes an action performed by Jane. *See also* participle.

grammar the whole body of rules that seeks to account for the way in which a language works, classifying its linguistic forms (nouns, verbs, adjectives, etc.) and describing the ways in which they are used in sentences and the changes to which they may be subjected. Linguists also use the word grammar to mean the system of rules by which a person can get to know and speak his or her native language. In its most modern usage, the word grammar denotes an abstract system of rules that generate or produce all the sentences of a language that are recognized as being correct by the native speakers of that language.

grammatical of or concerning **grammar**; in accordance with the rules embodied in the grammar of a language. A grammatical sentence is one that is considered to be correct in its observance of such rules.

hyphenate to spell a word with a hyphen or to use a hyphen to divide a word at the end of a line when there is not enough room to get the whole word in.

hyphenation and justification the process of laying out typed or printed matter on a page so that the lines of text align with each other on both the left- and the right-hand sides and, if necessary, words are divided at the end of a line to ensure that the spaces between the words are as even as possible. Hyphenation and justification are usually carried out by means of a special computer program on word processors and typesetting machines, known colloquially as an H & J program.

idiom a phrase or group of words whose meaning as a whole is different from what one would expect as a result of considering the meanings of the words individually. Typical English idioms are the phrases 'rain cats and dogs' and 'be up the creek without a paddle'.

independent clause a clause that can stand alone and form a complete sentence. Pairs of independent clauses that are linked by a logical connection rather than a conjunction are normally set off from each other by a semicolon. *See* the chapters on Comma and Semicolon.

indirect question a question contained in a noun clause that is the object of a verb of asking and is cast in the form of a statement. A typical indirect question is the sentence 'She asked him who he was.' *See* the chapters on Full Point; and Question Mark and Exclamation Mark.

indirect speech the reporting of someone's words through a recasting or paraphrase of them rather than by means of direct verbatim quotation. Also called indirect discourse or **reported speech**. *See* the chapter on Quotation marks.

interjection any of a class of words that are used to express an exclamation or a sudden outburst of emotion. Interjections are normally thought of as being outside the main pattern or structure of the sentence and often used to render a loud noise of any kind. *See* the chapter on Question Mark and Exclamation Mark.

intransitive verb a verb that is not usually followed by an object. Typical intransitive verbs are *come, go,* and *struggle* in their straightforward meanings. *See* **transitive verb**.

linguistic form any word, clause or sentence, or any part of these, that can be isolated for grammatical analysis or for the study or learning of a language.

linguistic unit a word or group of words that denote a single concept. The term covers such locutions as 'old man' or 'young woman'. This is a non-technical term not generally used by linguists.

main clause the principal clause of a sentence, which can in fact stand on its own. In 'I saw a man who said his name was Jim', the words 'I saw a man' represent the main clause and form a grammatically complete sentence.

masculine one of the genders of nouns, usually correlated in modern English with male animate things. *See* **gender**.

modify to alter or limit the effect of (a sentence, noun, verb, adjective or adverb). In the sentence 'He fights bravely', the adverb 'bravely' modifies the verb 'fights'.

neuter one of the genders of nouns, usually correlated in modern English with inanimate things. *See* **gender**.

non-specifying relative clause a type of relative clause that does not define the noun to which it refers but serves to add extra information about it. Non-specifying clauses are set off from the rest of the sentence by one or two commas. In this sentence, the commas mark off a non-specifying relative clause: 'The polar bear, which can weigh up to 450 kilograms, is ferocious.'

noun any of a class of words that denote people, places, living and non-living things, and abstract concepts. In English, nouns can be subdivided into countable nouns, such as *cat, bicycle, door*, etc.; uncountable, or mass, nouns, such as *sugar, disbelief, absent-mindedness*, etc.; and proper nouns, denoting people and places, such as *Suzanne, Fred Smith, London*, etc. Nouns are often preceded by a linguistic form called a determiner, which includes the definite article *the*, the indefinite article *a* (not used with uncountable nouns and rarely with proper nouns), and the possessive forms *my, your, his, her, its, our* and *their*. Nouns and their respective determiners are referred to by modern linguists as noun phrases and can be the subject (or agent) of a verb as well as the object of a transitive verb.

noun clause a subordinate clause that functions within a sentence like a noun and can be either the subject or object of a verb. A subordinate clause introduced by *that* after a verb of saying is typical of the modern noun clause.

onomatopoeic words words such as *crash, splash, bang*, etc., which are conceived of as imitating a sound.

open punctuation a relatively sparse use of punctuation marks, especially commas. The tendency in late 20th-century English has been to use open punctuation and to reduce the number of marks even more.

parenthesis a word, phrase, or clause that interrupts but does not belong to the structure and logic of a sentence. *See* the chapters on Comma, Dash and Parentheses.

parenthetical characteristic of, concerning, contained within, or representing a **parenthesis**.

participial phrase a phrase containing a present or past participle The phrase may or may not be part of an **absolute construction**. In the following sentences, the italicized portions are participial phrases: 'I saw Jane *lying on my bed*'; 'Jim having resigned, the task of running the company was given to Tom.'

participle an adjective formed from a verb. Participles can show tense in modern English but not person or number.

Past participles usually end in *-ed*, but there are many old irregular forms, such as *spoken*, from the verb *speak*. An example of a past participle is *smashed* in the sentence 'He found the vase smashed to pieces on the floor.' Present participles end in *-ing* and can be confused with a gerund. In the sentence 'The sight of Jane walking down the street with Tony made me very angry', *walking* is a present participle because it is an adjective modifying the noun 'Jane'. *See also* **gerund**.

period fault excessive use of the full point where other lighter punctuation marks would be more appropriate. This is an error recognized chiefly by United States writers. *See* the chapter on Full Point.

phrase any group of words lacking a finite verb. Phrases often lie outside the main sentence structure and are consequently parenthetical word-groups set off by commas.

points of suspension another name for an ellipsis. *See* the chapter on Ellipsis.

possessive case another name for the **genitive case**.

preposition any of a class of words that are placed in front of a noun or noun phrase in order to establish a link between the noun phrase and some other part of the sentence. In 'The book is on the desk', the word 'on' is a preposition that links the words 'desk' and 'book' and in so doing specifies the whereabouts of the book.

prefix *see* **affix**.

punctuation mark any of the symbols used to denote pauses or break points in a sentence. Punctuation marks include the comma, semicolon, colon, full point, and dash. Exclamation and question marks are technically not pause marks, but tones of voice written down.

quotation a phrase or passage from a book, play, speech or piece of conversation or dialogue that is presented word-for-word within quotation marks. *See* **direct speech** and the chapter on Quotation Marks.

relative clause an adjectival clause, introduced by *who, which or* that, which serves to modify a noun, known as the antecedent. Relative clauses can be either **specifying** or **non-specifying**.

reported speech another name for **indirect speech**. *See also* **direct speech** and the chapter on Quotation Marks.

reporting clause a clause such as 'he said', 'she asserted', as used with direct **quotation** or **indirect speech**.

restrictive comma a comma (often one of a pair) that adds information by which a preceding word is restricted, specified or narrowed down, as in this sentence: 'He went to university at Cambridge, Massachusetts.'

rhetorical of or concerning rhetoric as an art form, the use of language or discourse to persuade, elucidate, influence or entertain. The word is used in grammar to describe a kind of punctuation that is designed to achieve a certain rhetorical effect. The use of the term rhetorical has been extended to cover dramatic and stylistic effects in punctuation. Modern punctuation has moved away from such devices, which often lead to the overuse of punctuation marks.

salutation the phrase used to address the recipient at the beginning of a letter, as in 'Dear John', 'Dear Sir', 'Sir', etc.

sentence a series of words that can stand alone to make a declaration, issue a statement or command or to ask a question. It usually consists of a subject, a predicate and a finite verb. A typical sentence begins with a capital letter and ends with a full point, question mark or exclamation mark. *See also* the chapter on Full Point.

sentence modifier an adverb or adverbial phrase that modifies a whole sentence. An example of a sentence modifier is the word 'admittedly', as in 'Admittedly, he was confused at the time.'

specifying relative clause an adjectival relative clause that defines or specifies its antecedent. Specifying relative clauses are not set off by commas. The words in italics in the following sentence form a specifying relative clause: 'The cows *that are good producers of milk* are not sent to the abattoir; the rest are slaughtered for their meat.'

stop any of the punctuation marks that were used to mark a pause. Traditionally, they include the full point, colon, semicolon and the comma. Some people also include the question mark and the exclamation mark, but strictly these are not stops but tones.

subordinate clause a clause that cannot stand on its own but serves as an adjective, noun or adverb relating to parts of the main clause. The subordinate clause in italics in the following sentence is an adverbial clause telling us when the action of the main clause took place: '*While I was getting an ice cream*, a gang of boys stole my bicycle.'

subordinating conjunction a conjunction that introduces a subordinate clause. Examples are *because, if, until, while*.

suffix *See* affix.

syntactical of or concerning syntax. In relation to punctuation, the term refers to the use of punctuation marks to set off one syntactical element from another inside a sentence.

syntax the grammatical arrangement of the words in any given sentence of a language, or the rules or system that governs such an arrangement.

tag question a short question added onto the end of a sentence to confirm the truth of the sentence by requiring an expected answer. Thus *isn't she?* in 'She's Welsh, isn't she?' is a tag question that invites the answer 'yes', thereby confirming the truth of the assertion.

transitive verb a verb that usually takes a noun, noun phrase or noun clause as an object, as in 'He bought a blue car', in which bought is the past tense of *buy*, a transitive verb. Other such verbs are, for example, *take, spread, throw, make, prove*, and many more. *See* **intransitive verb**.

verb any of a large category of words that denote the occurrence or performance of an action or the existence of a state or condition. Typical verbs are *sit, jump, throw*, etc. In modern linguistics, a verb phrase is the whole of the sentence following the subject noun phrase.

vocative comma another name for a **comma of address**.